Her Own Accord

SELECTED AND EDITED BY
Denise Ahlquist, Nancy Carr, Joseph Coulson
Louise Galpine, Summer McDonald, and Donald H. Whitfield

CONTRIBUTORS
Kelsey Crick
Liz Friedman
Carlee Green
Mary Klein
Tom Pilcher
Audrey Schlofner
Christina Schubert
Josh Sniegowski
Samantha Stankowicz
Vinita Venkatraman
Mary Williams

Cover image: Carrie Moyer, *Four Dreams in an Open Room*, 2013. Acrylic and glitter on canvas, 66 × 56 in. © Carrie Moyer. Courtesy of DC Moore Gallery, New York.

Carrie Moyer is a Brooklyn-based artist who has exhibited widely over the last twenty years. She is best known for abstract paintings that are simultaneously opulent and graphic, influenced by a background in design and queer activism. Moyer also cofounded, with photographer Sue Schaffner, the long-standing public art project Dyke Action Machine!, which was active in New York from 1991 to 2008. The recipient of numerous awards, she is currently an associate professor of art at Hunter College, New York, and is represented by DC Moore Gallery, New York.

Cover graphic design: Tom Pilcher

Interior design: THINK Book Works

Her Own Accord

*American Women on Identity,
Culture, and Community*

THE GREAT BOOKS FOUNDATION
A nonprofit educational organization

Published and distributed by

THE GREAT BOOKS FOUNDATION
A nonprofit educational organization

35 E. Wacker Drive, Suite 400
Chicago, IL 60601
www.greatbooks.org

Shared Inquiry™ is a trademark of the Great Books Foundation. The contents of this publication include proprietary trademarks and original materials and may be used or quoted only with permission and appropriate credit to the Foundation.

Copyright © 2016 by The Great Books Foundation
Chicago, Illinois
All rights reserved
ISBN 978-1-939014-38-2 (print)   978-1-939014-39-9 (ebook)

First printing
9 8 7 6 5 4 3 2 1

Library of Congress Cataloging-in-Publications Data has been applied for.

About the Great Books Foundation

The Great Books Foundation is an independent, nonprofit educational organization that creates reading and discussion programs for students and adults with the conviction that literacy and critical thinking help form reflective and well-informed citizens. We believe that civil and open discussion of the world's enduring literature promotes empathy, understanding, and community, and by working to develop reading and thinking skills, we advance the ultimate promise of democracy—participation for all.

The Great Books Foundation was established in 1947 to promote liberal education for the general public. In 1962, the Foundation extended its mission to children with the introduction of Junior Great Books®. Since its inception, the Foundation has helped thousands of people throughout the United States and in other countries begin their own discussion groups in schools, libraries, and community centers. Today, Foundation instructors conduct hundreds of workshops each year, in which educators and parents learn to lead Shared Inquiry™ discussion.

Notes by the author are not bracketed; notes by the Great Books Foundation, an editor, or a translator are [bracketed].

Contents

Introduction — xi

Identity — 1

"What Do Women Want?" — 5
Kim Addonizio

At Odds — 7
Julia Serano

Ending Poem — 17
Aurora Levins Morales and Rosario Morales

Even the Queen — 19
Connie Willis

Rowing — 37
Anne Sexton

Family — 39

I Go Back to May 1937 — 43
Sharon Olds

Freedom Fighter — 45
Perri Klass

My Father's Chinese Wives — 65
Sandra Tsing Loh

Stories Don't Have Endings — 79
Janice Gould

The Box House and the Snow — 85
Cristina Henríquez

Relationships — 97

A Boy My Sister Dated in High School — **101**
Emily Mitchell

Apple Picking — **105**
Laura Negrete

Drinking Coffee Elsewhere — **109**
ZZ Packer

The Burning Heart — **131**
Louise Glück

Re-forming the Crystal — **133**
Adrienne Rich

Work — 135

Mind-Body Story — **139**
Nina Barrett

One Out of Twelve: Writers Who Are Women in Our Century* — **155**
Tillie Olsen

Baby Gotta Eat, Parts I–V — **173**
Kima Jones

Lowering Your Standards for Food Stamps — **187**
Sheryl Luna

Color Blind or Color Brave? — **189**
Mellody Hobson

Reeling for the Empire — **195**
Karen Russell

Politics — 221

"Recitatif" — **225**
Toni Morrison

When the World as We Knew It Ended — **245**
Joy Harjo

Bad Feminist: Take One — **247**
Roxane Gay

*Selection from a longer essay.

Woodchucks Maxine Kumin	**257**
Reading Lessons Edwidge Danticat	**259**
Ways of Conquest Denise Levertov	**273**
About Shared Inquiry	**275**
Discussion Questions	**277**
Acknowledgments	**303**

Introduction

In a world that is often at odds with the presence of women, it is a matter of survival to believe in "us." To fiercely hold on to our right to exist, not just as mothers, daughters, sisters, nieces, and wives, but simply as who we are and who we desire to be—as individuals, who also happen to be women.

Contemporary culture has fallen in love again with storytelling. And women's stories, in their beauty and complexity, have the power to shape minds and shift views. Those stories remind us that we are still here. And not only are we here in mind, body, and spirit, but with each passing day we grow stronger—creating, demanding, and staking out a space that is uniquely our own and of our own determination, all as women. Our stories reveal resilience and determination, passion and commitment, forgiveness and hope.

I grew up in a small town in India with my sister. Our father was an educator and he taught us to dream big. To be a girl was not a sentence of incapability. I am trained as a scientist and an engineer.

I celebrated my fortieth year by turning to a life given to community. I switched careers and began to work with the Chicago-based nonprofit Apna Ghar, which works with immigrant women faced with gender violence. It remains, to this day, one of the most transformative experiences of my life and career. I met women who had been battered and bruised while also facing the challenge of navigating a foreign world. Courageously, they held on to hope for a better life and were raising good children to be the best citizens of tomorrow.

Today I work at Chicago Foundation for Women, where we believe that all women and girls should have the opportunity to achieve their potential and live in safe, just, and healthy communities. We have

Introduction

seen many progressive gains in our thirty-year history, but every day the challenges persist. Progress is not happening fast enough.

Despite my father's forward thinking, the daily experiences of women and girls uncover the reality that we are still plagued by bias. Every day, all around the world, without regard to race, class, education, sexuality, or profession, women and girls are reminded that the very nature of who they are has the potential to bar them from opportunities, access, advancement, and safety.

What does bias look like in these times? It is defunded programs that help women in need to access birth control or childcare assistance. It is being paid less than men because of our gender and our race. It is unpredictable scheduling or wage theft of poor women and immigrant women because no one is there to advocate for our needs and rights. It is gender-based violence and sexual harassment because media and culture reinforce the notion that women and girls exist only for the male gaze and male consumption.

At Chicago Foundation for Women, we focus on expanding opportunity and removing barriers by investing in organizations that work to foster the success of women and girls—enhancing economic security, providing access to health and health information, and ensuring freedom from violence.

But, it is not enough to get women into industries that pay a living wage or out of abusive relationships. We need to do more. We need more. We need a complete shift, a total overhaul of how we think of women and girls and their place in the world. And one of the most effective ways to spark that change is to know one's journey. That is why stories are so powerful and so necessary.

Though we are often bound by our collective womanness, there is no universal narrative of who women are and what our lives look like. That is both exhilarating and terrifying. *Her Own Accord* addresses those nuances—of living, loving, existing, desiring, and being female. It gives insight to how family, relationships, work, identity, and politics all fuse together or intertwine to make up a fraction of who we are. And for that reason many of the pieces in *Her Own Accord* touch upon multiple themes.

The women's movement has been working for decades to change gender inequities, and while nothing has come easily, much

Introduction

progress has been made. It is the stories, the books, our collective voices, and shared histories that remind us to breathe, to celebrate and rejoice in who we are, where we have been, and where we aspire to go—as women. Our stories sustain us.

Her Own Accord reminds us that our presence is an act of resistance; our stories are movements within themselves.

—K. Sujata

K. Sujata is the president and CEO of Chicago Foundation for Women (CFW). As a grant-making institution, CFW connects need, money, and solutions to improve the lives of women and girls throughout metropolitan Chicago. In its thirty-year history, CFW has granted $26 million to ensure all women and girls have the opportunity to achieve their full potential and live in safe, just, and healthy communities.

Identity

The pieces gathered in this first section turn a particular focus to questions of selfhood and identity. As these writers explore sexuality, gender identity, group identity, ethnic and racial identity, and the growth of identity through childhood and adolescence, they ask us to consider how the self can be made and remade.

In "'What Do Women Want?'" (2000), **Kim Addonizio** (1954–) takes Freud's unanswered question and replies in her own terms. In the poem, the speaker focuses her desire on a single item of clothing and proffers the apparently simple answer, "a red dress."

Biologist, trans feminist, and author of the book *Whipping Girl* (2007), **Julia Serano** (1967–) transitioned from male to female and writes frequently about transgender identities and perspectives. In "At Odds" (2007), she explores her childhood and adolescence, focusing on what it was like to come of age as a trans person in an environment that offered little help in negotiating her experiences.

"Ending Poem" (1986), written by **Aurora Levins Morales** (1954–) and her mother **Rosario Morales** (1930–2011), presents voices speaking of different geographical, ethnic, and linguistic affinities, leaving the reader to consider what constitutes the self across time and distance.

In "Even the Queen" (1992), **Connie Willis** (1945–) depicts an extended family of women responding to a young woman's unexpected decision in a world where "the Liberation" has abolished menstruation. Willis asks us to think about how biology and science affect women's lives, as well as the various meanings of "liberation."

In her posthumously published poem "Rowing" (1975), **Anne Sexton** (1928–1974) traces a woman's journey from childhood, through adolescence, and into adulthood. But she leaves ambiguous the rower's motivation and destination.

"What Do Women Want?"
Kim Addonizio

I want a red dress.
I want it flimsy and cheap,
I want it too tight, I want to wear it
until someone tears it off me.
I want it sleeveless and backless,
this dress, so no one has to guess
what's underneath. I want to walk down
the street past Thrifty's and the hardware store
with all those keys glittering in the window,
past Mr. and Mrs. Wong selling day-old
donuts in their café, past the Guerra brothers
slinging pigs from the truck and onto the dolly,
hoisting the slick snouts over their shoulders.
I want to walk like I'm the only
woman on earth and I can have my pick.
I want that red dress bad.
I want it to confirm
your worst fears about me,
to show you how little I care about you
or anything except what
I want. When I find it, I'll pull that garment
from its hanger like I'm choosing a body
to carry me into this world, through
the birth-cries and the love-cries too,
and I'll wear it like bones, like skin,
it'll be the goddamned
dress they bury me in.

At Odds

Julia Serano

The thing that I remember most vividly about my junior high school years isn't my classes, hanging out with friends, extracurricular activities, or teen crushes. Rather, it is lying in bed, trying to fall asleep but not being able to. I had a monster case of insomnia—most nights it was at least an hour and a half (often longer) from the time when I first slipped under the covers to the time I would eventually drift off to sleep. Having been raised Catholic, I couldn't help but think of the time I spent each night ravaged by my own thoughts as a form of penance. I was being punished by my thoughts, for my thoughts. And as much as I wanted my nightly torture to stop, I didn't dare tell anybody about my insomnia. It was but one of many secrets I kept. My secrets were like Russian nested dolls—secrets within secrets—each one merely a shell that protected the secret just underneath it. And all of the secrets were designed to hide my most private, innermost core secret, the one that gave rise to my insomnia and my secretiveness in the first place: I wanted to be a girl.

Admittedly, "wanted" isn't really the right word. It's not that I consciously wished that I could be a girl, or that I felt that my life would be better or easier had I been born female. No, it was that, for some unknown reason, I simply couldn't stop thinking about being a girl. Like sleepiness, hunger, or thirst, the feelings I had about it would just flood my mind from time to time, without any warning, and despite countless conscious attempts on my part to ignore or repress them.

Initially, when I first became aware of these thoughts, I followed them. I indulged them. I would wrap curtains or blankets around my body as if they were dresses, and stare at myself in the mirror, impressed by how much I looked like a girl. Or I'd act out stories in my bedroom, in which the boy protagonist would suddenly be transformed into a girl, who would then go off on her own adventures, solve her own mysteries.

One day, after having enacted stories along these lines for a number of weeks, I paused for a moment to ask myself the one question that I had been avoiding the whole time: *Why do I enjoy pretending to be a girl so much?*

The world seemed to stop when I asked myself that question. I remember sitting on the edge of my bed, my body slowly growing cold. I had to admit to myself that this wasn't merely innocent exploration, like all those other times when I pretended to be a doctor or an animal or a character from *Star Wars*. Pretending to be a girl didn't quite feel like pretending. It felt real. Too real. A moment earlier, I had been just another kid playing make-believe, and now suddenly I was harboring a dangerous secret. And I felt very, very alone.

In the aftermath of that realization, I was consumed by all sorts of emotions, but the two that stood out most were fear and embarrassment. My fear came in many forms. I was scared about how devastated my parents might be if they found out, or how badly my friends and classmates would tease me if they knew what I was thinking. I worried that my thoughts about being a girl would never go away, that they would haunt me for the rest of my life, that the anxiety and restlessness they had inspired in me would never cease. But the thing I feared most of all was how God might judge me because of my desire.

The fact that I turned to God at this point in my life had less to do with my upbringing than it did with the fact that I felt as if I had no one else to share my secret with. Since God was supposedly omniscient, I didn't have to come out to him—he already knew what I was thinking and doing. And because I was eleven years old at the time, and had no access to any information related to what I was going through, the idea of turning to someone who might be able to solve my problem was immensely comforting. I would pray to him every night, begging him to turn me into a girl. I fantasized about simply waking up one morning as a girl and having no one in my life be surprised—they would act as if nothing had changed, as if the memories of me as a boy had been suddenly purged from their minds. Or I'd imagine that, during a routine doctor's visit, the pediatrician would realize something wasn't right with me. He'd order all these tests, and when the results finally came back, he'd say that there had been a mistake, and that I had really been a girl all along.

Of course, none of this ever happened. And as time went on, I started to seriously consider the possibility that maybe there hadn't been a mistake, that maybe I was supposed to be a boy after all. Maybe that was what God intended for me. And if God wanted me to be a boy, then my dreams of becoming a girl were no longer innocent fantasies. They were sins. I began to cultivate a preteen paranoia that God was testing me, like he did in those Old Testament stories about Abraham and Job that the nuns had taught me. And if God was testing me, then he obviously wanted me to resist this temptation, to sacrifice my own wants and desires as an offering to him. So, instead of praying to God to turn me into a girl, I prayed that he would stop the thoughts altogether. I tried to bargain with him by refusing to indulge my fantasies about being a girl, by spending my insomniac hours reciting rosary after rosary, by whispering the Act of Contrition to myself every time the girl thoughts popped into my head.

But nothing changed. If anything, denying the girl thoughts seemed to only make them more intense, not less. Despite all my prayers and begging, God never intervened. And the silence was deafening. I was desperate. Exhausted. Angry. Rather than continuing to confide in him, I began to ask myself what kind of God would purposely torture a young child like this. What kind of God would allow me, an isolated, frightened preteen, to become so consumed with the fear of burning in hell for all eternity that I couldn't sleep at night, that I couldn't concentrate during the day? I decided that I would not follow a god who required blind worship, who played cat-and-mouse games with children. I stopped praying and gave myself permission to experience the girl thoughts, to indulge them to a certain extent. While I still felt that it wasn't safe to share my secret desire with others, I convinced myself that anything I did within the privacy of my own room wouldn't hurt anyone.

It took many years—even decades—for me to begin to dismantle the overwhelming sense of embarrassment that I felt about my desire. This wasn't simply embarrassment about wanting to change my sex; it had more to do with my wanting specifically to be a girl. Although I grew up in the wake of the feminist movement of the 1960s and '70s, when it was common to hear sound bites like "Women and men are equal" and "Girls can do anything boys can do," I found that such comments often had little bearing on the world I inhabited, where teachers and parents frequently expected boys to outperform girls at most tasks; where schoolchildren relentlessly teased young boys in gym class whenever team captains picked girls ahead of them; where the cartoons I watched typically featured male superheroes and relegated female characters to the role of damsel in distress. For all the explicit talk about equal rights at the time, young boys were still expected and encouraged to adhere to two unspoken rules: Do not let girls beat you at anything, and do not appear girlish in any way or under any circumstances.

And I was way beyond girlish; I wanted to *be* a girl. Even after deciding that it was safe for me to act out, behind closed doors, my fantasies about being female, I still wasn't able to move beyond the shame that I felt about my desire. In many ways, my embarrassment was exacerbated by being brought up as a male. While girls my age had to manage blatantly sexist attitudes in an immediate and tangible way, at least they were sometimes able to partake of the relative safety of all-female environments and receive positive messages about femaleness from the women role models in their lives. As I would learn many years later, the very experience of living in the world as a woman necessitates that one develop self-defense mechanisms and self-empowering attitudes in order to deflect all of the demeaning antifemale and antifeminine sentiments one encounters regularly.

But back then, I was still living life as an extremely closeted boy who wanted to be a girl. As such, I had no role models, no script to follow, no one in my life whom I could ask questions, no one to offer me empowering advice. Nobody ever took me aside and told me that who I was and what I wanted were okay. Instead, I was thrown to the wolves. Without any support or protection, I was left exposed to the blatant misogyny that exists in many all-male spaces. I remember wanting to simply shrink into nothingness whenever I stepped inside boys' locker rooms, where junior high (and later high school) boys regularly tried to outdo one another with their crass, sexist comments—everything from preschool sentiments like "Girls are stupid" to adult-male clichés like "Women are only good for one thing." Every demeaning quip stung me like a barbed needle. As a female-identified child, being forced to endure boyhood felt like bleeding to death from a million small cuts.

Somehow I had to reconcile my deep, subconscious desire to be female with the unceasing stream of messages I received that insisted that women were the lesser sex. Some women who have been taught to feel ashamed of their own sexual urges will sometimes turn to rape fantasies—imagining themselves being taken against their will—as a way of exploring their sexual desires without having to feel guilty about them. Perhaps for that very same reason, my early teenage fantasies about being female always began with my being turned into a girl against my will. I would be kidnapped by some imagined nemesis or random psychopath, who would turn me into a girl as a way of punishing or torturing me. During the precise moment of my transformation, I would always feel a strange combination of both humiliation and elation. Since I was not able to transcend the shame that I felt at the time for wanting to be female, I found ways to incorporate it into my fantasies. Like most coping mechanisms, it wasn't particularly healthy for my self-esteem, but it at least helped me to make some sense out of all of my contradictory feelings, and to survive the most isolated period of my life.

As I moved through puberty, I began to incorporate love interests into these fantasies. Rather than my being abducted alone, the villain in my fantasy would also capture a girl whom I happened to have a crush on. Then he would offer me an ultimatum: he would threaten to kill her unless I agreed to be turned into a girl. Of course, I always gallantly chose the latter, and afterward, the girl would fall in love with me, despite my female anatomy, because I had just saved her life. These visions were twisted transgender takes on fairy tales, seamlessly combining sex change with chivalry and living happily ever after. In retrospect, what amazes me most about my fantasies is that they always ended both with my getting the girl *and* with my becoming a girl—an inventive plot twist, considering that it would still be a couple of years before I would hear the word "lesbian."

Ironically, it was my attraction to girls—a rather mundane desire given the fact that, physically speaking, I was a teenage boy—that confused me most. I had been dealing with the girl thoughts for about two years before my sexual attraction kicked in. And while my desire to be female was inexplicable in many ways, at least there seemed to be some sort of precedent for it, based on what I had seen on TV. Granted, this was in the late 1970s, when TV depictions of transgenderism were highly distorted and blurred all distinctions between effeminate gay men, transvestites, and transsexuals. But at least the shows I had seen suggested that some men did choose to live their lives as women, and that the main reason why they did so was that they were attracted to men. While I definitely didn't want to be "gay"—which, unlike "lesbian," had been tossed around the schoolyard as an insult since I was in second grade—I logically assumed that my desire to be female was a sign that I was going to end up being attracted to boys. And while TV images of gay men who became transsexual women may have been nothing more than inaccurate and unflattering caricatures, at least they offered me some kind of template that I could work from. As weird as it may seem, those images offered me the remote possibility that I might someday achieve a semblance of gender normalcy.

But once I began developing crushes on girls, my gender seemed to become doubly convoluted. Not only was my girl identity at odds with my boy body, but my sexual orientation was at odds with my desire to be female. These conflicting desires seemed to create two disparate paths for me, each leading toward an unfathomable and inadequate future. Either I could explore my attraction to girls by passing as a straight boy (which would require me to remain closeted about my desire to be female), or I could indulge my desire to be female by running away and starting a new life as a woman someplace else (which seemed to foreclose any possibility of meeting a girl who would be willing and able to fall in love with me). Both desires were strong—irrepressible—but at the same time it seemed as though I could only choose one.

I think I went back and forth on this issue for quite a while. Then, when I was fifteen, I went to my baseball league's all-star game with a handful of my male friends who also hadn't made the team. We were sitting in the bleachers when three girls came over and started a conversation. Next thing I knew, the boys and girls were chatting in a teenager-flirty sort of way. Everyone except for me. I just sat there. Silent. Observing. From the outside, I must have seemed very distant and removed from what was happening. But on the inside, I was totally consumed by what was going on. The scene inspired in me one of the most intense feelings that I had ever experienced—an intuition. A *knowing*. It seemed so clear to me right then that I should have been on the other side of that conversation, standing with those girls. I should have been one of them. And as those girls walked away, I remember thinking that I was going to have a sex change when I grew up. I didn't even know what that was, exactly. It didn't really matter. All that mattered was that I would get to be a girl. While the very phrase "sex change" sounded bizarre, foreign, alien, I figured that it couldn't be any more surreal than how I felt every day of my life—always pretending to be a boy and simultaneously imagining that I was a girl.

However, the profound truth that I experienced that day slowly began to give way to the realities of my day-to-day existence. Puberty began to reshape my body: my voice got a bit deeper, hair started growing out of my face, and I became more muscular without even trying. The girl thoughts never went away, mind you; it's just that my own biology seemed to betray me. Like gravity, my body seemed to keep pulling me back down to earth.

My junior year of high school, I asked a girl I really liked to the prom. The following year, we dated more seriously. She was my first love. While she didn't end up becoming my happily ever after, we did have a lot of wonderful times together. For the most part, I was ecstatic about being in a relationship with someone whose company I enjoyed so much—although sometimes, when the girl thoughts were strong, I would be overcome by sadness, because I knew what was happening. By default, I was choosing one of the two paths. And for better or for worse, this was the path of least resistance. It didn't involve sex change operations or sharing my dangerous secret with anyone. It was the safer path by far. But as much as I enjoyed exploring love and sexual attraction, I couldn't help but feel, with each step I took, that I was leaving a part of myself behind.

Fast forward roughly fifteen years, to the fall of 2000. I'm in a Mexican restaurant in Oakland, California, sharing chips and salsa with my fiancée, Dani. I'm telling her about the two disparate life paths that I had always envisioned for myself when I was younger—one that led to a relatively normal life, with a wife, a decent career, close friends and family, and so forth; and the other, where I ran away to live as a woman. She smiles and says, "And then what?"

"What do you mean?"

"After you became a woman. What would happen then?"

"To be honest, at the time, I never really thought about what would happen after that."

"That's ridiculous. Being a woman isn't a life path."

We both laugh. Shortly afterward, a waiter approaches us and says, "Hello, ladies, are you ready to order?" Dani subtly rolls her eyes at me before ordering, as if to say, *Again?* This has been happening more and more often lately, even though my appearance hasn't changed much. I'm still wearing the same sweat jackets, T-shirts, jeans, and sneakers that I've worn most of my life. It's just that I am no longer censoring myself. And as I have become more comfortable just being myself, and less concerned about what other people think of me, I find that people no longer assume that I'm a straight guy. Instead, they pick up on my femininity and assume that I'm a gay man, or they read me as a tomboy (as the waiter was apparently doing now).

There was a time in my late teens and early twenties when I would have been mortified by the very idea of strangers reading me as female. I would have taken it as a sign that my secret—the one I worked so hard to keep hidden—was leaking out for everyone to see. Now it doesn't bother me. I've finally stopped pretending to be male. While I haven't become a woman, per se, I am calling myself transgender. For the most part, Dani is pretty cool with it all. Granted, sometimes it can be difficult for her to be in a relationship with someone whose gender is in flux. But the idea of my becoming more feminine, or even female, in itself isn't really a problem for her, as she's identified as a dyke for most of her adult life. Ironically, we met shortly after she had begun to call herself bisexual.

I remember staring out the restaurant window, thinking about my teenage years, back when I believed that openly expressing my gender and spending my life with someone I loved were somehow mutually exclusive desires. Yet here I am, sharing my deepest and most dangerous secrets with my female life partner. Sometimes we do that to ourselves—we pit our desires against one another. We insist unnecessarily on seeing one aspect of our personality as being at odds with the rest of ourselves. Earlier in my life, it never occurred to me that I might someday fulfill both desires simultaneously.

Dani and I continue talking and eating, neither of us quite aware that one day, not too far down the path we now share, I will make the decision to transition. I will tell her this late one rainy night as we lie side by side in bed together. She will squeeze my hand when I tell her, and we will talk through the morning. I will tell her that I've imagined myself becoming female millions of times before, but this time will be very different. There will be no dreams about running off to a faraway city where nobody knows me, no fantasies of being forced into femaleness against my will.

For the first time in my life, I am able to imagine myself transitioning, right here, in Oakland, with her by my side. I picture all of it happening for real, in the life we share. And somehow now, it finally just seems right.

Ending Poem

Aurora Levins Morales and Rosario Morales

I am what I am.
A child of the Americas.
A light-skinned mestiza of the Caribbean.
A child of many diaspora, born into this continent at a crossroads.
I am Puerto Rican. I am U.S. American.
I am New York Manhattan and the Bronx.
A mountain-born, country-bred, homegrown jíbara child,
up from the shtetl, a California Puerto Rican Jew
A product of the New York ghettos I have never known.
I am an immigrant
and the daughter and granddaughter of immigrants.
We didn't know our forbears' names with a certainty.
They aren't written anywhere.
First names only or mija, negra, ne, honey, sugar, dear

I come from the dirt where the cane was grown.
My people didn't go to dinner parties. They weren't invited.
I am caribeña, island grown.
Spanish is in my flesh, ripples from my tongue, lodges in my hips,
the language of garlic and mangoes.
Boricua. As Boricuas come from the isle of Manhattan.
I am of latinoamerica, rooted in the history of my continent.
I speak from that body. Just brown and pink and full of drums inside.

I am not African.
Africa waters the roots of my tree, but I cannot return.

I am not Taína.
I am a late leaf of that ancient tree,
and my roots reach into the soil of two Americas.
Taíno is in me, but there is no way back.

I am not European, though I have dreamt of those cities.
Each plate is different.
wood, clay, papier mâché, metals basketry, a leaf, a coconut shell.
Europe lives in me but I have no home there.

The table has a cloth woven by one, dyed by another,
embroidered by another still.
I am a child of many mothers.
They have kept it all going

All the civilizations erected on their backs.
All the dinner parties given with their labor.

We are new.
They gave us life, kept us going,
brought us to where we are.
Born at a crossroads.
Come, lay that dishcloth down. Eat, dear, eat.
History made us.
We will not eat ourselves up inside anymore.

And we are whole.

Even the Queen

Connie Willis

The phone sang as I was looking over the defense's motion to dismiss. "It's the universal ring," my law clerk Bysshe said, reaching for it. "It's probably the defendant. They don't let you use signatures from jail."

"No, it's not," I said. "It's my mother."

"Oh." Bysshe reached for the receiver. "Why isn't she using her signature?"

"Because she knows I don't want to talk to her. She must have found out what Perdita's done."

"Your daughter Perdita?" he asked, holding the receiver against his chest. "The one with the little girl?"

"No, that's Viola. Perdita's my younger daughter. The one with no sense."

"What's she done?"

"She's joined the Cyclists."

Bysshe looked inquiringly blank, but I was not in the mood to enlighten him. Or in the mood to talk to Mother. "I know exactly what Mother will say," I told him. "She'll ask me why I didn't tell her, and then she'll demand to know what I'm going to do about it, and there is nothing I *can* do about it, or I obviously would have done it already."

Bysshe looked bewildered. "Do you want me to tell her you're in court?"

"No." I reached for the receiver. "I'll have to talk to her sooner or later." I took it from him. "Hello, Mother," I said.

"Traci," Mother said dramatically, "Perdita has become a Cyclist."

"I know."

"Why didn't you tell me?"

"I thought Perdita should tell you herself."

"Perdita!" She snorted. "She wouldn't tell me. She knows what I'd have to say about it. I suppose you told Karen."

"Karen's not here. She's in Iraq." The only good thing about this whole debacle was that thanks to Iraq's eagerness to show it was a responsible world community member, and its previous penchant for self-destruction, my mother-in-law was in the one place on the planet where the phone service was bad enough that I could claim I'd tried to call her but couldn't get through, and she'd have to believe me.

The Liberation has freed us from all sorts of indignities and scourges, including assorted Saddams, but mothers-in-law aren't one of them, and I was almost happy with Perdita for her excellent timing. When I didn't want to kill her.

"What's Karen doing in Iraq?" Mother asked.

"Negotiating a Palestinian homeland."

"And meanwhile her granddaughter is ruining her life," she said irrelevantly. "Did you tell Viola?"

"I *told* you, Mother. I thought Perdita should tell all of you herself."

"Well, she didn't. And this morning one of my patients, Carol Chen, called me and demanded to know what I was keeping from her. I had no idea what she was talking about."

"How did Carol Chen find out?"

"From her daughter, who almost joined the Cyclists last year. *Her* family talked her out of it," she said accusingly. "Carol was convinced the medical community had discovered some terrible side effect of ammenerol and were covering it up. I cannot believe you didn't tell me, Traci."

And I cannot believe I didn't have Bysshe tell her I was in court, I thought. "I told you, Mother. I thought it was Perdita's place to tell you. After all, it's her decision."

"Oh, Traci!" Mother said. "You cannot mean that!"

In the first fine flush of freedom after the Liberation, I had entertained hopes that it would change everything—that it would somehow do away with inequality and patriarchal dominance and those humorless women determined to eliminate the word "manhole" and third-person singular pronouns from the language.

Of course it didn't. Men still make more money, "herstory" is still a blight on the semantic landscape, and my mother can still say, "Oh, *Traci*!" in a tone that reduces me to preadolescence.

"*Her* decision!" Mother said. "Do you mean to tell me you plan to stand idly by and allow your daughter to make the mistake of her life?"

"What can I do? She's twenty-two years old and of sound mind."

"If she were of sound mind, she wouldn't be doing this. Didn't you try to talk her out of it?"

"Of course I did, Mother."

"And?"

"And I didn't succeed. She's determined to become a Cyclist."

"Well, there must be something we can do. Get an injunction or hire a deprogrammer or sue the Cyclists for brainwashing. You're a judge, there must be some law you can invoke—"

"The law is called personal sovereignty, Mother, and since it was what made the Liberation possible in the first place, it can hardly be used against Perdita. Her decision meets all the criteria for a case of personal sovereignty: it's a personal decision, it was made by a sovereign adult, it affects no one else—"

"What about my practice? Carol Chen is convinced shunts cause cancer."

"Any effect on your practice is considered an indirect effect. Like secondary smoke. It doesn't apply. Mother, whether we like it or not, Perdita has a perfect right to do this, and we don't have any right to interfere. A free society has to be based on respecting others' opinions and leaving each other alone. We have to respect Perdita's right to make her own decisions."

All of which was true. It was too bad I hadn't said any of it to Perdita when she called. What I had said, in a tone that sounded exactly like my mother's, was "Oh, *Perdita*!"

"This is all your fault, you know," Mother said. "I *told* you you shouldn't have let her get that tattoo over her shunt. And don't tell me it's a free society. What good is a free society when it allows my granddaughter to ruin her life?" She hung up.

I handed the receiver back to Bysshe.

"I really liked what you said about respecting your daughter's right to make her own decisions," he said. He held out my robe. "And about not interfering in her life."

"I want you to research the precedents on deprogramming for me," I said, sliding my arms into the sleeves. "And find out if the Cyclists have been charged with any free choice violations—brainwashing, intimidation, coercion."

The phone sang, another universal. "Hello, who's calling?" Bysshe said cautiously. His voice became suddenly friendlier. "Just a minute." He put his hand over the receiver. "It's your daughter Viola."

I took the receiver. "Hello, Viola."

"I just talked to Grandma," she said. "You will not believe what Perdita's done now. She's joined the Cyclists."

"I know," I said.

"You *know*? And you didn't tell me? I can't believe this. You never tell me anything."

"I thought Perdita should tell you herself," I said tiredly.

"Are you kidding? She never tells me anything either. That time she had eyebrow implants, she didn't tell me for three weeks, and when she got the laser tattoo she didn't tell me at all. Twidge told me. You should have called me. Did you tell Grandma Karen?"

"She's in Baghdad," I said.

"I know," Viola said. "I called her."

"Oh, Viola, you didn't!"

"Unlike you, Mom, I believe in telling members of our family about matters that concern them."

"What did she say?" I asked, a kind of numbness settling over me now that the shock had worn off.

"I couldn't get through to her. The phone service over there is terrible. I got somebody who didn't speak English, and then I got cut off, and when I tried again they said the whole city was down."

Thank you, I breathed silently. Thank you, thank you, thank you.

"Grandma Karen has a right to know, Mother. Think of the effect this could have on Twidge. She thinks Perdita's wonderful. When Perdita got the eyebrow implants, Twidge glued LEDs to hers, and I almost never got them off. What if Twidge decides to join the Cyclists, too?"

"Twidge is only nine. By the time she's supposed to get her shunt, Perdita will have long since quit." I hope, I added silently. Perdita had had the tattoo for a year and a half now and showed no signs of tiring of it. "Besides, Twidge has more sense."

"It's true. Oh, Mother, how could Perdita do this? Didn't you tell her about how awful it was?"

"Yes," I said. "And inconvenient. And unpleasant and unbalancing and painful. None of it made the slightest impact on her. She told me she thought it would be fun."

Bysshe was pointing to his watch and mouthing, "Time for court."

"Fun!" Viola said. "When she saw what I went through that time? Honestly, Mother, sometimes I think she's completely braindead. Can't you have her declared incompetent and locked up or something?"

"No," I said, trying to zip up my robe with one hand. "Viola, I have to go. I'm late for court. I'm afraid there's nothing we can do to stop her. She's a rational adult."

"Rational!" Viola said. "Her eyebrows light up, Mother. She has Custer's Last Stand lased on her arm."

I handed the phone to Bysshe. "Tell Viola I'll talk to her tomorrow." I zipped up my robe. "And then call Baghdad and see how long they expect the phones to be out."

I started into the courtroom. "And if there are any more universal calls, make sure they're local before you answer."

Bysshe couldn't get through to Baghdad, which I took as a good sign, and my mother-in-law didn't call. Mother did, in the afternoon, to ask if lobotomies were legal.

She called again the next day. I was in the middle of my Personal Sovereignty class, explaining the inherent right of citizens in a free society to make complete jackasses of themselves. My students weren't buying it.

"I think it's your mother," Bysshe whispered to me as he handed me the phone. "She's still using the universal. But it's local. I checked."

"Hello, Mother," I said.

"It's all arranged," Mother said. "We're having lunch with Perdita at McGregor's. It's on the corner of Twelfth Street and Larimer."

"I'm in the middle of class," I said.

"I know. I won't keep you. I just wanted to tell you not to worry. I've taken care of everything."

I didn't like the sound of that. "What have you done?"

"Invited Perdita to lunch with us. I told you. At McGregor's."

"Who is 'us,' Mother?"

"Just the family," she said innocently. "You and Viola."

Well, at least she hadn't brought in the deprogrammer. Yet. "What are you up to, Mother?"

"Perdita said the same thing. Can't a grandmother ask her granddaughters to lunch? Be there at twelve thirty."

"Bysshe and I have a court calendar meeting at three."

"Oh, we'll be done by then. And bring Bysshe with you. He can provide a man's point of view."

She hung up.

"You'll have to go to lunch with me, Bysshe," I said. "Sorry."

"Why? What's going to happen at lunch?"

"I have no idea."

On the way over to McGregor's, Bysshe told me what he'd found out about the Cyclists. "They're not a cult. There's no religious connection. They seem to have grown out of a pre-Liberation women's group," he said, looking at his notes, "although there are also links to the pro-choice movement, the University of Wisconsin, and the Museum of Modern Art."

"What?"

"They call their group leaders 'docents.' Their philosophy seems to be a mix of pre-Liberation radical feminism and the environmental primitivism of the eighties. They're floratarians and they don't wear shoes."

"Or shunts," I said. We pulled up in front of McGregor's and got out of the car. "Any mind-control convictions?" I asked hopefully.

"No. A bunch of suits against individual members, all of which they won."

"On grounds of personal sovereignty."

"Yeah. And a criminal one by a member whose family tried to deprogram her. The deprogrammer was sentenced to twenty years, and the family got twelve."

"Be sure to tell Mother about that one," I said, and opened the door to McGregor's.

It was one of those restaurants with a morning-glory vine twining around the maître d's desk and garden plots between the tables.

"Perdita suggested it," Mother said, guiding Bysshe and I past the onions to our table. "She told me a lot of the Cyclists are floratarians."

"Is she here?" I asked, sidestepping a cucumber frame.

"Not yet." She pointed past a rose arbor. "There's our table."

Our table was a wicker affair under a mulberry tree. Viola and Twidge were seated on the far side next to a trellis of runner beans, looking at menus.

"What are you doing here, Twidge?" I asked. "Why aren't you in school?"

"I am," she said, holding up her LCD slate. "I'm remoting today."

"I thought she should be part of this discussion," Viola said. "After all, she'll be getting her shunt soon."

"My friend Kensy says she isn't going to get one, like Perdita," Twidge said.

"I'm sure Kensy will change her mind when the time comes," Mother said. "Perdita will change hers, too. Bysshe, why don't you sit next to Viola?"

Bysshe slid obediently past the trellis and sat down in the wicker chair at the far end of the table. Twidge reached across Viola and handed him a menu. "This is a great restaurant," she said. "You don't have to wear shoes." She held up a bare foot to illustrate. "And if you get hungry while you're waiting, you can just pick something."

She twisted around in her chair, picked two of the green beans, gave one to Bysshe, and bit into the other one. "I bet Kensy doesn't. Kensy says a shunt hurts worse than braces."

"It doesn't hurt as much as not having one," Viola said, shooting me a Now-Do-You-See-What-My-Sister's-Caused? look.

"Traci, why don't you sit across from Viola?" Mother said to me. "And we'll put Perdita next to you when she comes."

"*If* she comes," Viola said.

"I told her one o'clock," Mother said, sitting down at the near end. "So we'd have a chance to plan our strategy before she gets here. I talked to Carol Chen—"

"Her daughter nearly joined the Cyclists last year," I explained to Bysshe and Viola.

"*She* said they had a family gathering, like this, and simply talked to her daughter, and she decided she didn't want to be a Cyclist after all." She looked around the table. "So I thought we'd do the same thing with Perdita. I think we should start by explaining the significance of the Liberation and the days of dark oppression that preceded it—"

"*I* think," Viola interrupted, "we should try to talk her into just going off the ammenerol for a few months instead of having the shunt removed. If she comes. Which she won't."

"Why not?"

"Would you? I mean, it's like the Inquisition. Her sitting here while all of us 'explain' at her. Perdita may be crazy, but she's not stupid."

"It's hardly the Inquisition," Mother said. She looked anxiously past me toward the door. "I'm sure Perdita—" She stopped, stood up, and plunged off suddenly through the asparagus.

I turned around, half expecting Perdita with light-up lips or a full-body tattoo, but I couldn't see through the leaves. I pushed at the branches.

"Is it Perdita?" Viola said, leaning forward.

I peered around the mulberry bush. "Oh, my God," I said.

It was my mother-in-law, wearing a black abaya and a silk yarmulke. She swept toward us through a pumpkin patch, robes billowing and eyes flashing. Mother hurried in her wake of trampled radishes, looking daggers at me.

I turned them on Viola. "It's your grandmother Karen," I said accusingly. "You told me you didn't get through to her."

"I didn't," she said. "Twidge, sit up straight. And put your slate down."

There was an ominous rustling in the rose arbor, as of leaves shrinking back in terror, and my mother-in-law arrived.

"Karen!" I said, trying to sound pleased. "What on earth are you doing here? I thought you were in Baghdad."

"I came back as soon as I got Viola's message," she said, glaring at everyone in turn. "Who's this?" she demanded, pointing at Bysshe. "Viola's new live-in?"

"No!" Bysshe said, looking horrified.

"This is my law clerk, Mother," I said. "Bysshe Adams-Hardy."

"Twidge, why aren't you in school?"

"I *am*," Twidge said. "I'm remoting." She held up her slate. "See? Math."

"I see," she said, turning to glower at me. "It's a serious enough matter to require my great-grandchild's being pulled out of school *and* the hiring of legal assistance, and yet you didn't deem it important enough to notify *me*. Of course, you *never* tell me anything, Traci."

She swirled herself into the end chair, sending leaves and sweet-pea blossoms flying and decapitating the broccoli centerpiece. "I didn't get Viola's cry for help until yesterday. Viola, you should never leave messages with Hassim. His English is virtually nonexistent. I had to get him to hum me your ring. I recognized your signature, but the phones were out, so I flew home. In the middle of negotiations, I might add."

"How *are* negotiations going, Grandma Karen?" Viola asked.

"They *were* going extremely well. The Israelis have given the Palestinians half of Jerusalem, and they've agreed to time-share the Golan Heights." She turned to glare momentarily at me. "*They* know the importance of communication." She turned back to Viola. "So why are they picking on you, Viola? Don't they like your new live-in?"

"I am *not* her live-in," Bysshe protested.

I have often wondered how on earth my mother-in-law became a mediator and what she does in all those negotiation sessions with Serbs and Catholics and North and South Koreans and Protestants and Croats. She takes sides, jumps to conclusions, misinterprets everything you say, refuses to listen. And yet she talked South Africa into a Mandelan government and would probably get the Palestinians to observe Yom Kippur. Maybe she just bullies everyone into submission. Or maybe they have to band together to protect themselves against her.

Bysshe was still protesting. "I never even met Viola till today. I've only talked to her on the phone a couple of times."

"You must have done something," Karen said to Viola. "They're obviously out for your blood."

"Not mine," Viola said. "Perdita's. She's joined the Cyclists."

"The Cyclists? I left the West Bank negotiations because you don't approve of Perdita joining a biking club? How am I supposed to explain this to the president of Iraq? She will *not* understand, and neither do I. A biking club!"

"The Cyclists do not ride bicycles," Mother said.

"They menstruate," Twidge said.

There was a dead silence of at least a minute, and I thought, It's finally happened. My mother-in-law and I are actually going to be on the same side of a family argument.

"All this fuss is over Perdita's having her shunt removed?" Karen said finally. "She's of age, isn't she? And this is obviously a case where personal sovereignty applies. You should know that, Traci. After all, you're a judge."

I should have known it was too good to be true.

"You mean you approve of her setting back the Liberation twenty years?" Mother said.

"I hardly think it's that serious," Karen said. "There are anti-shunt groups in the Middle East, too, you know, but no one takes them seriously. Not even the Iraqis, and they still wear the veil."

"Perdita is taking them seriously."

Karen dismissed Perdita with a wave of her black sleeve. "They're a trend, a fad. Like microskirts. Or those dreadful electronic eyebrows. A few women wear silly fashions like that for a little while, but you don't see women as a whole giving up pants or going back to wearing hats."

"But Perdita . . ." Viola said.

"If Perdita wants to have her period, I say let her. Women functioned perfectly well without shunts for thousands of years."

Mother brought her fist down on the table. "Women also functioned *perfectly well* with concubinage, cholera, and corsets," she said, emphasizing each word with her fist. "But that is no reason to take them on voluntarily, and I have no intention of allowing Perdita—"

"Speaking of Perdita, where is the poor child?" Karen said.

"She'll be here any minute," Mother said. "I invited her to lunch so we could discuss this with her."

"Ha!" Karen said. "So you could browbeat her into changing her mind, you mean. Well, I have no intention of collaborating with you. *I* intend to listen to the poor thing's point of view with interest and an open mind. Respect, that's the key word, and one you all seem to have forgotten. Respect and common courtesy."

A barefoot young woman wearing a flowered smock and a red scarf tied around her left arm came up to the table with a sheaf of pink folders.

"It's about time," Karen said, snatching one of the folders away from her. "Your service here is dreadful. I've been sitting here ten minutes." She snapped the folder open. "I don't suppose you have Scotch."

"My name is Evangeline," the young woman said. "I'm Perdita's docent." She took the folder away from Karen. "She wasn't able to join you for lunch, but she asked me to come in her place and explain the Cyclist philosophy to you."

She sat down in the wicker chair next to me.

"The Cyclists are dedicated to freedom," she said. "Freedom from artificiality, freedom from body-controlling drugs and hormones, freedom from the male patriarchy that attempts to impose them on us. As you probably already know, we do not wear shunts."

She pointed to the red scarf around her arm. "Instead, we wear this as a badge of our freedom and our femaleness. I'm wearing it today to announce that my time of fertility has come."

"We had that, too," Mother said, "only we wore it on the back of our skirts."

I laughed.

The docent glared at me. "Male domination of women's bodies began long before the so-called 'Liberation,' with government regulation of abortion and fetal rights, scientific control of fertility, and finally the development of ammenerol, which eliminated the reproductive cycle altogether. This was all part of a carefully planned takeover of women's bodies, and by extension, their identities, by the male patriarchal regime."

"What an interesting point of view!" Karen said enthusiastically.

It certainly was. In point of fact, ammenerol hadn't been invented to eliminate menstruation at all. It had been developed for shrinking malignant tumors, and its uterine-lining-absorbing properties had only been discovered by accident.

"Are you trying to tell us," Mother said, "that men forced shunts on women? We had to *fight* everyone to get ammenerol approved by the FDA!"

It was true. What surrogate mothers and anti-abortionists and the fetal rights issue had failed to do in uniting women, the prospect of not having to menstruate did. Women had organized rallies, petitions, elected senators, passed amendments, been excommunicated, and gone to jail, all in the name of Liberation.

"Men were *against* it," Mother said, getting rather red in the face. "And the religious right and the tampon manufacturers, and the Catholic Church—"

"They knew they'd have to allow women priests," Viola said.

"Which they did," I said.

"The Liberation hasn't freed you," the docent said loudly. "Except from the natural rhythms of your life, the very wellspring of your femaleness."

She leaned over and picked a daisy that was growing under the table. "We in the Cyclists celebrate the onset of our menses and rejoice in our bodies," she said, holding the daisy up. "Whenever a Cyclist comes into blossom, as we call it, she is honored with flowers and poems and songs. Then we join hands and tell what we like best about our menses."

"Water retention," I said.

"Or lying in bed with a heating pad for three days a month," Mother said.

"*I* think I like the anxiety attacks best," Viola said. "When I went off the ammenerol, so I could have Twidge, I'd have these days where I was convinced the space station was going to fall on me."

A middle-aged woman in overalls and a straw hat had come over while Viola was talking and was standing next to Mother's chair. "I had these mood swings," she said. "One minute I'd feel cheerful and the next like Lizzie Borden."

"Who's Lizzie Borden?" Twidge asked.

"She killed her parents," Bysshe said. "With an ax."

Karen and the docent glared at both of them. "Aren't you supposed to be working on your math, Twidge?" Karen said.

"I've always wondered if Lizzie Borden had PMS," Viola said, "and that was why—"

"No," Mother said. "It was having to live before tampons and ibuprofen. An obvious case of justifiable homicide."

"I hardly think this sort of levity is helpful," Karen said, glowering at everyone.

"Are you our waitress?" I asked the straw-hatted woman hastily.

"Yes," she said, producing a slate from her overalls pocket.

"Do you serve wine?" I asked.

"Yes. Dandelion, cowslip, and primrose."

"We'll take them all."

"A bottle of each?"

"For now. Unless you have them in kegs."

"Our specials today are watermelon salad and *chou-fleur gratiné*," she said, smiling at everyone. Karen and the docent did not smile back. "You handpick your own cauliflower from the patch up front. The floratarian special is sautéed lily buds with marigold butter."

There was a temporary truce while everyone ordered. "I'll have the sweet peas," the docent said, "and a glass of rose water."

Bysshe leaned over to Viola. "I'm sorry I sounded so horrified when your grandmother asked if I was your live-in," he said.

"That's okay," Viola said. "Grandma Karen can be pretty scary."

"I just didn't want you to think I didn't like you. I do. Like you, I mean."

"Don't they have soyburgers?" Twidge asked.

As soon as the waitress left, the docent began passing out the pink folders she'd brought with her. "These will explain the working philosophy of the Cyclists," she said, handing me one, "along with practical information on the menstrual cycle." She handed Twidge one.

"It looks just like those books we used to get in junior high," Mother said, looking at hers. "*A Special Gift*, they were called, and they had all these pictures of girls with pink ribbons in their hair, playing tennis and smiling. Blatant misrepresentation."

She was right. There was even the same drawing of the fallopian tubes I remembered from my middle school movie, a drawing that had always reminded me of *Alien* in the early stages.

"Oh, yuck," Twidge said. "This is disgusting."

"Do your math," Karen said.

Bysshe looked sick. "Did women really *do* this stuff?"

The wine arrived, and I poured everyone a large glass. The docent pursed her lips disapprovingly and shook her head. "The Cyclists do not use the artificial stimulants or hormones that the male patriarchy has forced on women to render them docile and subservient."

"How long do you menstruate?" Twidge asked.

"Forever," Mother said.

"Four to six days," the docent said. "It's there in the booklet."

"No, I mean, your whole life or what?"

"A woman has her menarche at twelve years old on the average and ceases menstruating at age fifty-five."

"I had my first period at eleven," the waitress said, setting a bouquet down in front of me. "At school."

"I had my last one on the day the FDA approved ammenerol," Mother said.

"Three hundred and sixty-five divided by twenty-eight," Twidge said, writing on her slate. "Times forty-three years." She looked up. "That's five hundred and fifty-nine periods."

"That can't be right," Mother said, taking the slate away from her. "It's at least five thousand."

"And they all start on the day you leave on a trip," Viola said.

"Or get married," the waitress said.

Mother began writing on the slate. I took advantage of the cease-fire to pour everyone some more dandelion wine.

Mother looked up from the slate. "Do you realize with a period of five days, you'd be menstruating for nearly three thousand days? That's over eight solid years."

"And in between there's PMS," the waitress said, delivering flowers.

"What's PMS?" Twidge asked.

"Premenstrual syndrome was the name the male medical establishment fabricated for the natural variation in hormonal levels that signals the onset of menstruation," the docent said. "This mild and entirely normal fluctuation was exaggerated by men into a debility." She looked at Karen for confirmation.

"I used to cut my hair," Karen said.

The docent looked uneasy.

"Once I chopped off one whole side," Karen went on. "Bob had to hide the scissors every month. And the car keys. I'd start to cry every time I hit a red light."

"Did you swell up?" Mother asked, pouring Karen another glass of dandelion wine.

"I looked just like Orson Welles."

"Who's Orson Welles?" Twidge asked.

"Your comments reflect the self-loathing thrust on you by the patriarchy," the docent said. "Men have brainwashed women into thinking menstruation is evil and unclean. Women even called their menses 'the curse' because they accepted men's judgment."

"I called it the curse because I thought a witch must have laid a curse on me," Viola said. "Like in *Sleeping Beauty*."

Everyone looked at her.

"Well, I did," she said. "It was the only reason I could think of for such an awful thing happening to me." She handed the folder back to the docent. "It still is."

"I think you were awfully brave," Bysshe said to Viola, "going off the ammenerol to have Twidge."

"It was awful," Viola said. "You can't imagine."

Mother sighed. "When I got my period, I asked my mother if Annette had it, too."

"Who's Annette?" Twidge said.

"A Mouseketeer," Mother said and added, at Twidge's uncomprehending look. "On TV."

"High-rez," Viola said.

"*The Mickey Mouse Club*," Mother said.

"There was a high-rezzer called *The Mickey Mouse Club*?" Twidge said incredulously.

"They were days of dark oppression in many ways," I said.

Mother glared at me. "Annette was every young girl's ideal," she said to Twidge. "Her hair was curly, she had actual breasts, her pleated skirt was always pressed, and I could not imagine that she could have anything so *messy* and undignified. Mr. Disney would never have allowed it. And if Annette didn't have one, I wasn't going to have one either. So I asked my mother—"

"What did she say?" Twidge cut in.

"She said every woman had periods," Mother said. "So I asked her, 'Even the Queen of England?' And she said, 'Even the Queen.'"

"Really?" Twidge said. "But she's so old!"

"She isn't having it now," the docent said irritatedly. "I told you, menopause occurs at age fifty-five."

"And then you have hot flashes," Karen said, "and osteoporosis and so much hair on your upper lip you look like Mark Twain."

"Who's—" Twidge said.

"You are simply reiterating negative male propaganda," the docent interrupted, looking very red in the face.

"You know what I've always wondered?" Karen said, leaning conspiratorially close to Mother. "If Maggie Thatcher's menopause was responsible for the Falklands War."

"Who's Maggie Thatcher?" Twidge said.

The docent, who was now as red in the face as her scarf, stood up. "It is clear there is no point in trying to talk to you. You've all been completely brainwashed by the male patriarchy." She began grabbing up her folders. "You're blind, all of you! You don't even see that you're victims of a male conspiracy to deprive you of your biological identity, of your very womanhood. The Liberation wasn't a liberation at all. It was only another kind of slavery."

"Even if that were true," I said, "even if it had been a conspiracy to bring us under male domination, it would have been worth it."

"She's right, you know," Karen said to Mother. "Traci's absolutely right. There are some things worth giving up anything for, even your freedom, and getting rid of your period is definitely one of them."

"Victims!" the docent shouted. "You've been stripped of your femininity, and you don't even care!" She stomped out, destroying several squash and a row of gladiolas in the process.

"You know what I hated most before the Liberation?" Karen said, pouring the last of the dandelion wine into her glass. "Sanitary belts."

"And those cardboard tampon applicators," Mother said.

"I'm never going to join the Cyclists," Twidge said.

"Good," I said.

"Can I have dessert?"

I called the waitress over, and Twidge ordered sugared violets. "Anyone else want dessert?" I asked. "Or more primrose wine?"

"I think it's wonderful the way you're trying to help your sister," Bysshe said, leaning close to Viola.

"And those Modess ads," Mother said. "You remember, with those glamorous women in satin brocade evening dresses and long white gloves, and below the picture was written, 'Modess, because...' I thought Modess was a perfume."

Karen giggled. "I thought it was a brand of *champagne*!"

"I don't think we'd better have any more wine," I said.

The phone started singing the minute I got to my chambers the next morning, the universal ring.

"Karen went back to Iraq, didn't she?" I asked Bysshe.

"Yeah," he said. "Viola said there was some snag over whether to put Disneyland on the West Bank or not."

"When did Viola call?"

Bysshe looked sheepish. "I had breakfast with her and Twidge this morning."

"Oh." I picked up the phone. "It's probably Mother with a plan to kidnap Perdita. Hello?"

"This is Evangeline, Perdita's docent," the voice on the phone said. "I hope you're happy. You've bullied Perdita into surrendering to the enslaving male patriarchy."

"I have?" I said.

"You've obviously employed mind control, and I want you to know we intend to file charges." She hung up.

The phone rang again immediately, another universal. "What is the good of signatures when no one ever uses them?" I said, and picked up the phone.

"Hi, Mom," Perdita said. "I thought you'd want to know I've changed my mind about joining the Cyclists."

"Really?" I said, trying not to sound jubilant.

"I found out they wear this red scarf thing on their arm. It covers up Sitting Bull's horse."

"That is a problem," I said.

"Well, that's not all. My docent told me about your lunch. Did Grandma Karen really tell you you were right?"

"Yes."

"Gosh! I didn't believe that part. Well, anyway, my docent said you wouldn't listen to her about how great menstruating is, that you all kept talking about the negative aspects of it, like bloating and cramps and crabbiness, and I said, 'What are cramps?' and she said, 'Menstrual bleeding frequently causes headaches and discomfort,' and I said, 'Bleeding? Nobody ever said anything about bleeding!' Why didn't you tell me there was blood involved, Mother?"

I had, but I felt it wiser to keep silent.

"And you didn't say a word about its being painful. And all the hormone fluctuations! Anybody'd have to be crazy to want to go through that when they didn't have to! How did you stand it before the Liberation?"

"They were days of dark oppression," I said.

"I *guess*! Well, anyway, I quit and now my docent is really mad. But I told her it was a case of personal sovereignty, and she has to respect my decision. I'm still going to become a floratarian, though, and I don't want you to try to talk me out of it."

"I wouldn't dream of it," I said.

"You know, this whole thing is really your fault, Mom! If you'd told me about the pain part in the first place, none of this would have happened. Viola's right! You never tell us *anything*!"

Rowing

Anne Sexton

A story, a story!
(Let it go. Let it come.)
I was stamped out like a Plymouth fender
into this world.
First came the crib
with its glacial bars.
Then dolls
and the devotion to their plastic mouths.
Then there was school,
the little straight rows of chairs,
blotting my name over and over,
but undersea all the time,
a stranger whose elbows wouldn't work.
Then there was life
with its cruel houses
and people who seldom touched—
though touch is all—
but I grew,
like a pig in a trenchcoat I grew,
and then there were many strange apparitions,
and nagging rain, the sun turning into poison
and all of that, saws working through my heart,
but I grew, I grew,
and God was there like an island I had not rowed to,
still ignorant of Him, my arms and my legs worked,
and I grew, I grew,
I wore rubies and bought tomatoes

Anne Sexton

and now, in my middle age,
about nineteen in the head I'd say,
I am rowing, I am rowing
though the oarlocks stick and are rusty
and the sea blinks and rolls
like a worried eyeball,
but I am rowing, I am rowing,
though the wind pushes me back
and I know that that island will not be perfect,
it will have the flaws of life,
the absurdities of the dinner table,
but there will be a door
and I will open it
and I will get rid of the rat inside of me,
the gnawing pestilential rat.
God will take it with his two hands
and embrace it.

As the African says:
This is my tale which I have told,
if it be sweet, if it be not sweet,
take somewhere else and let some return to me.
This story ends with me still rowing.

Family

The five selections in this section share a strong focus on family relationships. The featured writers explore and reimagine the connections among a wide range of family members—children, parents, siblings, spouses—while paying particular attention to the lifelong impact of these crucial relationships.

In her poem "I Go Back to May 1937" (1987), **Sharon Olds** (1942–) presents a speaker picturing her parents at their respective college gates, about to graduate—and considers what, if anything, the speaker should say to them about their future lives.

Pediatrician **Perri Klass** (1958–) writes both fiction and nonfiction. In her story "Freedom Fighter" (2001), she portrays two female friends who reunite for a road trip and confront the different choices each has made about career and children.

"My Father's Chinese Wives" (1994), a short story by **Sandra Tsing Loh** (1962–), describes the sometimes surprising effects of a father's late-life remarriage to a mail-order bride from his native China.

In her story "Stories Don't Have Endings" (1989), **Janice Gould** (1949–) interweaves her narrator's memories of her Maidu childhood, sexuality, and bereavement to explore the connections between a family's past, present, and future. What constitutes a family, and how that evolves, stands as a central theme in Gould's piece.

"The Box House and the Snow" is a 2006 short story by Panamanian American writer **Cristina Henríquez** (1977–). When a family home is inundated during a rare snowfall, the subsequent media attention and perceived threat to the physical structure of the house stoke tensions between a father, mother, and daughter.

I Go Back to May 1937

Sharon Olds

I see them standing at the formal gates of their colleges,
I see my father strolling out
under the ochre sandstone arch, the
red tiles glinting like bent
plates of blood behind his head, I
see my mother with a few light books at her hip
standing at the pillar made of tiny bricks,
the wrought-iron gate still open behind her, its
sword-tips aglow in the May air,
they are about to graduate, they are about to get married,
they are kids, they are dumb, all they know is they are
innocent, they would never hurt anybody.
I want to go up to them and say Stop,
don't do it—she's the wrong woman,
he's the wrong man, you are going to do things
you cannot imagine you would ever do,
you are going to do bad things to children,
you are going to suffer in ways you have not heard of,
you are going to want to die. I want to go
up to them there in the late May sunlight and say it,
her hungry pretty face turning to me,
her pitiful beautiful untouched body,
his arrogant handsome face turning to me,
his pitiful beautiful untouched body,
but I don't do it. I want to live. I
take them up like the male and female

Sharon Olds

    paper dolls and bang them together
    at the hips, like chips of flint, as if to
    strike sparks from them, I say
    Do what you are going to do, and I will tell about it.

Freedom Fighter

Perri Klass

Jan and Marcie go away for the weekend. Two women, friends since college twenty years ago, sit in a car driving north out of Boston. One of them is so pregnant that it's her last chance to go away for a weekend; in another week, she comments to her friend, she'll be in that ninth month, that month when you aren't supposed to go too far from the hospital. "Well, you should know," her friend replies, a reference to the fact that the pregnant one is also an obstetrician, a professional giver of advice to the pregnant.

"Well, you know," Jan, the pregnant one, says honestly, "there's always a certain amount of do as I say, not as I do." The truth is, she is already slightly over that borderline; it's a tiny bit reckless to be going out of town. But this is her third baby, a third safe and boringly uneventful pregnancy (from her professional obstetric point of view). Jan's babies don't come early; she expects this one to arrive, as the other two did, in the week after the due date—and her due date, needless to say, is professionally accurate. So it's just a theoretical recklessness, really; Jan knows perfectly well that she will trundle her pregnant belly back to Boston at the end of the weekend and she and her husband, Alan, will wait out another four weeks or so.

"Your patients must look at you and think, That woman sure knows what she's talking about," says Marcie, her friend, not pregnant, not planning ever to be pregnant again. "Do as she says, do as she does, you're all in this together." *But not me, not ever again* is what her voice suggests. There they are, the two of them, like some bad movie about women's choices: Marcie who got pregnant and dropped out of college and married and divorced and lived hard and poor, Jan who plodded on through medical school and married at almost thirty and will soon have three children spaced at neat three-year intervals, while Marcie, her grownup son now off in college, is rich and successful and busy with love affairs. "I would think it would be excellent for business," Marcie says. "You're a walking billboard for your own profession."

In fact, Jan's patients all comment on it when Jan walks into the room. "Doctor, I didn't know you were expecting!" "You're going to have a baby," they say, or just, "When are you due?"

She smiles. She nods. She does their pelvic exams, leaning forward over her belly, which is the largest thing about her these days.

"So is this your first?" they ask, these clinic mothers, who mostly had their firsts before the age of twenty—and sometimes their seconds as well. Jan cannot help it, she thinks of this as their unconscious but devastating tribute to class distinctions, to the fact that she is obviously in her late thirties but without makeup, with her hair cut short and left in its natural state and color, even her clothes, these professional natural fabrics. When they look at her, these mothers see an overgrown yuppie schoolgirl, ready now for that carefully planned, long-deferred first baby.

"My third," she says, with a certain smugness. And though they smile, for the most part they lose interest there and then. *Oh,* Jan imagines them thinking with bored familiarity, *why, she's one of us after all—probably doesn't even use birth control.* But how dare they sum her up like this, when she has spent more than a decade working on a good but stressed marriage (her job, his job, the kids, all the women's magazine problems)—how dare anyone at all take Jan and Alan and their third baby for granted? The third baby; even her parents seem to have lost interest. And after all she's done for them, too—the MD, the two perfect grandchildren. How dare they face the prospect of a third with such matter-of-fact, here-we-go-again equanimity?

It feels good to be moving, to be in motion away from her family, her children, her parents, her patients, her life. Even away from Alan, just for a little while. Jan leans back and closes her eyes and pats her pregnant belly, and thinks about how often she has imagined running away with her belly, with her baby, how often she has wanted to escape with this pregnancy out of the noisy, busy matrix of her life.

Evenings at home, Jan often sits on the couch and talks to the third. Plans their elopement. We'll run away together to someplace where the scenery is strange and the topography is as new to me as it and everything else will be to you. The Southwest, the Yukon, the Low Country. Where seldom is heard a discouraging word. And there I'll hold you in my arms and turn slowly around beneath a strange lone cactus, a towering redwood, a tree dripping Spanish moss. And there I'll sit in a rocking chair on the porch or before the crackling fire and put you to my breast. My love.

So this will have to do. A weekend with Marcie, who is not pregnant and does not plan ever to be pregnant again. Who is unmarried, whose son is in college, an almost unimaginable stage now for Jan, whose children are still young. Carry me far away, Marcie. Talk to me of things I know nothing about, and listen while I draw to your attention the wonder of my own adventure. I want to appreciate you, and I want to be appreciated. And I want a little fun before the oxytocin kicks in and the contractions start and the prolactin starts me lactating and I become once again the creature of the hormones I know so much about. A little fun—is that too much to ask?

"I wish we had a convertible," Jan and Marcie will say to each other, any number of times. What they actually have is Jan's family Volvo, nice and reliable in a crash but lumbering along emptily behind the two of them, two ladies in the front seat of a station wagon. It's Jan's car, but Marcie prefers to drive and Jan prefers to lean back and be driven, and as she is driven along, she fiddles with the radio, switching back and forth between two oldies stations, and when she happens to hit a song about cars, driving, racing, she turns up the volume and they sing along. "Little Deuce Coupe," "Mustang Sally," "Oh Lord, won't you buy me . . ."

This is one of the things you can't remember from one pregnancy to the next—like the feeling of labor, Jan reflects as Marcie switches lanes abruptly, cutting off a red Jeep Cherokee. This sense of an almost full-size baby packed in there and elbowing, this peculiar intimacy, like two large adults trying to sleep together on a camp cot on a hot night. Every move this baby makes, Jan is on the receiving end—a positional wiggle, an exuberant cascade of kicks. She lies back in her seat, free to incline it without having her children yell their complaints from the back. The baby has shifted this past week, fallen slightly down and forward, and Jan has to lean backwards when she walks. Not so easy on the ice, but it's spring; the Boston winter is over, there's no more ice on the sidewalks. And even when she's not pregnant, Jan of course does not go to work in high-heeled shoes, not with those professional natural fabrics.

Secretly, in her own mind, Jan is what maybe everyone is everywhere, all the time: a rebel, an iconoclast, a strange and estranged and angry freedom fighter. *If you knew me really,* she believes, when she stops to think about it, *you would be shocked. By my true fantasies, my true preferences, my true beliefs.* I cannot quite put a name to those beliefs of hers, cannot quite explain why she feels entitled to this certainty that she is something rich and strange.

So look: she is having a third baby; her body has been overtaken, as bodies get overtaken, especially in the third trimester, with the longings and weight and movements of an alien other. It is, believe me, a wanted, planned, discussed, and deliberate pregnancy. So why does her abdomen give her this smug and yet slightly angry feeling that she is a rebel, an infiltrator, a guerilla? Why does she think that completing the triad of the 1950s TV family (think *My Three Sons,* think either half of the Brady Bunch), is a revolutionary gesture?

Speaking of revolutionary gestures, look at her now. Not the Brady Bunch but rather Thelma and Louise, says her husband, with what seems to be genuine indulgence but could also be interpreted as deep forbearance, the forbearance of a man who does not actually think that it is fair and fifty-fifty to leave him home with two children while she takes her stomach off for a long weekend on the road with an old girlfriend. But Alan is a nice guy, and of course he recognizes, as how can he not, that she is the one shlepping the stomach for nine months, not to mention throwing up in the morning and all the rest, though, respecting his greater delicacy as the non-doctor who doesn't really want to know too many details, she hasn't mentioned the stress incontinence or the constipation. Go ahead, Alan tells her, as magnanimous as a man is when he knows that all his wife's female friends will consider him model, will reproach their own husbands with comparisons. Go ahead and take your weekend on the road.

Marcie is in from out of town, passing through Boston on her way to New York. It was her suggestion, a little hesitant, maybe a little bit of a challenge of the I-don't-imagine-you'd-be-able-to-do-this-but-it-would-sure-be-fun variety. Yes, Jan thought, it would sure be fun. And she began to fantasize about exactly this scene, her very pregnant self escaping, just for a couple of days, from all the rules and boundaries of her complicated, responsible life. Then too, of course, proving to Marcie that even pregnant with her third child, she, Jan, is still something of a free agent. Still capable of a small deviation. Once again the way two friends can polarize each other: I represent a straight-arrow career and working on your marriage and young children at home and one more on the way; you stand for a troubled romantic life, a struggle to raise a child all alone, that child now in college and your business really taking off. They entertain each other, Jan and Marcie, with stories from their lives, but they also tiptoe round; Jan does not come down too heavily with her meticulously scheduled bourgeois domesticity, Marcie does not say, Thank God it's not me, starting over with a new baby, just when I have so much else to do.

Jan and Marcie stop to do some shopping. As they drive into the Outlet Capital of New England, the rain starts to fall. Marcie picks a parking lot almost at random, and the two of them stroll together through aisles of household goods, Scandinavian ski sweaters, glossy shoes. The stores are lumped together into mini-malls with no obvious connections, and they are peopled by serious shoppers, groups of women off the big tour buses, down from Canada, up from Connecticut, which sit idling in the parking lots. FULLY AIR CONDITIONED, the buses announce on this chilly spring day. RESTROOM EQUIPPED FOR YOUR CONVENIENCE. COMFORT COACHES WITH VIDEO SCREENS to take you shopping. Jan watches a woman pile up six or seven children's snowsuits and finds herself imagining the troop of children, neatly arranged stepwise, smallest to largest, waiting at home.

Guiltily, she tries to stir her own interest: a snowsuit for Matthew, age three and a half, big enough for next winter? You'll never find it at a better price. But she cannot imagine buying it now, for a winter that seems so impossibly remote, far on the other side of a long hot summer to come, on the other side of this baby, for heaven's sake. When winter comes, she will have a six-month-old. How can this be? Anyway, surely one of Abby's old snowsuits must be around somewhere, the right size for Matthew? Matthew rampages briefly through her mind, full speed ahead. A snowsuit, Mom? Are you kidding? What about a Ninja sword? For Abby she does not even consider buying a winter coat; Abby is six and reserves the right to make all important clothing decisions for herself.

Jan sees Marcie watching her watch the woman with all the snowsuits. Is Marcie waiting for her to start in on dreary talk about Matthew's size and Abby's hand-me-downs?

"Let's hit the lingerie shop," she tells Marcie firmly.

Is there something a little comic, a little tasteless, about a hugely pregnant woman sorting through the racks of teddies and merry widows and camisoles, fingering the silk and satin? Jan accompanies Marcie into the no-frills communal dressing room firmly resolved to try nothing on. She may buy herself a cotton flannel nightgown, but then again she may not, and no trying on is needed. But there in the dressing room is a gaggle of high school girlfriends egging one another on: Try the one with the super pushup bra built in—try it in black—no, try it in red!

A male name is invoked: what Joey D. will think of that red super pushup number! All the girls scream. Marcie, slipping into a sleeveless saffron silk gown, regards them with some interest.

"Do I detect the notes of an impending ceremonial loss of virginity?" she asks Jan very quietly.

"Really?" Jan looks the group over; her professional bias, of course, not to say sampling error, but to her they all look old enough to be her patients—that is, old enough to be sexually active.

"Only one way to find out," Marcie murmurs. She slips the matching saffron robe over her gown and regards herself in a poorly lit three-way mirror. "I like a nice feather trim—tickles you while you sleep" is all she says as Jan looks at her well-exercised body with envy. Jan can barely imagine what it would be like to try on an article of clothing as a lark, to deck yourself out and admire the result. In a month she will have this baby, and then, of course, she gets to have her body back.

Marcie, in her slinky saffron silk and feathers, turns her back to the three-way mirror and faces the group of high school girls. "So, ladies," she says pleasantly, "special occasion coming up? Joey D. himself, as it might be?"

The girls stare at her, blank-faced, all giggling stopped. Marcie shrugs. "I myself have two lovers in two different cities these days," she remarks to Jan.

"Like an airline pilot," Jan offers. "Is it as much fun as it sounds?"

"You'd be good at it—you like schedules," Marcie says.

No, I don't particularly like schedules, Jan wants to say. Or rather, *Hey, there's more to me than schedules and stomach.*

The high school girls are dressed again in their own clothes, and are giggling again, shaking with suppressed laughter, barely polite enough to wait till they are out of the dressing room to start in—the outfit with the feathers! the two lovers like an airline pilot! And off they go.

Jan is hurt by the "you like schedules" and feels silly to be hurt. She checks out a crowded rack of assorted items at the back of the dressing room, holding up clothes that strike her as particularly ornate. "Can you imagine?" she asks, holding up against her something that looks like a bathing suit made entirely of black lace with emerald-green ribbon garters hanging down from it.

She finds a robe, a silk kimono, crowded among velour gowns with zippers and hoods on one end of the rack. She holds the robe out to Marcie, who reaches and takes the two sleeves in her hands as if to dance with it. Midnight-blue silk with flocks of gray geese flying across it; Marcie wraps the robe over her saffron ensemble. She is five foot eight, but the robe puddles on the floor at her feet. Good, she nods. "This one's a keeper." Obscurely, Jan feels forgiven.

The sales clerk is apologetic when Marcie goes to make her purchase: the robe shouldn't really be here at all. It's a man's robe, as you can see—she points to the extra inches of fabric. It was supposed to go to our other store, the one in the Bargain Barn complex. I can show you some very nice silk robes—

But Marcie pays cash. A lot of cash; even after all the discounts, the robe costs almost two hundred dollars. Marcie actually has hundred-dollar bills in her wallet; Jan looks on, impressed. For years and years Marcie lived on the edge financially. Never any child support from the brief and bad marriage that produced her son. Some really historically terrible jobs: night hallway monitor in a residential home for emotionally disturbed teenagers, proofreader of discount coupon books. Jan used to wonder about offering money, not that she had a great deal herself during those years. Finally she did offer, one difficult winter when Marcie's son had a series of ear infections and they had no health insurance, and Marcie said no but let Jan mail her sample antibiotics pilfered from the hospital supply. Jan actually felt more uncomfortable about that than she would have felt about sending a check, but she mailed off several care packages of powdered amoxicillin samples. She wonders now whether Marcie even remembers this, or whether it was just one more penny-saving exigency in a life that was nothing but scrimping and trying to get by. Certainly for years, when Marcie would call, Jan tried always to say, This is a bad time, I'm busy, can I call you back in a little while? Never actually saying, Let it be my nickel. It's kind of a trip now, watching Marcie with her bankroll, especially since she's still wearing the robe.

Marcie works as a consultant to hotel restaurants. Flies all over the country, sometimes all over the world. Stays free in any city she goes to. This is a business she sort of lucked into five years ago; to Jan, on the phone (her nickel), it sounded like yet another not-very-promising job. *Yes, sure, it'll be interesting.* And then eventually Marcie went into partnership with the guy who founded the business, and then last year he retired and she bought him out. Jan cannot help being impressed with the serendipity of it all; she herself does a job that required some pronounced early-on decision making—set your goals and work step by step to achieve them. Marcie had no idea that hotel consulting was her destiny, and look at her now.

Indeed, look at her now. Jan sits across the table from her oldest friend as they eat hamburgers. In answer to a casual question about how her appetite has been affected by her pregnancy, Jan realizes with stricken self-consciousness that she has run on far too much.

Nausea the first trimester, still some heartburn, can't tolerate cruciferous vegetables very well. Marcie looks pained, and who can blame her? Actually, what this baby likes is ice cream. Evenings, Jan allows herself a little dish, her calcium, her reward for gaining less weight this time than with either of the other two, for going to the gym right into the second trimester, until she finally gave it up with a sigh of relief that lasted for weeks. After the ice cream she leans back to give the baby more scope, and the calisthenics begin. Without benefit of exercise machines, the baby works each muscle group.

"How's Ricky?" Jan asks, determined to turn the conversation back. I talk your ears off about mine; now tell me about yours. Remember when he had the ear infections and I would mail you the drug samples?

"He's fine." Said with a certain firmness, as if period, end of sentence.

"He's still liking college?"

"College is fine."

"What's he majoring in again?"

Marcie looks her in the eye. "I don't really want to talk about him. I know he wouldn't like to think I was using his life as fodder for my friendships."

Jan, stung and more than a little bit hurt, can only nod emphatically.

Back in the car, heading north again, she thinks about why she feels so smartly put in her place. The truth is, she would like to talk—she has been waiting, she now feels, for weeks to say various things to Marcie, to take her life apart and examine it and say what she cannot say to her husband and would not say to a friend or colleague who lived nearby. To regard herself and her family with wonder and irony rather than take them for granted and assume that family life is the lot of us all, that you just have to choose between the Volvo station wagon and the minivan. Marcie might shake her head and wonder why Jan is doing this, but Jan would appreciate a little wonder, even a little shock, even a little awe. Maybe it's not *your* revolutionary gesture, but it's a revolutionary gesture nonetheless. When you make radical and sudden changes, that's revolution. Movement, tumult, change.

The baby moves tumultuously inside her, maybe reacting to the hamburger, and Jan closes her eyes.

Jan and Marcie find a place to stay. They've parked in a famously quaint fishing village, prowled the colonially cute main street, and resisted any number of "country" souvenirs, things in the shape of geese or made of gingham. In fact, they've been on a goose quest, inspired by Marcie's new flock-of-geese robe; they've been, as Marcie puts it, exploring the goose motif. Finding goose items everywhere, keeping score, investigating each and every store till one of them finds the goose. It's been a terrific afternoon; they are having a blast. In fact, they say that to each other all afternoon: what a blast. It's drizzling, but only a little. And they find a room in a bed-and-breakfast first crack out of the box, a VACANCY sign right there by the side of the road.

Maude's, the place is called. Not actually Maude's Cozy Nook or anything like that, but that's about the size of it: lace at the windows and an antique teddy bear carefully propped against an old black flatiron on a sea chest. The room has two nice white wooden beds, thick quilts.

Jan thinks about her fantasies of taking this third baby away somewhere—of course, not to someone's antique-filled bed-and-breakfast nook. Getting spit-up on the feather beds. Pushing the antique bear aside to change diapers on the chest. She looks around the room.

"No place I have ever lived has ever looked like this," she says. "Or ever will."

Marcie looks around too, less impressed. "Why would you need so much old lace and Victoriana? Maude is Maude."

"Sometimes I wish that I could have some small arranged space in my life. Some room that looks the way it looks for *effect*, you know?"

When they go walking on the beach that night after supper, the moon is full and low. There are boulders to climb, but Jan can't climb them. Her belly is too big; she's way off balance. She sits down carefully on a rock, and Marcie goes on ahead a little, almost out of sight. Jan draws up her legs, balances deliberately. Thinks briefly of two patients who have been on her mind, reviews her children, the two at home, the one here with her, rubs her now slightly protruding umbilicus, which has been forced out of its refuge by the pressure from inside. Then starts to think of all the things she has to get done Monday. Abby's new shoes for soccer; the plumber about the long-standing leak in the downstairs bathroom so it can maybe get fixed before the new baby comes, so she can maybe discourage the older children from always using the upstairs bathroom.

"Enough!" Jan says it out loud. She belches slightly, a pregnant belch, after the indulgence of too much lobster, too much melted butter. *Here I am on a rock in the moonlight, beside the Atlantic Ocean. Let me be in this moment, just me and my belly. I am a freedom fighter, I am my secret self. Let the salt-filled wind come howling in off the wild Atlantic and sweep over me—anything is possible!* She lumbers to her feet, tilts a little, thinks for one crazy moment she's going right off the boulder. Her well-trained medical mind instantly provides an entire scenario; she lies broken and injured on the wet sand, and then—oh, melodrama—the baby starts to come!

"Need a hand?" Marcie has appeared on the next rock. She stands so well balanced, so sure of her footing. She can even extend a hand, and Jan grips it gratefully, steadying herself.

Jan calls home for the first time. As they stroll back through town, heading for Maude's, inevitably they pass a pay phone. And inevitably Jan thinks with a faint qualm of home and hearth. "Do you mind?" she asks, feeling self-conscious, feeling silly for feeling self-conscious. After all, there is no phone in their bower at Maude's.

As Jan punches in the long series of numbers necessary to call her home number and charge it to her phone card, Marcie gestures: Do you want me to walk on, give you privacy? Jan grimaces no, shakes her head; it's only Alan—who needs privacy? Yet she feels self-conscious, feels like she is playing an unenviable part, obliged to check in, can't be away for twelve hours without calling home. Some freedom fighter.

She imagines a very quick conversation about nothing: I'm on a street corner in Maine, how're you, how're the kids, we're fine, thanks for sending me off. When Alan answers he is preoccupied with some sports event he is watching on television, his own indulgence with the kids in bed and Jan away, and their conversation is indeed brief and functional. But somehow all through that quick conversation, she is most conscious of Marcie's ironic eye. As they set off for the bed-and-breakfast, Jan finds she is tensed, waiting for some patronizing remark.

"Why don't we stop at the convenience store and get cookies?" Marcie says.

"How will Maude feel if we get crumbs on the objets d'art?"

"We won't tell Maude," Marcie says. "We'll lie in our beds and eat cookies and go to sleep without brushing our teeth."

Marcie stops for a hitchhiker. They're driving north, through what is a fairly heavy rain. They lingered over brunch, packed up, moved on with somewhat deliberate aimlessness. Actually, Jan has been rather enjoying the hypnotizing back-and-forth of the windshield wipers, the persistence of the drops drumming on the pane. It's conducive to conversation; as Marcie drives them steadily on, they talk easily about the shapes of their lives. Marcie's fantasy of what she will do if she makes a lot of money in the stock market: live on a boat in the Caribbean, learn to scuba dive. Would you want to stop working? Jan asks, and Marcie says, If I had the money, I'd stop in a minute. Wouldn't you? Well, no, Jan says, or at least she isn't sure. It's all this *stuff* she's accumulated, she goes on, thinking about it as she speaks: the skill with her hands, the training of the brain. It would seem a pity to let go of it, though there's no question it would also mean letting go of a lot of stress—and she begins to tell Marcie about the dreams she has of patients with sudden disasters, about the nights she cannot sleep for thinking and agonizing over a clinical decision made earlier in the day. The Caribbean, did you say, Marcie? Sounds kind of appealing. Just the kind of conversation Jan had imagined, the kind you can have only when you step slightly outside your life.

Then Marcie swerves over onto the shoulder and a very wet young woman is getting into the back seat, stuffing a small backpack in beside her.

"Put on your seat belt," Jan says automatically; that's what she's always saying to the people in that back seat.

"Thank you, ma'am, I surely will." A southern voice, remarkably out of place after all the Yankee accents they've been hearing. Jan turns around to look more closely at this person Marcie has invited into her car. This very wet person. She's a heavyset girl, looks college age, wearing a sodden thick sweater and jeans. Trying to polish her wet glasses on the sweater and getting nowhere, just smearing the lenses. Jan hands her a tissue.

"Thank you, ma'am."

"Are you in school around here?" Marcie asks, and Jan thinks of Marcie's son, far away at college. Understands why Marcie could not pass up a wet young hitchhiker, understands who Marcie was imagining by the side of the road.

"No, ma'am, I'm not in school right now. I've been working down in Lancaster. I surely do appreciate your stopping."

"Where can we take you?" Marcie asks.

"Where are y'all going?"

It turns out she wants to get to Portland, to the bus station. She's left her au pair job and is heading home. She doesn't say why, and they don't ask. Jan suspects that Marcie is determined to see her safely on her way, but why not, Portland is in the direction they are driving anyway.

Their passenger's name is Ellie, and when they stop for coffee and get out of the car, she does a small double take as she sees clearly that Jan is pregnant. And Jan, with her professional eye, sees equally clearly that Ellie is pregnant, though much, much less far along.

"I have to pee," Jan says to her. "When you're pregnant, you have to pee all the time." The girl looks startled.

The diner bathroom holds only one. Jan comes out to find Ellie waiting, pasty faced.

Jan squeezes her pregnant self into the booth across from Marcie, and they sip their coffee.

"Are you okay with taking her into Portland?" Marcie asks, sounding actually a little apologetic.

"Sure." They look up from their heavy white diner cups and smile at each other. It's not so bad to be taking care of someone together, even for a little while.

Ellie slides in beside Marcie, and the waitress swoops down on them. They are the only people in the diner. Ellie's color is a little better, and she is staring at a tall glass case stacked with oversize cakes and pies.

"Want something to eat?" Jan asks. "Our treat." She is thinking about her patients, about people who get pregnant before they can ever plan not to get pregnant. And then about Abby, her smart, confident six-year-old back in Boston.

For Abby's sake, and for Ricky's sake, and maybe even for Ellie's own sake, they insist on treating Ellie: Order whatever you want. A slice of German chocolate cake, a slice of banana cream pie, and a large Diet Pepsi. She gobbles down the food. Her hair is almost dry now, loopy brown tendrils around her pleasant plump face. She looks very, very young—so young, in fact, that finally Jan asks her age.

Ellie looks surprised. "Nineteen next July, ma'am."

"Are your parents going to be okay about having you come home?"

Marcie looks at her in surprise: Why so nosy? What's not to be okay? But Jan does this for a living, talks to girls and young women and not-so-young women about how they feel about being pregnant, about what their parents and boyfriends and husbands will say. *Prenatal care whether you want it or not,* she thinks, watching Ellie stir the remnants of her soda around in the glass with the straw.

"They'll be surprised, that's all. They expected me to stay in this here job until the end of the summer."

"But they have a place for you? They'll . . . take you in?"

"Well, I surely hope so, ma'am."

"Have you been to a doctor?" Jan thinks angrily that probably the au pair job did not include health insurance, whatever else it may have included. Is it possible that this poor girl is running away from a home where she was molested, even raped? You do hear stories.

Ellie is looking down at the table. Her voice is very soft as she answers, "When I get home I will."

Jan can feel her desire to ask more questions. All her customary locutions come to mind: are you in a relationship with the father, is he supportive, do you have a place to take the baby home to? But she does not pursue these questions, any of them. All she says is, "I'm sure you're going to be fine. But you have to take care of yourself, you know."

Ellie begins to sniffle a little, and there are tears at the corners of her eyes. Jan opens her purse, pulls out a tissue. There in the purse she sees a brown plastic drugstore vial: her own prenatal vitamins, the last month's installment. She takes the vial out and hands it over.

"They're vitamins. They're what the doctor will give you at that first appointment. If you take one every day, it will help you take care of yourself. Of your baby too."

Ellie is staring at her in confusion. Marcie is staring at her in confusion. Jan feels more than a little confused herself; she is hardly the type to go passing medications around casually. But Ellie looks at the bottle dubiously for a minute, then opens it and takes out a white torpedo.

Jan leans over and takes one out as well. The two of them swallow their pills in unison.

"Keep the bottle," Jan tells her. "One a day, remember."

Jan conks out. After they finally find the Portland bus station and drop Ellie off, they head north, out of the city.

"I've been there," Marcie says. "Almost nineteen, knocked up, too dumb to spell my own name."

"I hope there's someone waiting for her at the other end of that bus ride."

Marcie honks impatiently at a wavering station wagon. "I tucked a hundred dollars into the front pocket of her backpack. Just in case."

"So at least she gets home with a little money and some prenatal vitamins. She could have done worse."

The station wagon switches into the right lane, and Marcie goes zooming past. "Good Lord!" she says, almost reverently. "How ever can you do all this again?"

Jan thinks with distant affection of her busy home, puttering along without her. Folds her arms around her belly: *No, you are not to prove a point, you are not a complication; you are my little love, my treasure.*

"I've got that afternoon pregnant drowsy feeling."

"Go ahead and sleep. I like the idea of driving your pregnant self northward through the rain. Into the unknown."

Jan reaches over and clasps her friend's shoulder. "Oh, Marce, I'm so glad we did this. What a hoot."

"What a hoot," Marcie agrees. Jan is already falling asleep.

Jan and Marcie look for a hotel room. They've frittered away the rainy afternoon: a brief walk in a wet piny woods, a visit to a pottery store, afternoon tea overlooking a marina. Now Marcie has turned inland, away from the coast road, and they've agreed to settle somewhere for the night. Jan imagines another quaint little bed-and-breakfast; Marcie says maybe a regular motel this time, with a functional shower. Maude had a claw-footed tub only.

But they can't find anyplace. They must already, so quickly, have gotten away from tourist land. No bed-and-breakfast signs, no motels, no nothing. Jan suggests they backtrack, but Marcie says she would hate the feeling of retracing their steps. Instead she takes one determined turn after another, following some instinct that does not appear to be serving her very well.

"Oh well," Jan says, "we could always hit the highway and drive all the way south, be in Boston by midnight."

"Bad idea." Marcie sounds as if she means it. And of course it is a bad idea.

Jan finds herself beginning to gabble, to cover up the marked silence of not finding any hotels, not knowing precisely where they are. "You know, if it was me at home with the kids and Alan away for the weekend, I would feel obliged to stage some kind of special dinner. It's what I always do, like I'm trying to prove what a great job I can do all on my own. Alan doesn't have any of that. He'll probably bring in Chinese takeout and they'll eat right out of the containers. Unless maybe he took them out for the afternoon, if it wasn't this rainy in Boston, and then he'll just take them for burgers or something. You know? He doesn't want me to come home and exclaim over what an amazing performance he put on over the weekend, but I always seem to be trying to impress him, you know what I mean?"

"Maybe that's important to you—impressing people." Marcie's voice is flat. She turns the car sharply onto a small road leading off to the right; no turn signal, no slowing down, no nothing. Another road without any sign of hotels or restaurants.

"It would be important to me right now to find a bathroom," Jan says with as much dignity as she can muster. She is suddenly imagining her life to come, with an infant in her arms, trying to orchestrate a special dinner. The baby crying, the older children squabbling. *What have I done? Why am I here in this car in the middle of nowhere? What am I going back to?*

"A bathroom it is!" There is jubilation in Marcie's voice; a well-illuminated restaurant is coming up on the left. The Ponderosa turns out to be a heavily western-themed steakhouse, with wagon wheels hanging from the ceiling, lariats on the wall. And an excellent, well-lit, well-heated, spacious women's bathroom.

"Next time we'll have to go west," Marcie says as they tear into the dinner rolls. "Rope us a steer. Ride the range."

Jan imagines herself on a horse, her belly nestled neatly in the curve of the horse's neck. Quite a sight it would be, even if she knew how to ride.

After they eat, Marcie asks the waitress if there are any hotels in the area. The waitress asks the manager. The manager asks one of the dishwashers. There's a boardinghouse about two miles up the road where there might be a room; otherwise there's nothing till you get over near the coast.

Jan calls home again. There's a pay phone in the vestibule of the Ponderosa, and Jan calls home while Marcie is using that nice comfortable ladies' room. She finds herself wondering how she will be able to explain this weekend to Alan, who would never go away for a weekend without a goal and object. Skiing, the beach; even once, long ago, a wine-tasting weekend. Alan likes comfortable hotels and he likes getting things right. Being able to say he saw the foliage at its peak. Not bumbling around in Maine in the rain from diner to western steakhouse to heaven knows where.

"How're you, how're the kids?"

"Hi, wait a minute," he says, right off the bat, his voice hushed and troubled. She can tell he doesn't want the kids to overhear him talking. He's probably taking the phone into the kitchen, closing the door. "Something happened today that upset me a lot. I took the kids over to have brunch at the Blue Moon, and they gave us a table right in the window, and I started seeing these kids from Abby's class going by—all of them girls, all dressed up and carrying presents."

Jan thinks fast. "Clea's house!" she says, placing it on her mental map: right up the street from the restaurant.

"Yeah, exactly. It was a big party at Clea's house. I don't think Abby noticed—she was sitting with her back to the window—but I saw them go by, one after another."

"But how can Clea have a party and not invite Abby? She's been over to our house, Abby goes over there."

"She came to Abby's party!" They say it in perfect unison, over the phone to each other, but they don't laugh.

"I couldn't resist," Alan says. "After brunch I loaded the kids up in the car and I cruised around the block, and Clea's house was all decorated with balloons and streamers. And I saw that kid Jessica going by, and Rachel Sloane, and a couple of others I didn't recognize."

"But Abby didn't see anything?"

"I don't think so. But isn't she sure to hear about it in school?"

"Well, maybe not," Jan says. She is astonished by how angry she is.

"She's going to feel terrible. They were all her friends, and they were all dressed up. I couldn't help thinking it would have been a chance for her to wear that dress with the berries on it that she loves so much."

"And her shiny shoes," Jan says.

"Why would Clea not invite her? Do you think they had a fight?"

"Clea is a horrible child, and her mother is totally tedious," Jan says firmly. "If I never have to hear about acupressure and herbal healing again from that woman, I will be very relieved."

"But you don't think—you don't think Abby is somehow generally excluded? You don't think she's some kind of outsider at school?"

"No," Jan says, trying to make it true by saying it. "No, I don't think so. But I think she'd be hurt to know there was a party and she wasn't invited."

Marcie comes striding out into the vestibule, revved up and ready for the road.

"I know it's silly," Alan says, not sounding at all like he knows it's silly, "but I'm so angry at that kid I can't think about anything else. At Clea."

"She's a horrible, horrible child." Jan sees Marcie looking at her with a puzzled expression. "Remember when she used to wet her pants and we gave Abby that little talk about not making fun of her? Well, that's what she is, she's a peepee-headed little slug. And her mother is a submoron."

It takes them another ten minutes of this before they're through. Marcie has gone outside the restaurant, and Jan finds her there, waiting patiently by the life-size plastic bronco. She wants to apologize; she feels silly about the way her life at home has spilled over into their evening, silly about the way her brain is frantically turning over and over the insult to Abby, the possibility of Abby's hearing about the party on Monday and coming home dejected and disturbed, and worst of all, the possibility that in fact this is the harbinger of some general social outcast state, the end of Abby's happy childhood. The dress with the berries—Jan thinks of her daughter's pleasure in dressing up. Would it have killed Clea to include her, to give that innocent trusting girl an extra chance to wear her precious berry dress before she outgrows it?

"I'm sorry," Jan says abruptly. "I seem to be a little unbalanced right now."

"Some little fleabitten hobgoblin with poor bladder control did something mean to Abby?"

"I'd like to kill her," Jan says as they get into the car. "And her miserable mother too."

Marcie and Jan stay in a boardinghouse. It's a boardinghouse, all right, not a motel. In the summer, according to the lady in the housecoat who shows them to their room, college kids rent rooms by the week and work over by the shore; there's a special shuttle bus to take them back and forth. Now she just has a couple of people staying. The room has two iron single beds, each with a thin pillow and a brown woolen blanket. A linoleum floor. A wood veneer desk peeling at the edges. A chair with a woven seat. And a typed list of house rules on the back of the door.

They've paid her thirty dollars in advance and parked in her driveway. Jan goes out to use the bathroom, comes back to the room to find Marcie in her midnight-blue silk robe, cross-legged on one of the beds.

"You give the room a certain something," Jan tells her, collapsing enormously onto her bed.

"It needs a certain something. We've come a long way from Maude's."

"Rather more Mavis than Maude," Jan says.

"There's a very profound truth in there somewhere. Let's not dig it out."

In fact, both of them are peculiarly delighted to be there. Jan lies back and lets the baby kick; Marcie comes and stands over her and feels the activity.

"Impressive," she says.

She reads aloud from the list of rules, Mavis's list. No persons of the opposite sex in rooms. One towel provided, to be changed on Friday. No noise after eleven, twelve on weekends, special arrangements to be made by anyone wishing to come in late. Please have consideration for others and leave the bathroom as you would wish to find it.

"All the possible lives there are," Jan says woozily. Students living in a boardinghouse and working at the shore. Southern girls stranded, pregnant, in Maine, taking the bus back home. Obstetricians delivering babies and having babies. Hotel consultants. Mavis and Maude. You get embedded. You embed yourself. You escape, but you don't escape. You don't want to escape.

She rubs her belly. Soon, soon. "This is my revolutionary gesture," she says.

"Yes," Marcie agrees.

Jan rolls on her side and inspects her friend, regal and beautiful, admirable and unknowable. "What's yours? Your revolutionary gesture?"

Marcie gestures widely, as if to say—indicating her robe, perhaps—the money spent carelessly out of her wallet, or perhaps more broadly, us here together, this weekend, this room. Or perhaps, more broadly yet, life is made of revolutionary gestures. All the possible lives.

My Father's Chinese Wives

Sandra Tsing Loh

My father doesn't want to alarm us. But then again, it would not be fair to hide anything either. The fact is, at seventy, he is going to try and get married again. This time to a Chinese wife. He thinks this would be more suitable than to someone American, given his advanced age.

He has written his family in Shanghai, and is awaiting response. He is hoping to be married within six months.

Let us unpeel this news one layer at a time.

Question: At this point, is my father even what one would consider marriageable?

At age seventy, my father—a retired Chinese aerospace engineer—is starting to look more and more like somebody's gardener. His feet shuffle along the patio in their broken sandals. He stoops to pull out one or two stray weeds, coughing phlegmatically. He wears a hideous old crew-neck tennis sweater. Later, he sits in a rattan chair and eats leathery green vegetables in brown sauce, his old eyes slitted wearily.

He is the sort of person one would refer to as "Old Dragon Whiskers." And not just because it is a picturesque Oriental way of speaking.

"I am old now," he started saying, about ten years after my mother had died of cancer. "I'm just your crazy old Chinese father." He would rock backwards in his chair and sigh. "I am an old, old man . . ."

At times he almost seems to be overacting this lizardy old part. He milks it. After all, he still does the same vigorous exercise regime—forty-five minutes of pull-ups, something that looks like the twist, and much bellowing—he did ten years ago. This always performed on the most public beaches possible, in his favorite Speedo—one he found in a dumpster.

"Crazy old Chinese father" is, in truth, a code word, a rationalization for the fact that my father has always had a problem . . . spending money. Why buy a briefcase to carry to work, when an empty Frosted Flakes cereal box would do? Papers slip down neatly inside, and pens can be clipped conveniently on either side.

Why buy Bounty paper towels when, at work, he can just walk down the hall to the washroom, open the dispenser, and lift out a stack? They're free—he can bring home as many as we want!

If you've worn the same sweater for so many years that the elbows wear out, turn it around! Get another decade out of it! Which is why to this day, my father wears only crew-neck, not V-neck sweaters . . .

Why drive the car to work when you can take the so-convenient RTD bus? More time to read interesting scientific papers . . . and here they are, in my empty Frosted Flakes box!

"Terrific!" is my older sister Kaitlin's response when I phone her with the news. Bear in mind that Kaitlin has not seen my father since the mid-'80s, preferring to nurse her bad memories of him independently, via a therapist. She allows herself a laugh, laying aside her customary dull hostility for a moment of more jocular hostility. "So who does he think would want to marry *him*?"

"Someone Chinese," I answer.

"Oh good!" she exclaims. "That narrows down the field . . . to what? Half a billion? Nah, as always, he's doing this to punish us.

"Think about it," Kaitlin continues with her usual chilling logic. "He marries a German woman the first time around. It's a disaster. You and I represent that. Because he's passive aggressive and he's cheap. But no, to him, it's that rebellious Aryan strain that's the problem.

"You take an Asian immigrant just off the boat, on the other hand. This is a person who has just fled a Communist government and a horrible life working in a bicycle factory for ten cents a month and no public sanitation and repeated floggings every hour on the hour. After that, living with our father might seem like just another bizarre interlude. It could happen."

Kaitlin scores some compelling points, but nonetheless . . .
I'm bothered for a different reason . . .

Perhaps it is because in describing the new wife, he has used only that one adjective: *Chinese*. He has not said: "I'm looking for a smart wife," or even "a fat wife," he has picked "Chinese." It is meant to stand for so much.

Asian. Asian women. Asian *ladies*.

I think back to a college writing workshop I once attended. (No credit and perhaps that was appropriate.) It was long before my current "administrative assistant" job at Swanson Films. (Makers of the ten-minute instructional video *Laughterobics! Featuring Meredith Baxter-Birney*, among other fine titles.)

Anyway, the workshop contained thirteen hysterical women—and one Fred. Fred was a wealthy Caucasian sixty-something urologist; he was always serene and beautifully dressed and insistent upon holding the door open for me "because you're such a lovely lady." I always wore jeans and a USC sweatshirt, sometimes even sweatpants, so at first I did not know what he meant.

We women, on the other hand, were a wildly mixed group—writing anything from wintery Ann Beattie-esque snippets to sci-fi romance/porn novels ("She would be King Zenothar's concubine, whether she liked it or not"). We attacked each other's writing accordingly. People were bursting into tears every week, then making up by emotionally sharing stories about mutual eating disorders.

But there was one moment when all thirteen women were of like minds. It was that moment when Fred would enter the classroom, laden with xeroxes, blushing shyly as a new bride. We would all look at each other as if to say, "Oh my God, Fred has brought in work *again*."

As though springing from a murky bottomless well, each week new chapters would appear from this semi-epistolary novel Fred was penning about an elderly doctor named Fred who goes on sabbatical for a year to Japan and there finds love with a twenty-three-year-old Japanese medical student named Aku who smells of cherry blossoms.

There were many awkward scenes in which Fred and Aku were exploring each other's bodies as they lay—as far as I gather—upon the bare floor, only a *tatami* mat for comfort. (Fred would always italicize the Japanese words, as if to separate and somehow protect them from other, lesser words.) But it was all beautifully pure and unlike the urban squalor we find in America—the rock music, the drugs, the uncouth teenagers.

Anyway, I recall the one line that I have never since been able to blot from my mind. I cannot think of it without a bit of a shiver. Nor the way he read it, in that hoarse, tremulous voice . . .

"I put my hand in hers, and her little fingers opened like the petals of a moist flower."

It is a month later and, as in a dream, I sit at the worn Formica family dining table with my father, photos and letters before us.

Since my father has written to Shanghai, the mail has come pouring in. I have to face the fact that my father is, well, hot. "You see?" he says. "Seven women have written! Ha!" He beams, his gold molar glinting. He is drinking steaming green tea from a beaker, which he handles with a *Beauty and the Beast* potholder.

Remarkably, my father doesn't make the least effort to mask his delight, no matter how inappropriate. He is old now. *He can do whatever the hell he wants*, is how I now understand it. With a sigh, I turn to the photos. In spite of myself, I am wowed!

Tzau Pa, Ling Ling, Sui Pai, Chong Zhou . . . "twenty-eight, administrative assistant," "forty-seven, owner of a seamstress business," "thirty-nine, freelance beautician." The words jump off the pages, both in English and Chinese translations. These women are dynamos, achievers, with black curly hair, in turtlenecks, jauntily riding bicycles, seated squarely on cannons before military museums, standing proudly with three grown daughters.

One thing unites them: they're all ready to leap off the mainland at the drop of a hat.

And don't think their careers and hobbies are going to keep them from being terrific wives. Quite the opposite. Several already have excellent experience, including one who's been married twice already. The seamstress has sent him two shorts and several pairs of socks; there is much talk of seven-course meals and ironing and terrific expertise in gardening.

Superachievement is a major theme that applies to all. And the biggest star of all is my father. He clears his throat and gleefully reads from a letter by one Liu Tzun:

> Dr. Chow, your family has told me of your great scientific genius and of your many awards. I respect academic scholarship very highly, and would be honored to meet you on your next visit.

"You see?" my father chuckles. "They have a lot of respect for me in China. When I go there, they treat me like President Bush! Free meals, free drinks . . . I don't pay for anything!"

"He had his chance. He got married once, for twenty-five years. He was a terrible husband and a worse father."

Kaitlin is weighing in. All jokes are off. Her fury blazes away, further aggravated by the fact that she is going through a divorce and hates her $50,000-a-year job. Her monthly Nordstrom bills are astronomical. MCI is positively crackling.

"He's a single man," I say. "Mum's been gone for twelve years now—"

"And now he gets a second try—just like that?" Kaitlin exclaims. "Clean slate? Start right over? Buy a wife? It makes me sick. He is totally unqualified to sustain a marriage. A family structure of any kind collapses around him. Do you even remember one happy Christmas?"

Twinkling lights and tinsel suddenly swirl before me and looking deeper, through green foliage, I see my mother looking beautiful and crisp in lipstick and pearls, her wavy auburn hair done . . . except for the fact that she is hysterical, and my father, his face a mask of disgust so extreme it is almost parodic, is holding his overpriced new V-neck tennis sweater from Saks out in front of him like it is a dead animal—

"I try to block it out," is what I say.

"Well I was six years older than you so I can't." Kaitlin's pain is raw. "Why does he deserve to be happy . . . now? He made Mama miserable in her lifetime—he was so cheap! I think she was almost glad to go as soon as she did. A seventy-dollar dress, leaving the heater on overnight, too much spent on a nice steak dinner—he could never let anything go! He could never just let it go! He just could . . . not . . . let . . . things . . . go!"

Meanwhile . . .
On its own gentle time clock, unsullied by the raging doubts of his two daughters . . .
My father's project bursts into flower.
And forty-seven-year-old Liu—the writer of the magic letter—is the lucky winner! Within three months, she is flown to Los Angeles. She and my father are married a week later.
I do not get to meet her right away, but my father fills me in on the stats. And I have to confess, I'm a little surprised at how modern she is, how urban. Liu is a divorcée with, well, with ambitions in the entertainment business. Although she speaks no English, she seems to be an expert on American culture. The fact that Los Angeles is near Hollywood has not escaped her. This is made clear to me one Sunday evening, three weeks later, via telephone.
"I know you have friends in the entertainment business," my father declares. He has never fully grasped the fact that I am a typist and that Swanson Films' clients include such Oscar contenders as Kraft Foods and Motorola.
"Aside from having knitted me a new sweater and playing the piano," my father continues, "you should know that Liu is an excellent singer—" Turning away from the phone, he and his new wife exchange a series of staccato reports in Mandarin, which mean nothing to me.
"I'm sure that Liu is quite accomplished," I reply, "it's just that—"
"Oh . . . she's terrific!" my father exclaims, shocked that I may be calling Liu's musical talent into question. "You want to hear her sing? Here, here, I will put her on the phone right now . . ."
Creeping into my father's voice is a tremulous note that is sickeningly familiar. How many times had I heard it during my childhood as I was being pushed toward the piano, kicking and screaming? How many times—
But that was twenty years ago. I gulp terror back down. I live in my own apartment now, full of director's chairs, potted ficuses, and

Matisse posters. I will be fine. My father has moved on to a totally new pushee . . .

Who picks up the phone, sighs—then bursts out triumphantly: "Nee-ee hoo-oo, tieh-hen see bau-hau jioo . . . !"

> I have left you and taken the Toyota, Dr. Chow—so there!

Five weeks later, Liu just packs up her suitcase, makes some sandwiches, and takes off in the family Toyota. She leaves her note on the same Formica table at which she'd first won his heart.

My father is in shock. Then again, he is philosophical.

"Liu—she had a lot of problems. She said she had no one to talk to. There were no other Chinese people in Tarzana. She wanted me to give her gifts. She was bored. You know I don't like to go out at night. But I tell her, 'Go! See your friends in Chinatown.' But Liu does not want to take the bus. She wants to drive! But you know me, your cheap father. I don't want to pay her insurance. That Liu—she was a very bad driver—"

"Ha!" is Kaitlin's only comment.

Summer turns to fall in Southern California, causing the palm trees to sway a bit. The divorce is soon final, Liu's settlement including $10,000, the microwave, and the Toyota.

Never one to dwell, my father has picked a new bride: Zhou Ping, thirty-seven, homemaker from Qang-Zhou province. I groan.

"But no . . . Zhou Ping is very good," my father insists. He has had several phone conversations with her. "And she comes very highly recommended, not, I have to say, like Liu. Liu was bad, that one. Zhou Ping is sensible and hardworking. She has had a tough life. Boy! She worked in a coal mine in Manchuria until she was twenty-five. The winters there were very, very bitter! She had to make her own shoes and clothing. Then she worked on a farming collective, where she raised cattle and grew many different kinds of crops—by herself!"

"I'm sure she's going to fit in really well in Los Angeles," I say.

Zhou Ping is indeed a different sort. The news, to my astonishment, comes from Kaitlin. "I received . . ." her voice trails off, the very words seeming to elude her. "A *birthday card*. From Papa . . . and *Zhou Ping*."

My sister continues in a kind of trance of matter-of-factness, as if describing some curious archaeological artifact. "Let's see, on the front is a picture with flowers on it. It's from Hallmark. Inside is gold lettering, cursive, that says 'Happy Birthday!' At the bottom, in red pen, it says . . . 'Love, Zhou Ping and *your* Dad.'"

"Your 'Dad'?"

"I think Zhou Ping put him up to this. The envelope is not addressed in his handwriting. Nonetheless . . ." Kaitlin thinks it over, concurs with herself. "Yes. Yes. I believe this is the first birthday card I've ever received from him in my life. The first. It's totally bizarre."

A week later, Kaitlin received birthday gifts in the mail: a sweater hand-knit by Zhou Ping, and a box of "mooncakes." She is flipping out. "Oh no," she worries, "now I really have to call and thank her. I mean, the poor woman probably has no friends in America. Who knows what he's having her do? We may be her only link to society!"

Kaitlin finally does call, managing to catch Zhou Ping when my father is on the beach doing his exercises (which he always does at eleven and three). Although Zhou Ping's English is very broken, she somehow convinces Kaitlin to fly down for a visit.

It will be Kaitlin's first trip home since our mother's passing. And my first meeting of either of my stepmothers.

I pull up the familiar driveway in my Geo. Neither Kaitlin nor I say anything. We peer out the windows.

The yard doesn't look too bad. There are new sprinklers, and a kind of irrigation system made by a network of ingeniously placed rain gutters. Soil has been turned, and thoughtfully. Cypresses have been trimmed. Enormous bundles of weeds flank the driveway, as if for some momentous occasion.

We ring the doorbell. Neither of us has had keys to the house in years.

The door opens. A short, somewhat plump Chinese woman in round glasses and a perfect bowl haircut beams at us. She is wearing a bright yellow "I hate housework!" apron that my mother was once given as a gag gift—and I think never wore.

"Kat-lin! Jen-na!" she exclaims in what seems like authentic joy, embracing us. She is laughing and almost crying with emotion.

In spite of myself, giggles begin to well up from inside me as if from a spring. I can't help it: I feel warm and euphoric. Authentic joy is contagious. Who cares who this woman is: no one has been this happy to see me in ages.

"Wel-come home," Zhou Ping says, with careful emphasis. She turns to Kaitlin, a shadow falling over her face. "I am glad you finally come home to see your Daddy," she says in a low, sorrowful voice. She looks over her shoulder. "He old now."

Then, as if exhausted by that effort, Zhou Ping collapses into giggles. I sneak a glance over at Kaitlin, whose expression seems to be straining somewhere between joy and nausea. Pleasantries lunge out of my mouth: "It's nice to finally meet you!" "How do you like America?" "I've heard so much about your cooking!"

My father materializes behind a potted plant. He is wearing a new sweater and oddly formal dress pants. His gaze hovers somewhere near the floor.

"Hul-lo," he declares, attempting a smile. "Long time no see!" he exclaims, not making eye contact, but in Kaitlin's general direction.

"Yes!" Kaitlin exclaims back, defiant, a kind of winged Amazon in perfect beige Anne Klein II leisurewear. "It certainly is!"

My father stands stiffly.

Kaitlin blazes.

"It's good to see you!" he finally concludes, as though this were something he learned in English class.

Feeling, perhaps, that we should all leave well enough alone, the Chow family, such as we are, moves on through the house. It is ablaze with color—the sort of eye-popping combinations one associates with Thai restaurants and Hindu shrines. There are big purple couches, peach rugs, a shiny brass trellis, and creeping Charlies everywhere.

All this redecorating came at no great expense, though. "See this rug?" my father says proudly, while Zhou Ping giggles. "She found it in a dumpster. They were going to throw it away!" "Throw it away!" she exclaims. "See? It very nice."

Over their heads, Kaitlin silently mouths one word to me: "Help."

Beyond, the Formica dining room table is set. Oddly. There are little rice bowls, chopsticks, and a sheet of plain white paper at each place setting. It is good to know some definite event has been planned. Kaitlin, my father, and I are so unaccustomed to being in a room together that any kind of definite agenda—AKA: "We'll eat dinner, and then we'll leave"—is comforting.

My father goes off to put some music on his new CD player. "That bad Liu made me buy it!" he explains. "But it's nice." Zhou Ping bustles into the kitchen. "Dinner ready—in five minute!" she declares.

Kaitlin waits a beat, then pulls me aside into the bathroom and slams the door.

"This is so weird!" she hisses.

We have not stood together in this bathroom for some fifteen years. It seems different. I notice that the wallpaper is faded, the towels are new—but no, it's something else. On one wall is my mother's framed reproduction of the brown Dürer etching called *Praying Hands* which she had always kept in her sewing room. Right next to it, in shocking juxtaposition, is a green, red, blue, and yellow Bank of Canton calendar from which a zaftig Asian female chortles.

"I can't go through with this!" Kaitlin continues in stage whisper. "It's too weird! There are so many memories here, and not good ones!"

And like debris from a hurricane, the words tumble out:

"I go by the kitchen and all I can see is me standing before the oven clock at age five with tears in my eyes. He is yelling: 'What time is it? The little hand is most of the way to four and the big hand is on the eight! It was 3:18 twenty-two minutes ago—so what time is it now? What's eighteen plus twenty-two? Come on—you can do it in your head! Come on! Come on!'

"I go by the dining room and I see him hurling my Nancy Drew books across the floor. They slam against the wall and I huddle against Mum, screaming. 'Why do you waste your time on this when your algebra homework isn't finished? You . . . good for nothing! You're nothing, nothing—you'll never amount to anything!'

"I go by the bedroom—"

"Please—" I have this sickening feeling like I am going to cry, that I'm going to just lose it. I want to just sit down in the middle of the floor and roll myself into a ball. But I can't. Kaitlin's rage is like something uncontainable, a dreadful natural force, and I am the gatekeeper. I feel if I open the door, it will rush out and destroy the house and everyone in it. "Please," is what I end up whispering. "Please. Let's just eat. We'll be done in an hour. Then we can go home. I promise. You won't have to do this again for another ten years—or maybe ever."

At dinner, endless plates of food twirl their way out of the kitchen, Zhou Ping practically dancing underneath. Spinach, teriyaki-ish chicken, shrimp, some kind of egg thing with peas, dumplings packed with little pillows of pork.

And amazingly, there is no want of conversational material. Photos from Shanghai are being pulled out of envelopes and passed around of her family, his family . . .

I do recognize three or four Chinese relatives—a cousin, an aunt, a grand-uncle? Their names are impossible for me to remember. We had met them in China during our last trip as a family. I was fifteen; it was right before our mother started to get sick.

Shanghai is a distant, confused memory for me, of ringing bicycle bells and laundry lines hanging from buildings. What I do remember is how curious my father's family had seemed about Kaitlin and me, his odd American experiment, oohing over our height and touching our auburn hair. There were many smiles but no intelligible conversation, at least to our ears. We probably won't see any of these people again before we die.

Zhou Ping, though, is determined to push through, to forge a bridge between us. She plunges ahead with her bad English, my father almost absent-mindedly correcting her.

Their lives are abuzz with activity. Zhou Ping is taking piano lessons at the community college. My father is learning Italian and French off the Learning Channel—he sets his alarm for four in the morning. "So early!" Zhou Ping hoots. They listen to Karl Haas's *Listening to Good Music* on the classical station at ten. "Mot-sart—he

Sandra Tsing Loh

very nice!" They have joined the Bahais, a local quasi-religious group. "I must cook food all the time!" My father suddenly puts his spoon down. He is chewing slowly, a frown growing.

"This meat . . ." he shakes his head, "is very greasy."

He turns to Zhou Ping and the lines at both sides of his mouth deepen. His eyes cloud. He says something to her in Chinese, with a certain sharp cadence that makes my spine stiffen . . .

Zhou Ping's face goes blank for a moment. Her eyes grow big. My stomach turns to ice.

How will she respond? By throwing her napkin down, bursting into tears, running from the room? Will she knock the table over, plates sliding after each other, sauces spilling, crockery breaking? Will we hear the engine turn over as she drives off into the night, to leave us frightened and panicked?

It is none of these things.

Zhou Ping's head tilts back, her eyes crinkle . . .

And laughter pours out of her, peal after peal after peal. It is a big laugh, an enormous laugh, the laugh of a woman who has birthed calves and hoed crops and seen harsh winters decimate countrysides. Pointing to our father, Zhou Ping turns to us with large glittering eyes and says words which sound incredible to our ears:

"Your Papa—he so funny!"

My jaw drops. No one has ever laughed out loud at this table, ever. We laughed behind closed doors, in our bedrooms, in the bathroom, never before my father. We laughed sometimes with my mother, on those glorious days when he would be off on a trip—

But Kaitlin is not laughing. She is trembling; her face is turning red.

"Why are you always so angry?" Kaitlin cries out in a strangled voice. It is the question that she has waited thirty years to ask. "Why were you so angry?"

There is shocked silence. My father looks weary and embarrassed. He smiles wanly and shrugs his thin shoulders.

"No really," Kaitlin insists. "All those years. With Mama. Why?"

"I don't know," my father murmurs. "People get angry."

And I know, in that moment, that he doesn't have an answer. He literally doesn't. It's as if anger was this chemical which reacted on him for twenty years. Who knows why, but like some kind of spirit, it has left him now. The rage is spent. He is old now. He is old.

Dusk has fallen, and long shadows fall across the worn parquet floor of the dining room. After a moment of silence, my father asks Zhou Ping to sing a song. The hausfrau from Qang-Zhou opens her mouth and, with an odd dignity, sings simply and slowly. My father translates:

> From the four corners of the earth
> My lover comes to me
> Playing the lute
> Like the wind over the water

He recites the words without embarrassment, almost without emotion. And why shouldn't he? The song has nothing to do with him personally: it is from some old Chinese fable. It has to do with missing someone, something, that perhaps one can't even define anymore.

As Zhou Ping sings, everyone longs for home. But what home? Zhou Ping—for her bitter winters? My father—for the Shanghai he left forty years ago? Kaitlin and I? We are even sitting in our home, and we long for it.

Stories Don't Have Endings
Janice Gould

Stories don't have endings. That's the problem for me. When I look on my life, the things that have happened, I can't find any way to wrap things up. I was too lonely. I lived in an absence of relationship. When I got tired of a place I moved on. And I brought everything with me, all my hope and despair, packed neatly into my guitar case and sung out again through the strings. Songs I refuse to sing anymore.

Even my mom's death, there's no ending there. I'm waiting to resume something with her, an unfinished dialogue. Things weren't always so good in the past as they might be one day out among the new stars of our universe. I want to see my mom again, sitting on some big, flat, granite slab in a meadow, warm sun, blue of the noon sky, and my sisters there too. And a cold, clear river running by, shallow enough to wade in, yellow sandy bottom. It might be that way.

And where will my dad be? I don't know. I leave him in his pink negligee and blond wig, standing in the kitchen warming his coffee. Even if I knew I wanted to, I can't bring him into our circle. He is too complicated and I still have a child's fear of the abnormal.

Don't tell me I can't use that word! I know all about it.

I can accept him for the ways he came through for my mom in the end. It sounds mean for me to say, but it must have taken him a load of courage to lie down with my mother after she had received extreme unction, and hold her hand. How many years had it been since he lay with her on the same bed? My mom held her own for a day and a half after that. We bathed her, my older sister and I, turning her gently, and water streamed away from the hot mass of tumor that had erupted beneath her skin. Maidu skin, creamy brown, soft as velvet.

Like I say, things weren't always good between my mom and me. There were years of intense struggle. Struggle for what? For control on my mom's part, for autonomy on mine. I suppose autonomy. I never achieved it. I gave in to her always. I was alert to her, even I guess when I imagined I wasn't. These days, I find myself hoping mama isn't watching from on high. But then I figure, well, it's time she knew the truth. So I strut around in my Levi's and black T-shirt, wearing my leather jacket. I don't turn her photo to the wall when I take my woman to bed and make love to her until she's crying out.

My mom knew she had a butch daughter. But it is a fine balance, a fine balance I had to maintain. When I slipped off into the butch side, boy, my mom would be mad. "Why are you carrying that girl's suitcases?" she'd ask indignantly. "She's big enough to carry her own. What are you trying to do, be the man? It looks ridiculous!"

Probably it did look ridiculous. There's a little door beneath my heart that opens on the word "shame," and every shameful moment of my life crawls over that doorway and down into that dark place.

She didn't want me to be my dad. I mean what I say. She didn't want me to be like him, dressing up in clothes of the opposite sex and pretending to be that sex, that gender. "It looks ridiculous!"

But when I wasn't trying to look like a boy I still looked like a boy in my brown cords and white shirt and cook's apron. That woman who came in the deli where I worked, she was after me, flirting. She thought I was a teenage boy, a Greek. My friends laugh when I tell that story. "An Adonis," they say. And I laugh too. But that woman saw what she wanted to see. She bought baklava from me, no wonder she thought I was Greek. And in those days I'd say to Rachel, "Come here and dance with me!" and we'd practice some steps to a hora, or some Greek dance, around the tables, me humming the melody. And Rachel was a beautiful girl with long, thick, black hair. That woman admired what a pretty couple we were.

"What is that boy's name?" she asked my boss, Mrs. Goldstein.

"Which boy?"

"That Greek boy."

"What Greek boy? We have no Greek boy."

The woman was looking confused. And I was standing behind them, realizing, "Yeah, that lady thinks I'm a boy."

And was she ever ashamed when Mrs. Goldstein looked at her in astonishment and said, "She's no boy!" That woman never came back in the deli after that.

But hell, maybe she was only disappointed because she couldn't introduce me to her sixteen-year-old niece, Susie. Who knows?

Which reminds me that I did "rob the cradle" once with a sixteen-year-old married girl. And she knew I was a woman. But that's another story. I stole her heart, her husband stole money from me. So everything is equal.

But those aren't the stories I was planning to tell. I was thinking about Hood River, the farm, the factories where I worked. I was remembering the long days in the fields, bailing hay. That was the summer. And autumn, there were rain showers in September clearing off to puffy clouds above the river, in a turquoise sky, autumn planting before supper, before the moon rose, full as a pumpkin.

I was anorexic in those days, slip-sliding on the factory floor in my proud boots, me on the second-to-last peeler on row six, the fast row where they put the youngest or the hardest-working women.

Hell, we all worked hard. Seven-and-a-half hours a day, loading the peeler with six pears every ten seconds. Speed up, slow down, break time, lunch time, off work. In hairnets and plastic aprons. I never once looked at myself in the mirror in the ladies' room. A matter of principle with me, a matter of superstition. The lunch buckets on shelves, last names printed on adhesive tape: Gray, Turner, Rideout, Springer. And my last name, Gallagher.

We'd go into the company cafeteria. Chili stew. And rain coming down hard outside, sound of wet gravel being crunched by truck tires, and truck engines churning, the hydraulic whirring of forklifts. Men's voices, hollering. After lunch I'd always go outside and walk around, rain or sun.

And as fall time came on, more rain, cold winds, and finally snow. Lights coming on around four in the afternoon as we were driving home from the cannery.

Janice Gould

Sometimes on Friday nights I'd go down to Stevenson with my friend Sharon. She was a half-breed like myself, but a Yakima. I was in love with her. She had five kids, was about ten years older than me.

And I had it bad for that woman. I guess everybody did. Still, her husband was always going off to the bar, or going out hunting on the weekends. I seldom saw him.

It's not much of a story. In short, a lot of time getting drunk, a lot of time talking with her, a lot of time singing. The kids would get tired and put blankets and pillows down on the living room floor and go to sleep. I guess they wanted to be near their mom, in the dark snowlit living room, that one yellow kitchen light over the sink, the coffee pot making an occasional blip.

Finish off a six-pack of beer, drink a pot of coffee, go pee every half hour, sober drunks. Two, three o'clock in the morning, me, my clitoris pounding against the tight crotch of my jeans and Sharon saying, "You should always do whatever you want to do." Lady, if you only knew what I want to do. And I reach out to touch her long Indian hair, just brushed.

She doesn't say a word, just looks at me.

But another time she says, "If you aren't comfortable sleeping on that settee, you can sleep with me. Jim won't be home tonight."

She is wearing nothing but a long yellow T-shirt. It must be near one in the morning. There is cold light on the snow, blue shadows of spruce and Douglas fir, a black, glistening night of stars and half-moon. I go to her room.

She is lying on her side, but her black hair is spread up over her pillow. I get in under the covers with my jeans and shirt on. I'm shivering. She is only a few inches from me.

And I lie there frozen, feeling her body heat, wanting to touch her, to take her in my arms, to put my lips to her lips, to feel her legs wrap around my legs. I want to hear her say my name. I want to tell her I love her.

I imagine how she'll recoil from me. "You queer! Get out of my bed!" And then that iciness, that look of disgust or amusement on her face whenever she looks at me and sees me looking at her.

Stories Don't Have Endings

"What are you, one of those lesbians? I better never catch you with my daughter."

So I lie there hating myself for feeling as I do, too much a coward to touch her, too much a coward to go away. Lonely. My hand nearly touching her hair.

"Sharon." My voice is less than a whisper. "Sharon!"

"Hmm?"

I don't say anything. I wait.

"Mom? Mommy?" It's her youngest daughter.

"What is it, baby?"

"Can I get in bed with you?"

"Sure, honey." She moves over toward me and lifts the sheets. Emily crawls in and curls up next to her.

"Hello, sweet lamb," whispers Sharon. "Were you scared?"

She goes on talking to Emily in a soft, warm voice. "Nothing's gonna hurt you. I love you. Do you know that?"

I hear her breathing into Emily's hair. I know her arm is around her small body, closing Emily into her heart and belly warmth.

Later I was ashamed of how jealous I felt, how I inched my body away from the two of them and cried.

But at 4:30 a.m. Sharon was up. "I'll make some breakfast for you." And she made me a sandwich of elk meat and a thermos of coffee for me to take to work.

And after that? I guess I never did go back. I quit my job at the cannery and got another job at a factory making fishing lures and "Li'l Chief Smokers." You know, for smoking salmon, elk, deer, wild burros. Whatever.

And I didn't see her again, though once I heard she was working, selling Christmas trees at The Dalles. I drove up there in a snowstorm, like a fool. Drove everywhere, looking for Christmas-tree lots. She and the kids were probably holed up in a motel room with one double bed and a kitchenette. I can imagine the kids watching TV, and her smoking, looking out the window with a far-off look on her face.

Stories. No endings. I dream of the river canyon, the Columbia River, riding our horses out by the bluffs, the northwest wind. In spring, misty rain, dogwood blossoming in a narrow cut of the canyon cliffs. And the smell of wet asphalt, two-lane highway. Smell of pine and oak.

The day I came home, back to California, it was so cold I got the sleeping bag out of my car and curled up in it on the front porch, waiting for my mom to come home. I didn't have a key to the house.

They were surprised to see me, my mom and my younger sister. I don't think I even hugged them. Probably not. I never gave anything with my body in those days. I was always stiff with people who tried to hug me.

We made coffee. We sat at the table, as always. Somehow I knew my mom was mad at me.

"So, what do you plan to do now," asked my mom, "now that you're home?" She looked impatient. She had fourteen years left.

I lied and told her my plans. School, job, a way to support myself, my own apartment, eventually. But I really didn't know. I didn't know.

I didn't know until those fourteen years were finished, and she had moved on to the next phase, wherever, whatever that is.

I keep feeling that I want to phone home and talk to her. That unfinished dialogue. A way to explain those things I hope she now knows.

The Box House and the Snow
Cristina Henríquez

Their house was a box. It was a perfect house. It was the father's favorite thing in the world. No one else he knew had a house quite like it and no one, he thought, ever would again. It was the sort of place that should go on the National Register of Best Houses, if such a thing existed. And if it didn't exist, it should be invented to honor this one house.

They lived in a valley between two mountains. There were forty-two other houses in their modest valley town. There were once forty-three other houses, but a few years earlier a whipping windstorm had its way with one of them and toppled it into a pile of matchsticks and glass. The man whose house had fallen had built the house himself, a feat he often boasted of at length to everyone in the town. So when it crumbled, though they were nothing but kind and supportive to his face, the people in the town whispered behind the man's back about how embarrassing it was that the house had collapsed like a bad soufflé, and they laughed with derision and agreed that the man's pridefulness had been met with just punishment. The father was among those whispering and laughing and agreeing, though it scared him to recognize a bit of himself in the man, since the father, too, was buoyed by pride. But when he confessed this fear to his wife, she assured him that there was a difference between arrogant pride and joyous pride, and that the father possessed the latter, which was the acceptable variety. The father felt better. He even hired a photographer to take a picture of him and his wife and their daughter in front of their perfect house, to commemorate his joyous pride.

The valley town was huddled in the middle of a tropical country. The people there were used to air that never dropped below eighty degrees, air that was sticky and warm every year of their lives. So they were more than a little surprised when, one April morning, they encountered a curious white substance covering nearly everything they could see. The substance was snow.

Later, this is the story they would collectively decide upon, the legend they would pass down to their children and their children's children: The snowstorm came at night while everyone was sleeping. The world was perfectly still. No breeze rustling the trees; no whispers ribboning through the air; no animals yawning; no people turning in their sleep, flinching from their dreams; no soft gurgling in the sewers below the streets. The moon was masked behind thick clouds. The world was black, caked on and opaque. Then, all at once, millions of snowflakes burst from the murky sky and fluttered to the earth. It was a pillow ripping open. It was a silent, exploding firework. It was as if God had been collecting mounds and fistfuls and armfuls of snow for centuries and, finally, could hold the white flakes no more. He tore a seam in the fabric of heaven and sent the snowflakes scampering forth. At first, the snow danced through the air doing cartwheels, doing flip-flops, doing triple full twists and Arabian front tucks. Later, carried by a new wind, it leapt in great tumbling clumps like paratroopers. As the night went on, it shot down in a nosedive, in a fury, as if thrust from the sky against its will, as if spit from the mouths of angels. And later still, in a last heroic push before the sun came up in the morning, the snow grew so dense that it gave the appearance of cascading walls of snow, a world made from snow, solid all the way through. There was so much of it that the entire night sky was blanched, and the earth below it surrendered. The world turned white.

But before the people in the valley town settled upon this story, they had to deal with the astonishment of that morning. When they first woke their shutters were closed, as they were every night, to block out the blinding morning sun. There was a chill in the air stiffer than usual, but not enough to provoke alarm. It was not until, one by one, the people climbed out of bed and opened their doors that they noticed the snow. People plunged into the waist-high sea of white that flooded into their doorways. They looked out from their houses for their neighbors, for trees, for wire trash cans, for street signs—for anything familiar—but found that only the top half of everything was visible. Against houses and buildings, the snow soared, swept up gently by the wind like a cresting wave frozen in time.

The phones were quiet.

The electricity was severed.

The sewers were frozen.

Inside their houses, people talked on and on and on among themselves, in complete disbelief, trying to comprehend the world outside their windows.

In the perfect house, the father was the first one awake. He found himself pressed against his wife when he opened his eyes. He was shivering. For a moment, he believed he was sick. He groped for his watch on the bedside table and held it in front of him but, because of the perfect darkness in the house, he could not see the face. For a moment, he believed he had gone blind. He curled his icy toes around his wife's ankle. He smoothed the standing hairs on his arms. He stared into pitch-blackness and then became scared. His wife's ankle was as cold as his toes. For a moment, he believed he was dead.

When finally he got up, the father pulled three pairs of socks over his feet and padded to the front door, stealing his way through the dark. The iciness of the wrought-iron door handle shocked him but when he opened the door, slowly, pulling it toward him, what he saw shocked him more: a bright white earth that stretched for miles. The snow that had built up against the door gently tumbled into the house. The father tried to nudge it out with his toe and in doing so, made a soft indentation at the bottom of the snow wall. He stared at the glittering snowscape. He took a step back into the house and closed the door.

The mother felt the cold slink in through her pores and spread like a vapor under her skin. In the night, she thought it was a dream. She pulled a sheet over her body and fought her way into a ball, holding her knees to her chest to stay bunched. She slept restlessly, trembling. She knew something was not right.

And then the father poked her in the morning. He whispered, Get up.

It's the middle of the night, she told him. It's dark.

It's not dark. It's just that the windows are covered.

Well then open the shutters. You always open the shutters when you get up.

The shutters are open.

What do you mean? the mother asked, sighing.

You'll see, the father said. He pulled her out of her ball.

What's going on? she asked.

The father slid socks over her feet as she sat on the bed. She was growing impatient.

You won't believe it, he told her. Then he dragged her through the house, guiding her with his hand.

I can't see a thing, she said.

The father opened the door for her. Light streamed into the house. He gave a dramatic bow. See this, he said.

The snow was big news. Reporters from all over were clamoring to cover it, but the problem was that they couldn't get into the town because the roads were blocked. The networks that could afford to sent helicopters to hover over the town. The shots were incomparable. The earth smoothed over, soft shimmering dimpled mounds. One network from Chile was so desperate to cover the story—which was being hailed as a miracle on par with tears from the statue of the Virgin Mary—that they diverted their traffic copter to the valley town. The result was sixty-six traffic accidents in Santiago in one day—a sort of anti-miracle.

The people in the town, eager to be on television, worked hard to clear pathways for the reporters to make their way in. They cleared streets using pots, pans, cookie sheets, watering cans, bowls, plastic bags, shoes, pillowcases, and couch cushions—anything they could find. The work was hard. They weren't prepared. They safety-pinned towels around their thighs and around their torsos to help keep their bodies warm. They swirled blankets around their shoulders and clutched them at the front to keep them closed. They lit their stoves and took turns warming their reddened hands over the hissing blue

The Box House and the Snow

flames. They picked up their phones for a dial tone—to call the stations and invite them in—but were greeted by silence on the other end. They pulled at their TV knobs, hoping to see themselves on the news, hoping to see a government emergency alert, but the TVs stayed asleep. They took photographs of the great white ocean that had swallowed them whole, forcing teeth-chattering smiles for the camera as they stood outside. Two enterprising families trampled on the snow, spelling out HOLA with their footprints, and this image, captured by the swarm of helicopters overhead, became the most famous of the miracle snow.

The father used a silver platter he and the mother had received for their wedding to push the snow aside, enough so he could walk out the door. The soles of his sandals stamped a pattern of diamonds on the white land as he walked. He stopped at his fence, an iron fence ornate with curlicues and swirls. Snow rested in the spaces of the design. The father poked his finger at the snow. It came loose like a cutout and fell quietly against the powder on the other side. But he had not ventured outside, as others had, for fun or novelty. The father turned and looked at his perfect house, ambushed by snow. He thought of the man whose house had blown down as punishment for his pride. The father told himself that if he could keep his house standing, it would be God's way of telling him he had a reasonable sort of pride, one for which he did not deserve to be punished. On the other hand, if something happened to the house, it would mean that the father was a sinner, since the wrong sort of pride was a sin. On top of that, there were the news cameras. If the house collapsed, almost everyone in the world would know it. Things were getting serious.

Inside, the father told the mother to gather dishrags and bath towels. The mother was sitting at the kitchen table with her knees pulled to her chest, trying to stay warm. She had checked on the daughter but let her keep sleeping. At this point, it seemed better than being awake. The mother raised her eyebrows as the father pointed to the wooden wall behind the sink.

Do you see how dark it is? he asked.

The mother turned to look. Something black blossomed in a patch above the sink.

It looks like a stain, she said.

It's water, the father said. It's seeping through.

But it rains here and the wood gets wet, the mother said.

The father shook his head. The snow is wrapped around the house like a boa constrictor. It's not the same as rain.

The mother was worried now but the father told her not to be. Get the dishrags and towels, he said. He showed her how to hold them up to the walls, how to use them to swab the water away.

The father woke the daughter next. Are you awake? he yelled. You have to get up! There's been a snowstorm, he said. He heard the daughter laugh from her room.

The father opened her bedroom door. It's true, he said.

But it doesn't snow here, the daughter argued.

I'm almost positive that's what it is. I've seen pictures before.

The daughter jumped up, giddy. Is it really? She rushed past the father to the front door. When she saw the snow, she shuddered and pulled her arms in through the sleeves of her nightgown. The air smelled like it had been laundered, fresh and wet. A bird sprang lightly into the snow, sinking in and flitting off again.

It's amazing, the daughter whispered.

Yes, okay, the father said, dragging her away from the door. That's enough of that. We need your help.

The father took a wooden chair from the kitchen and put it in what he estimated was the center of the house. Already the ceiling had begun to bow. The mother said she couldn't tell, but the father saw it. The roof was flat and the weight of the snow would collapse it.

The father told the daughter to put on her best socks and her warmest clothes. The mother, who could see what was coming next, protested. I'll stand on the chair myself, the mother said.

I've already taught you how to swab the walls, the father argued. I'll teach the girl.

It will take too long. Someone needs to get on the chair now and that's the girl.

The mother bit her tongue.

The father told the daughter to stand on the chair.

No way, she said.

Do it or I'll bury you in that snow, the father shouted.

That's terrible, the mother said. Don't say that to her.

The father sighed. You're right. I'm feeling a little crazy. I'm sorry. *Please* get up on the chair.

The daughter put her arms back through her nightgown's armholes and climbed up wordlessly, her dark hair swimming down her back.

Reach your arms up, the father said. His expression was grave, his eyes wide and expectant.

The daughter did as he asked, gazing at the ceiling as her hands neared the wood.

Can you touch? the father asked.

The daughter flattened her palms against the ceiling.

The mother said, Are you okay?

The daughter said, I guess.

The father said, Now don't move.

Very slowly, small paths began to open up all over the town like arteries, allowing people to get around to most places, allowing life to flow again. The reporters gave round-the-clock updates and when by that evening not a single new snowflake had fallen, most of them packed up and left.

As far as the father knew, no one else's house had suffered. They all had sloped roofs so the snow tumbled off. For the first time, the father saw his own house as something less than perfect. It was not invincible. He complained about this to the mother.

But the mother said, This only proves it's *more* perfect than the rest. Because with this house comes a challenge. And surviving the challenge will only make you stronger. Do other people have houses that will make them stronger?

No, the father admitted, pleased by this logic. The father was also inspired by this logic. He went out and found one of the few news teams left in town and told them he had a knockout story for them. He promised them the greatest house in the world. The news team was about to leave the scene. There was only so much they could say about snow and only so much they could speculate about how it got there and what might happen next. But at the offer to see the greatest house in the world, they thought, Why not?

Cristina Henríquez

The news team arrived as the mother was squeezing rags over the sink. She was exhausted but the clay between the wood was softening so she had to work quickly. More than once, the mother had slumped in the corner and covered her face with one of the rags. She said a prayer, moving her lips against the terry cloth. She asked God to lift the snow, to suck it back into the sky. She imagined streamers of snow running up into the clouds. The dry earth would return to itself layer by layer.

The daughter stood, perched on the wooden kitchen chair in the middle of the floor, her arms spread and raised overhead, palms flat and pressed into the wet wood, fingers splayed. She watched her mother huddle in the corner. She heard whispering but could not make out the words. The daughter itched one ankle with the toes of her other foot. She wore red woolen knee-high socks that her mother had bought once to make into stockings for Christmas but never had. Then the daughter heard the commotion outside. Who's here? she said.

Who's where? the mother asked.

The daughter nodded her head toward the door.

The mother peered out and then shrieked.

At the sound of the shriek, the father looked up and strode to the house. Isn't it magnificent? he said, motioning toward the news team. Now everyone will know about our house. The whole world will be able to see it.

I'm not wearing any makeup, the mother said, and skittered to the bathroom.

The father peered outside at the crew and then looked to the daughter. Whatever you do, do not move, he said. Even after the snow melts, the wood will get heavy with water. You have to hold it up. The whole world will be watching.

The daughter sighed.

Don't sigh, the father scolded.

I don't think it will fall, the daughter said.

Do you really want to find out? the father asked.

Although the father had not foreseen it, the story ended up being not so much about the house as about the daughter standing inside the house, literally holding it together with her own two hands. The news team requested interviews with the daughter, but the father insisted that she not be bothered. She needed to focus. Sometimes, though, the daughter yelled out requests for food or pleas that someone trade places with her because she was growing tired, even though the father pinched her legs when she did because he didn't want her to make him seem like a cruel father in front of the whole world, as he kept saying.

Failing the opportunity to interview the daughter, the news anchor at least wanted to interview the father. The father welcomed the attention.

How much longer will the girl have to hold up the ceiling? the news anchor asked. She wore a pink suit. She was a gumdrop in the snow.

The snow has almost melted, the father replied.

Why can't we talk to her?

I already told you.

Tell me again.

If you start talking to her, she will be distracted. It's important for her to focus. She's holding up the most perfect house in the world.

Would a perfect house be capable of collapsing?

It won't collapse. You'll see.

Then the father flashed a huge smile at the camera, showing his gums.

Cut, the news anchor said.

Did you get a shot of the house? the father asked.

Sure, the news anchor replied.

When it was time for bed, the father told the daughter to stay on the chair.

All night? the daughter said. You have to be kidding.

All night, the father replied, and the daughter did as she was told.

The mother had trouble sleeping that first night. She kept dreaming she was wet. She kept feeling water edging under her skin, under her nails, into her ears. She would wake and touch her skin until she was sure it was dry, and then fall asleep, fitfully, again. She dreamed she was stuck underwater. She was submerged in a tank, floating in pale gray water. She was holding her breath but her lungs were losing air. She dreamed she was in the mouth of a volcano, buoyed by lava. She could feel the volcano rumbling beneath her. She could feel the vibrations traveling through her toes to her knees to her hips to her shoulders. And then the volcano exploded. She was thrown out. But what it spewed wasn't lava and ash. It was snow. And the mother landed face-down on the ground, snow raining over her. She tried to get up but she couldn't. The snow pushed her down like hundreds of tiny hands. She tried to open her mouth to scream but it was filled with the flakes. She dreamed she was choking on snow.

By the morning of the second day, the news team had grown bored even with the story of the girl. They packed up and left. The father learned this when he went out to bid them good morning. He was disappointed to see they had gone, but turned his attention again to the house. Conditions were better than yesterday. The sun was out and the father had managed to push the snow away from the house in a ring. The problem now was the rivulet of water surrounding the house. It would creep in at the baseboards, he knew. He would tell the mother where to concentrate her efforts today.

The daughter had been holding up the ceiling all night. Once, she bent her elbows the tiniest bit to see what would happen and she felt it: the ceiling began to give way. She restraightened her arms. She knew then that the father was right: If she got down, the ceiling would fall. The house would be ruined. Her shoulders popped. Her wrists creaked under the weight, warning her in a language of aching—*please, we won't be able to take it much longer*. But the daughter had no choice.

When the father came back inside, the daughter asked for breakfast. The father sped past her, spoke to the mother, and sped back out again, into town.

Hey, the daughter yelled after him, but the father seemed not to hear.

In certain parts of town, the snow was melting fast, trickling along the edges of itself, running into sewers and soil and lower land. One woman's sandals, which she had left on her stoop the night before the storm, were washed away by the runoff, gliding down the street into an open manhole. Armed with a flashlight, her husband was underground for hours, searching for her shoes.

By nightfall tomorrow, the townspeople guessed, the snow would be gone. When the earth had had enough, there would be flooding, but it had flooded before and they would handle it as they always had. After the father left, the mother went out, too. The father had warned her repeatedly that one of them needed to stay at the house at all times to keep an eye on the daughter. And besides, the mother was supposed to be swabbing away. But the mother was restless and lonely in the house and when the father left, she wanted to go out, too.

I'll be gone for a little while, she told the daughter.

Can I come? the daughter asked.

The mother shook her head. I'll get you something if you'd like, she said.

I'm tired.

I know. It can't be much longer now.

I'm so tired.

The mother patted the top of the daughter's foot. Just hold on a little longer. I'll bring you a bag of marzipan.

The daughter was too exhausted to argue. Satisfied, the mother walked out the door, her feet crunching against the packed powder.

There was no telling how long the mother and father had been gone. But the daughter started to come undone. By now, the ceiling had lost almost all the snow, but the wood—saturated with water, soaked through by the unexpected winter—was nearly blackened and heavy with melting. The weight climbed into the daughter's bones. Her eyelids fluttered. She could no longer feel her hands. Her stockinged toes curled over the edge of the chair and her heels throbbed. Blood swelled in her neck and pooled in her shoulders. Her hips were cast forward, locked under the weight. It was as if the roof were fighting her, intent on crashing to the ground. She was beyond the point of crying out. She thought she couldn't do it. She thought it was too much. But she told herself: One more second now, one more second now, now it's just one more second. Fighting to keep herself going. And then, somewhere near the end of the day, the daughter started crying. Tears poured from her eyes the way the snow had gushed from the sky days earlier. Her entire body wept, sobbing with anguish.

When the father came back from town, he was relieved to see the house still intact. But he was unrelieved when he walked into the house. The daughter was still on the chair, her head lolling forward. The father hardly saw her. What he noticed instead was the water around his ankles. All over the floor. A calm layer, almost ten centimeters deep, filled the house from wall to wall. The father waded through it silently, the soft swish of water the only sound.

The mother came home then, too, and stood in the open door, water sliding out over her feet.

It's ruined, the father said softly. The water got through somehow. She let it through.

It could have come from anywhere, the mother said.

No. Everything around the house is dry. It came from the ceiling. I knew if it bowed enough, it would splinter. The water would come through.

The ceiling is still perfectly flat, the mother said, glancing up at it.

You could never see it, the father said. He knelt and lapped his hands through the water. It's ruined, he said again.

It will dry, the mother said.

The father shook his head. The ceiling will have to be rebuilt. The whole house.

If the father had raised his hands to his mouth, he would have tasted the salt of the daughter's tears, but he didn't. He simply scooped the water over and over with his hands, his back rounded, his head sinking farther into his chest.

Some books are damaged, the mother said. Only things on the floor!

It's the wood, the father said. It's too wet now. The walls are too soft. They'll fall in soon. She let it through, he whispered.

The daughter, her slender arms strained under the weight of the house, her tears long since dry, was too exhausted to speak. She simply stared at the father and held up the ceiling.

Relationships

How is our understanding of self shaped by our relations—especially sexual relations—with others? The pieces in this section offer a range of responses to this question, as the writers consider how factors such as ethnicity, class, and violence affect women's experiences of this fundamental part of human life.

In "A Boy My Sister Dated in High School" (2015), **Emily Mitchell** (1975–) depicts a woman's reaction to learning that her sister was slapped by a boyfriend in high school and kept the incident hidden for many years.

The poem "Apple Picking" (2004), by **Laura Negrete** (1982–), explores how the stories of Eve and the Virgin Mary shape gender relations within a Latino family and in the world at large.

"Drinking Coffee Elsewhere" (2003), by **ZZ Packer** (1973–), portrays a poor black woman from Baltimore who must simultaneously negotiate the challenging terrain of Yale University and her own attraction to a fellow female student.

In her poem "The Burning Heart," published in 1999, **Louise Glück** (1943–) uses Dante's account of doomed lovers Francesca and Paolo as the starting point for an interrogation of the mysteries of passion and destiny.

"Re-forming the Crystal" (1973), a poem by **Adrienne Rich** (1929–2012), investigates the complexities of sexual desire and asks how women might reclaim and use that energy for their own purposes.

A Boy My Sister Dated in High School

Emily Mitchell

A boy my sister dated in high school slapped her across the face during an argument. They were sitting in the front seat of his car, parked by the basketball court behind our house, and she made a sarcastic reply to something he had said and before she knew what was happening, he'd raised his hand and swung it, open palmed, against her cheek.

She didn't tell me about this until years later after we had both left home. When she told me, I felt at once angry and strangely guilty because the boy in question was extraordinarily good-looking and I remembered having been impressed in a shallow way that I never spoke about that my sister was dating someone so handsome. I was jealous of a lot of things about my sister in those days: her beauty and her ease with people, how spontaneously funny she could be, how well she was liked. She fit in at our school and in our town, in her own body, in a way that I could not seem to manage, quiet and bookish and peculiar as I was then and remain. Still, there was never a time when I didn't love her very much and when I wouldn't have done whatever I could to support and defend her.

Why didn't you tell me sooner? I asked, when she finally told me.

When the boy she was dating hit my sister, it made a sharp cracking sound, just like it does in the movies. She raised her hand and touched the side of her own face. The expanse of skin where he'd struck her buzzed and tingled, felt weirdly alive. It didn't hurt and even the actual slap itself hadn't really hurt. Instead, she was shocked, surprised because she had not expected this, and then confused about what she should do next.

She looked over at the boy she was dating, who had just hit her. He was leaning way back away from her against the car door as if he was afraid, either of her or of what he had just done. In his eyes was an expression of shock and remorse much more intense than anything she herself seemed to be feeling. He too had been surprised, and he looked like he might be about to cry. At that moment it came into her mind that maybe, in punishment for what he had done, the gods had magically frozen him in his current physical position: curled up like a frightened fetus with his eyes bugged out and his mouth hanging slightly open. Perhaps he would be stuck like that forever. In her mind she envisioned having to explain to the boy's mother how her son came to be paralyzed in this posture: *He hit me,* she would say, *and then, well, now he doesn't seem able to move or speak. I'm sorry.* She thought of him in various scenes over the course of his life to come—in school, at home, in church—still fixed in that attitude, and the absurdity of these images together with the amazement she still felt at what had just occurred made her suddenly snort with laughter.

Her laughter seemed to free the boy from his paralysis.

"Oh, god," he said. "I'm so sorry. I'm so, so sorry. I didn't mean . . ." He reached out toward her as though he wanted to take back what he'd done, but then he withdrew his hand. "I'm sorry," he said again. He hung his head.

"I guess you should take me home," my sister said. Suddenly she felt like crying. He nodded and started the car. When they pulled up in front of my parents' house, he turned off the engine. He looked over at her mournfully. She suddenly thought he was making a huge, self-centered melodrama out of something that wasn't really so important. He wanted to be a terrible, unforgivable villain. She did not want to give him that satisfaction.

"Look," she said. "I'm okay. It doesn't hurt. I'm not, like, scarred for life or anything."

"Really?" he asked.

"Really," she said. She leaned over and kissed him on the cheek. He clasped her hands gratefully. They smiled at each other because

A Boy My Sister Dated in High School

that was what they were used to doing. When they smiled, it felt as if a moment before they had been drowning in some cold, unpleasant sea, but now they were back on solid ground, back in the world they knew. A wave of relief swept over them.

"You were being kind of a bitch," he said.

"I was," she conceded. "And you were being a class-one a-hole." She opened the door and got out.

"Can I call you tomorrow?" he called after her.

"Yes," she said and went inside. She could hardly even feel where he had hit her at all anymore.

Because they had made up and because she wasn't hurt, she didn't feel like she needed to mention to anyone what had happened. If she said anything to our mother, she thought, Mom would only overreact. She would call the school, maybe the boy's parents. She would say things about violence against women and the patriarchy, the kind of embarrassing things that my sister had to do her best to ignore so that she would not be a total outcast in the conservative suburb where we lived. If she told our mother and she started making a fuss, it would definitely mean that she and the boy would break up and stop dating. They were both part of a big group of friends, and she didn't want to cause problems in that group over something that was really, truly no big deal but that might become a big deal if the parents were involved. It wasn't like she was some battered and abused woman, like you saw on television talk shows or heard about on local news. Probably, in a few months, she wouldn't even remember that it had happened.

So she said nothing and the boy never did it again and after a while they broke up for unrelated reasons and started dating other people without much drama or distress to either of them. They finished high school, went on to different colleges. They didn't keep in touch.

But during that time, unlike what she had expected, the memory of being hit by the boy didn't just fade away and vanish. It wasn't that she thought about it all the time or it ruined her life or she could never trust a man again or anything like that. From time to time it would come into her mind, that day, the moment of surprised confusion afterward. And she came to feel, especially as she got a little older, that she had let herself down by the way she had reacted. This was the feeling that grew incrementally inside her. She should not have tried to make him feel better by telling him it was no big deal. She should not have kept it from their friends just so they could all continue to get along. From the beginning she had failed to stand up for herself, and now she knew, or felt she knew, about herself that she would let someone do that to her and do nothing about it. She would be obliging. She would comply.

This guilt about how she hadn't stood up for herself was like a small stone that she had to carry around. That was how she pictured it. Small and round, but heavy. And she came to believe—she said, when she finally told me about it all those years later—that maybe if she told people about it, as she was doing now, it would get smaller and lighter; that sharing would diminish it, make it smaller, maybe even make it vanish.

And I thought, but did not say: maybe, or maybe it will make it multiply.

Apple Picking
Laura Negrete

1.
One Sunday Ama, Papá, Ruth, Rocio, Fausto, myself,
my cousin Manuel, and his wife Elena were gathered

in the living room. A Bible salesman had on display
an array of Bibles in front of us on the floor. There

were big Bibles, little Bibles, leather bound Bibles, children's
Bibles. Bibles, Bibles, Bibles. Each of them with its own religious

experience stamped on the cover. The salesman spoke of virgins
and the Passion. And then asked Manuel, "How did God make

your wife?" Manuel smirked and said, "From my rib." The
salesman sermoned about the woman's role as his eyes watched

my sisters and me and the newly married Elena. I was eight,
but even then, those words he spoke didn't sound right to me.

2.
A number of years ago a study was conducted in Mexico,
researchers asked men and women about their marital status.

Men responded *Estoy casado. Estoy*, a conditional state of being.
Women responded *Soy casada. Soy*, a permanent condition.

3.
Mamá Andrea is eighty-seven years old. A devout Catholic.
She walks with a hobble, a hunched back underneath layers

of clothes, a scapular around her neck that hangs snuggled between
her breasts, wrinkled from feeding eight children. They sag down

to her belly button. One day she proclaims, "If I could I would chop
these things off." In her hand a meat cleaver. "They are useless

and in the way." She has been bent over a featherless chicken
attempting to dismember it.

4.
Juan: *Felipe que a tu esposa María el dejaron un tereno.*
Yo creo que pronto va tener mas que tu.

Felipe: *Y de quien es María?*   *(jajajajajaja)*

5.
Here's the sex talk from my mother, "Laura, boys only want
one thing, don't give it to them."

6.
On her wedding day, my mother wore a blue dress not white
because she wasn't married the proper way. My mother

fue robaba by my father. He stole her from her house, from
her father's ownership. My father took her into his bed

and *la hizo suya*, he made her his.

7.
John: Phillip, I hear your wife Mary inherited some land.
Pretty soon, she's going to have more than you.

Phillip: And who does Mary belong to?   (hahahahahaha)

8.
Outside on the stone stoop Papá, Ruth, and Papá Juan
were gathered on a lovely summer day. Papá says to Ruth

"If you ever get pregnant at this age don't think of coming back
to this house." Papá Juan steps in and says, "Don't say that, Jesus.

One day she just might get up and leave this house for good."
Papá says, *"Pues, que Dios la bendiga."*   (Well, may God bless her)

9.
Our lady of Refuge, pray for us. Our lady of Angels, pray for us.
Nuestra Señora de San Juan, pray for us. Our lady of Altagracia,

pray for us. Our Lady of Fatima, pray for us. The most pure;
the most humble; the most faithful; the most devout; the most

obedient; the most merciful, pray for us. And the all mighty
Virgen de Guadalupe, *ruege por nosotros*.

10.
On our way back from Oaxaca, we had to stop in Mexico City.
Sarah's uncle suggested we go to the Basilica since our plane

didn't leave until the next day. I made my duty-bound pilgrimage
unintentionally. At the new Basilica with the souvenir shop

in the basement, I waited for mass to be over to go see you the only
blessed woman among all women. My dignity wanted to taste

your cherry sweet skin as it mixed with my own that burned
your throat like cheap whisky. You passed by so quickly as I stood

on the automated walkway. I barely got a glimpse of your face
looking down at me. I gazed at your image on the cloak

of Juan Diego, my breath pausing for a moment and I thought,
"If you ask me, it's you who ruined it for the rest of us. Not Eve."

Drinking Coffee Elsewhere

ZZ Packer

Orientation games began the day I arrived at Yale from Baltimore. In my group we played heady, frustrating games for smart people. One game appeared to be charades reinterpreted by existentialists; another involved listening to rocks. Then a freshman counselor made everyone play Trust. The idea was that if you had the faith to fall backward and wait for four scrawny former high school geniuses to catch you, just before your head cracked on the slate sidewalk, then you might learn to trust your fellow students. Russian roulette sounded like a better way to go.

"No way," I said. The white boys were waiting for me to fall, holding their arms out for me, sincerely, gallantly. "No fucking way."

"It's all cool, it's all cool," the counselor said. Her hair was a shade of blond I'd seen only on *Playboy* covers, and she raised her hands as though backing away from a growling dog. "Sister," she said, in an I'm-down-with-the-struggle voice, "you don't have to play this game. As a person of color, you shouldn't have to fit into any white, patriarchal system."

I said, "It's a bit too late for that."

In the next game, all I had to do was wait in a circle until it was my turn to say what inanimate object I wanted to be. One guy said he'd like to be a gadfly, like Socrates. "Stop me if I wax Platonic," he said. I didn't bother mentioning that gadflies weren't inanimate—it didn't seem to make a difference. The girl next to him was eating a rice cake. She wanted to be the Earth, she said. Earth with a capital *E*.

There was one other black person in the circle. He wore an Exeter T-shirt and his overly elastic expressions resembled a series of facial exercises. At the end of each person's turn, he smiled and bobbed his head with unfettered enthusiasm. "Oh, that was good," he said, as if the game were an experiment he'd set up and the results were turning out better than he'd expected. "Good, good, good!"

When it was my turn I said, "My name is Dina, and if I had to be any object, I guess I'd be a revolver." The sunlight dulled as if on cue. Clouds passed rapidly overhead, presaging rain. I don't know why I said it. Until that moment I'd been good in all the ways that were meant to matter. I was an honor roll student—though I'd learned long ago not to mention it in the part of Baltimore where I lived. Suddenly I was hard-bitten and recalcitrant, the kind of kid who took pleasure in sticking pins into cats; the kind who chased down smart kids to spray them with Mace.

"A revolver," a counselor said, stroking his chin, as if it had grown a rabbinical beard. "Could you please elaborate?"

The black guy cocked his head and frowned, as if the beakers and Erlenmeyer flasks of his experiment had grown legs and scurried off.

"You were just kidding," the dean said, "about wiping out all of mankind. That, I suppose, was a joke." She squinted at me. One of her hands curved atop the other to form a pink, freckled molehill on her desk.

"Well," I said, "maybe I meant it at the time." I quickly saw that this was not the answer she wanted. "I don't know. I think it's the architecture."

Through the dimming light of the dean's office window, I could see the fortress of the old campus. On my ride from the bus station to the campus, I'd barely glimpsed New Haven—a flash of crumpled building here, a trio of straggly kids there. A lot like Baltimore. But everything had changed when we reached those streets hooded by gothic buildings. I imagined how the college must have looked when it was founded, when most of the students owned slaves. I pictured men wearing tights and knickers, smoking pipes.

"The architecture," the dean repeated. She bit her lip and seemed to be making a calculation of some sort. I noticed that she blinked less often than most people. I sat there, intrigued, waiting to see how long it would be before she blinked again.

My revolver comment won me a year's worth of psychiatric counseling, weekly meetings with Dean Guest, and—since the parents of the roommate I'd never met weren't too hip on the idea of their Amy sharing a bunk bed with a budding homicidal loony—my very own room.

Shortly after getting my first C ever, I also received the first knock on my door. The female counselors never knocked. The dean had spoken to them; I was a priority. Every other day, right before dinnertime, they'd look in on me, unannounced. "Just checking up," a counselor would say. It was the voice of a suburban mother in training. By the second week, I had made a point of sitting in a chair in front of the door, just when I expected a counselor to pop her head around. This was intended to startle them. I also made a point of being naked. The unannounced visits ended.

The knocking persisted. Through the peephole I saw a white face, distorted and balloonish.

"Let me in." The person looked like a boy but it sounded like a girl. "Let me in," the voice repeated.

"Not a chance," I said. I had a suicide single, and I wanted to keep it that way. No roommates, no visitors.

Then the person began to sob, and I heard a back slump against the door. If I hadn't known the person was white from the peephole, I'd have known it from a display like this. Black people didn't knock on strangers' doors, crying. Not that I understood the black people at Yale. Most of them were from New York and tried hard to pretend that they hadn't gone to prep schools. And there was something pitiful in how cool they were. Occasionally one would reach out to me with missionary zeal, but I'd rebuff the person with haughty silence.

"I don't have anyone to talk to!" the person on the other side of the door cried.

"That is correct."

"When I was a child," the person said, "I played by myself in a corner of the schoolyard all alone. I hated dolls and I hated games, animals were not friendly and birds flew away. If anyone was looking for me I hid behind a tree and cried out 'I am an orphan—'"

I opened the door. It was a she.

"Plagiarist!" I yelled. She had just recited a Frank O'Hara poem as though she'd thought it up herself. I knew the poem because it was one of the few things I'd been forced to read that I wished I'd written myself.

The girl turned to face me, smiling weakly, as though her triumph was not in getting me to open the door but in the fact that she was able to smile at all when she was so accustomed to crying. She was large but not obese, and crying had turned her face the color of raw chicken. She blew her nose into the waist end of her T-shirt, revealing a pale belly.

"How do you know that poem?"

She sniffed. "I'm in your Contemporary Poetry class."

She said she was Canadian and her name was Heidi, although she said she wanted people to call her Henrik. "That's a guy's name," I said. "What do you want? A sex change?"

She looked at me with so little surprise that I suspected she hadn't discounted this as an option. Then her story came out in teary, hiccup-like bursts. She had sucked some "cute guy's dick" and he'd told everybody and now people thought she was "a slut."

"Why'd you suck his dick? Aren't you a lesbian?"

She fit the bill. Short hair, hard, roach-stomping shoes. Dressed like an aspiring plumber. And then there was the name Henrik. The lesbians I'd seen on TV were wiry, thin strips of muscle, but Heidi was round and soft and had a moonlike face. Drab henna-colored hair. And lesbians had cats. "Do you have a cat?" I asked.

Her eyes turned glossy with new tears. "No," she said, her voice quavering, "and I'm not a lesbian. Are you?"

"Do I look like one?" I said.

She didn't answer.

"OK," I said. "I could suck a guy's dick, too, if I wanted. But I don't. The human penis is one of the most germ-ridden objects there is." Heidi looked at me, unconvinced. "What I meant to say," I began again, "is that I don't like anybody. Period. Guys or girls. I'm a misanthrope."

"I am, too."

"No," I said, guiding her back through my door and out into the hallway. "You're not."

"Have you had dinner?" she asked. "Let's go to the Commons."

I pointed to a pyramid of ramen noodle packages on my windowsill. "See that? That means I never have to go to Commons. Aside from class, I have contact with no one."

"I hate it here, too," she said. "I should have gone to McGill, eh."

"The way to feel better," I said, "is to get some ramen and lock yourself in your room. Everyone will forget about you and that guy's dick and you won't have to see anyone ever again. If anyone looks for you—"

"I'll hide behind a tree."

"A revolver?" Dr. Raeburn said, flipping through a manila folder. He looked up at me as if to ask another question, but he didn't.

Dr. Raeburn was the psychiatrist. He had the gray hair and whiskers of a Civil War general. He was also a chain smoker with beige teeth and a navy wool jacket smeared with ash. He asked about the revolver at the beginning of my first visit. When I was unable to explain myself, he smiled, as if this were perfectly reasonable.

"Tell me about your parents."

I wondered what he already had on file. The folder was thick, though I hadn't said a thing of significance since Day One.

"My father was a dick and my mother seemed to like him."

He patted his pockets for his cigarettes. "That's some heavy stuff," he said. "How do you feel about Dad?" The man couldn't say the word "father." "Is Dad someone you see often?"

"I hate my father almost as much as I hate the word 'Dad.'"

He started tapping his cigarette.

"You can't smoke in here."

"That's right," he said, and slipped the cigarette back into the packet. He smiled, widening his eyes brightly. "Don't ever start."

I thought that that first encounter would be the last of Heidi or Henrik, or whatever, but then her head appeared in a window of Linsly-Chit during my Chaucer class. A few days later, she swooped down a flight of stairs in Harkness, following me. She hailed me from across Elm Street and found me in the Sterling Library stacks. After one of my meetings with Dr. Raeburn, she was waiting for me outside Health Services, legs crossed, cleaning her fingernails.

"You know," she said, as we walked through Old Campus, "you've got to stop eating ramen. Not only does it lack a single nutrient but it's full of MSG."

I wondered why she even bothered, and was vaguely flattered that she cared, but I said, "I like eating chemicals. It keeps the skin radiant."

"There's also hepatitis." She knew how to get my attention—mention a disease.

"You get hepatitis from unwashed lettuce," I said. "If there's anything safe from the perils of the food chain, it's ramen."

"But do you refrigerate what you don't eat? Each time you reheat it, you're killing good bacteria, which then can't keep the bad bacteria in check. A guy got sick from reheating Chinese noodles, and his son died from it. I read it in the *Times*." With this, she put a jovial arm around my neck. I continued walking, a little stunned. Then, just as quickly, she dropped her arm and stopped walking. I stopped, too.

"Did you notice that I put my arm around you?"

"Yes," I said. "Next time, I'll have to chop it off."

"I don't want you to get sick," she said. "Let's eat at Commons."

In the cold air, her arm had felt good.

The problem with Commons was that it was too big; its ceiling was as high as a cathedral's, but below it there were no awestruck worshippers, only eighteen-year-olds at heavy wooden tables, chatting over veal patties and Jell-O.

We got our food, tacos stuffed with meat substitute, and made our way through the maze of tables. The Koreans had a table. Each singing group had a table. The crew team sat at a long table of its own. We passed the black table. Heidi was so plump and moonfaced that the sheer quantity of her flesh accentuated just how white she was. The black students gave me a long, hard stare.

"How you doing, sista?" a guy asked, his voice full of accusation, eyeballing me as though I were clad in a Klansman's sheet and hood. "I guess we won't see you till graduation."

"If," I said, "you graduate."

The remark was not well received. As I walked past, I heard protests, angry and loud as if they'd discovered a cheat at their poker game. Heidi and I found an unoccupied table along the periphery, which was isolated and dark. We sat down. Heidi prayed over her tacos.

"I thought you didn't believe in God," I said.

"Not in the God depicted in the Judeo-Christian Bible, but I do believe that nature's essence is a spirit that—"

"All right," I said. I had begun to eat, and cubes of diced tomato fell from my mouth when I spoke. "Stop right there. Tacos and spirits don't mix."

"You've always got to be so flip," she said. "I'm going to apply for another friend."

"There's always Mr. Dick," I said. "Slurp, slurp."

"You are so lame. So unbelievably lame. I'm going out with Mr. Dick. Thursday night at Atticus. His name is Keith."

Heidi hadn't mentioned Mr. Dick since the day I'd met her. That was more than a month ago and we'd spent a lot of that time together. I checked for signs that she was lying; her habit of smiling too much, her eyes bright and cheeks full so that she looked like a chipmunk. But she looked normal. Pleased, even, to see me so flustered.

"You're insane! What are you going to do this time?" I asked. "Sleep with him? Then when he makes fun of you, what? Come pound your head on my door reciting the collected poems of Sylvia Plath?"

"He's going to apologize for before. And don't call me insane. You're the one going to the psychiatrist."

"Well, I'm not going to suck his dick, that's for sure."

She put her arm around me in mock comfort, but I pushed it off, and ignored her. She touched my shoulder again, and I turned, annoyed, but it wasn't Heidi after all; a sepia-toned boy dressed in khakis and a crisp plaid shirt was standing behind me. He thrust a hot-pink square of paper toward me without a word, then briskly made his way toward the other end of Commons, where the crowds blossomed. Heidi leaned over and read it: "Wear Black Leather— the Less, the Better."

"It's a gay party," I said, crumpling the card. "He thinks we're fucking gay."

Heidi and I signed on to work at the Saybrook dining hall as dishwashers. The job consisted of dumping food from plates and trays into a vat of rushing water. It seemed straightforward, but then I learned better. You wouldn't believe what people could do with food until you worked in a dish room. Lettuce and crackers and soup would be bullied into a pulp in the bowl of some bored anorexic; ziti would be mixed with honey and granola; trays would appear heaped with mashed potato snow women with melted chocolate ice cream for hair. Frat boys arrived at the dish-room window, en masse. They liked to fill glasses with food, then seal them, airtight, onto their trays. If you tried to prize them off, milk, Worcestershire sauce, peas, chucks of bread vomited onto your dish-room uniform.

When this happened one day in the middle of the lunch rush, for what seemed like the hundredth time, I tipped the tray toward one of the frat boys as he turned to walk away, popping the glass off so that the mess spurted onto his Shetland sweater.

He looked down at his sweater. "Lesbo bitch!"

"No," I said, "that would be your mother."

Heidi, next to me, clenched my arm in support, but I remained motionless, waiting to see what the frat boy would do. He glared at me for a minute, then walked away.

"Let's take a smoke break," Heidi said.

I didn't smoke, but Heidi had begun to, because she thought it would help her lose weight. As I hefted a stack of glasses through the steamer, she lit up.

"Soft packs remind me of you," she said. "Just when you've smoked them all and you think there's none left, there's always one more, hiding in that little crushed corner." Before I could respond she said, "Oh, God. Not another mouse. You know whose job that is."

By the end of the rush, the floor mats got full and slippery with food. This was when mice tended to appear, scurrying over our shoes; more often than not, a mouse got caught in the grating that covered the drains in the floor. Sometimes the mouse was already dead by the time we noticed it. This one was alive.

"No way," I said. "This time you're going to help. Get some gloves and a trash bag."

"That's all I'm getting. I'm not getting that mouse out of there."

"Put on the gloves," I ordered. She winced, but put them on. "Reach down," I said. "At an angle, so you get at its middle. Otherwise, if you try to get it by its tail, the tail will break off."

"This is filthy, eh."

"That's why we're here," I said. "To clean up filth. Eh."

She reached down, but would not touch the mouse. I put my hand around her arm and pushed it till her hand made contact. The cries from the mouse were soft, songlike. "Oh, my God," she said. "Oh, my God, ohmigod." She wrestled it out of the grating and turned her head away.

"Don't you let it go," I said.

"Where's the food bag? It'll smother itself if I drop it in the food bag. Quick," she said, her head still turned away, her eyes closed. "Lead me to it."

"No. We are not going to smother this mouse. We've got to break its neck."

"You're one heartless bitch."

I wondered how to explain that if death is unavoidable it should be quick and painless. My mother had died slowly. At the hospital, they'd said it was kidney failure, but I knew, in the end, it was my father. He made her so scared to live in her own home that she was finally driven away in an ambulance.

"Breaking its neck will save it the pain of smothering," I said. "Breaking its neck is more humane. Take the trash bag and cover it so you won't get any blood on you, then crush."

The loud jets of the steamer had shut off automatically and the dish room grew quiet. Heidi breathed in deeply, then crushed the mouse. She shuddered, disgusted. "Now what?"

"What do you mean, 'now what?' Throw the little bastard in the trash."

At our third session, I told Dr. Raeburn I didn't mind if he smoked. He sat on the sill of his open window, smoking behind a jungle screen of office plants.

We spent the first ten minutes discussing the *Iliad*, and whether or not the text actually states that Achilles had been dipped in the River Styx. He said it did, and I said it didn't. After we'd finished with the *Iliad*, and with my new job in what he called "the scullery," he asked questions about my parents. I told him nothing. It was none of his business. Instead, I talked about Heidi. I told him about that day in Commons, Heidi's plan to go on a date with Mr. Dick, and the invitation we'd been given to the gay party.

"You seem preoccupied by this soirée." He arched his eyebrows at the word "soirée."

"Wouldn't you be?"

"Dina," he said slowly, in a way that made my name seem like a song title, "have you ever had a romantic interest?"

"You want to know if I've ever had a boyfriend?" I said. "Just go ahead and ask if I've ever fucked anybody."

This appeared to surprise him. "I think that you are having a crisis of identity," he said.

"Oh, is that what this is?"

His profession had taught him not to roll his eyes. Instead, his exasperation revealed itself in a tiny pursing of his lips, as though he'd just tasted something awful and was trying very hard not to offend the cook.

"It doesn't have to be, as you say, someone you've fucked, it doesn't have to be a boyfriend," he said.

"Well, what are you trying to say? If it's not a boy, then you're saying it's a girl—"

"Calm down. It could be a crush, Dina." He lit one cigarette off another. "A crush on a male teacher, a crush on a dog, for heaven's sake. An interest. Not necessarily a relationship."

It was sacrifice time. If I could spend the next half hour talking about some boy, then I'd have given him what he wanted.

So I told him about the boy with the nice shoes.

I was sixteen and had spent the last few coins in my pocket on bus fare to buy groceries. I didn't like going to the Super Fresh two blocks away from my house, plunking government food stamps into the hands of the cashiers.

"There she go reading," one of them once said, even though I was only carrying a book. "Don't your eyes get tired?"

On Greenmount Avenue you could read schoolbooks—that was understandable. The government and your teachers forced you to read them. But anything else was antisocial. It meant you'd rather submit to the words of some white dude than shoot the breeze with your neighbors.

I hated those cashiers, and I hated them seeing me with food stamps, so I took the bus and shopped elsewhere. That day, I got off the bus at Govans, and though the neighborhood was black like my own—hair salon after hair salon of airbrushed signs promising arabesque hair styles and inch-long fingernails—the houses were neat and orderly, nothing at all like Greenmount, where every other house had at least one shattered window. The store was well swept, and people quietly checked long grocery lists—no screaming kids, no loud cashier-customer altercations. I got the groceries and left the store.

I decided to walk back. It was a fall day, and I walked for blocks. Then I sensed someone following me. I walked more quickly, my arms around the sack, the leafy lettuce tickling my nose. I didn't want to hold the sack so close that it would break the eggs or squash the hamburger buns, but it was slipping, and as I looked behind me a boy my age, maybe older, rushed toward me.

"Let me help you," he said.

"That's all right." I set the bag on the sidewalk. Maybe I saw his face, maybe it was handsome enough, but what I noticed first, splayed on either side of the bag, were his shoes. They were nice shoes, real leather, a stitched design like a widow's peak on each one, or like birds' wings, and for the first time in my life I understood what people meant when they said "wingtip shoes."

"I watched you carry them groceries out that store, then you look around, like you're lost, but like you liked being lost, then you walk down the sidewalk for blocks and blocks. Rearranging that bag, it almost gone to slip, then hefting it back up again."

"Uh-huh," I said.

"And then I passed my own house and was still following you. And then your bag really look like it was gone crash and everything. So I just thought I'd help." He sucked in his bottom lip, as if to keep it from making a smile. "What's your name?" When I told him, he said, "Dina, my name is Cecil." Then he said, "*D* comes right after *C*."

"Yes," I said, "it does, doesn't it."

Then, half question, half statement, he said, "I could carry your groceries for you? And walk you home?"

I stopped the story there. Dr. Raeburn kept looking at me. "Then what happened?"

I couldn't tell him the rest: that I had not wanted the boy to walk me home, that I didn't want someone with such nice shoes to see where I lived.

Dr. Raeburn would only have pitied me if I'd told him that I ran down the sidewalk after I told the boy no, that I fell, the bag slipped, and the eggs cracked, their yolks running all over the lettuce. Clear amniotic fluid coated the can of cinnamon rolls. I left the bag there on the sidewalk, the groceries spilled out randomly like cards loosed from a deck. When I returned home, I told my mother that I'd lost the food stamps.

"Lost?" she said. I'd expected her to get angry, I'd wanted her to get angry, but she hadn't. "Lost?" she repeated. Why had I been so clumsy and nervous around a harmless boy? I could have brought the groceries home and washed off the egg yolk, but instead I'd just left them there. "Come on," Mama said, snuffing her tears, pulling my arm, trying to get me to join her and start yanking cushions off the couch. "We'll find enough change here. We got to get something for dinner before your father gets back."

We'd already searched the couch for money the previous week, and I knew there'd be nothing now, but I began to push my fingers into the couch's boniest corners, pretending that it was only a matter of time before I'd find some change or a lost watch or an earring. Something pawnable, perhaps.

"What happened next?" Dr. Raeburn asked again. "Did you let the boy walk you home?"

"My house was far, so we went to his house instead." Though I was sure Dr. Raeburn knew that I was making this part up, I continued. "We made out on his sofa. He kissed me."

Dr. Raeburn lit his next cigarette like a detective. Cool, suspicious. "How did it feel?"

"You know," I said. "Like a kiss feels. It felt nice. The kiss felt very, very nice."

Raeburn smiled gently, though he seemed unconvinced. When he called time on our session, his cigarette had become one long pole of ash. I left his office, walking quickly down the corridor, afraid to look back. It would be like him to trot after me, his navy blazer flapping, just to get the truth out of me. *You never kissed anyone.* The words slid from my brain, and knotted in my stomach.

When I reached my dorm, I found an old record player blocking my door and a Charles Mingus LP propped beside it. I carried them inside and then, lying on the floor, I played the Mingus over and over again until I fell asleep. I slept feeling as though Dr. Raeburn had attached electrodes to my head, willing into my mind a dream about my mother. I saw the lemon meringue of her skin, the long bone of her arm as she reached down to clip her toenails. I'd come home from a school trip to an aquarium, and I was explaining the differences between baleen and sperm whales according to the size of their heads, the range of their habitats, their feeding patterns.

I awoke remembering the expression on her face after I'd finished my dizzying whale lecture. She looked like a tourist who'd asked for directions to a place she thought was simple enough to get to only to hear a series of hypothetical turns, alleys, one-way streets. Her response was to nod politely at the perilous elaborateness of it all; to nod and save herself from the knowledge that she would never be able to get where she wanted to go.

The dishwashers always closed down the dining hall. One night, after everyone else had punched out, Heidi and I took a break, and though I wasn't a smoker, we set two milk crates upside down on the floor and smoked cigarettes.

The dishwashing machines were off, but steam still rose from them like a jungle mist. Outside in the winter air, students were singing carols in their groomed and tailored singing-group voices. The Whiffenpoofs were back in New Haven after a tour around the world, and I guess their return was a huge deal. Heidi and I craned our necks to watch the year's first snow through an open window.

"What are you going to do when you're finished?" Heidi asked. Sexy question marks of smoke drifted up to the windows before vanishing.

"Take a bath."

She swatted me with her free hand. "No, silly. Three years from now. When you leave Yale."

"I don't know. Open up a library. Somewhere where no one comes in for books. A library in a desert."

She looked at me as though she'd expected this sort of answer and didn't know why she'd asked in the first place.

"What are you going to do?" I asked her.

"Open up a psych clinic. In a desert. And my only patient will be some wacko who runs a library."

"Ha," I said. "Whatever you do, don't work in a dish room ever again. You're no good." I got up from the crate. "C'mon. Let's hose the place down."

We put our cigarettes on the floor, since it was our job to clean it anyway. We held squirt guns in one hand and used the other to douse the floors with the standard-issue, eye-burning cleaning solution. We hosed the dish room, the kitchen, the serving line, sending the water and crud and suds into the drains. Then we hosed them again so the solution wouldn't eat holes in our shoes as we left. Then I had an idea. I unbuckled my belt.

"What the hell are you doing?" Heidi said.

"Listen, it's too cold to go outside with our uniforms all wet. We could just take a shower right here. There's nobody but us."

"What the fuck, eh?"

I let my pants drop, then took off my shirt and panties. I didn't wear a bra, since I didn't have much to fill one. I took off my shoes and hung my clothes on the stepladder.

"You've flipped," Heidi said. "I mean, really, psych-ward flipped."

I soaped up with the liquid hand soap until I felt as glazed as a ham. "Stand back and spray me."

"Oh, my God," she said. I didn't know whether she was confused or delighted, but she picked up the squirt gun and sprayed me. She was laughing. Then she got too close and the water started to sting.

"God damn it!" I said. "That hurt!"

"I was wondering what it would take to make you say that."

When all the soap had been rinsed off, I put on my regular clothes and said, "OK. You're up next."

"No way," she said.

"Yes way."

She started to take off her uniform shirt, then stopped.

"What?"

"I'm too fat."

"You goddamn right." She always said she was fat. One time I'd told her that she should shut up about it, that large black women wore their fat like mink coats. "You're big as a house," I said now. "Frozen yogurt may be low in calories, but not if you eat five tubs of it. Take your clothes off. I want to get out of here."

She began taking off her uniform, then stood there, hands cupped over her breasts, crouching at the pubic bone.

"Open up," I said, "or we'll never get done."

Her hands remained where they were. I threw the bottle of liquid soap at her, and she had to catch it, revealing herself as she did.

I turned on the squirt gun, and she stood there, stiff, arms at her side, eyes closed, as though awaiting mummification. I began with the water on low, and she turned around in a full circle, hesitantly, letting the droplets from the spray fall on her as if she were submitting to a death by stoning.

When I increased the water pressure, she slipped and fell on the sudsy floor. She stood up and then slipped again. This time she laughed and remained on the floor, rolling around on it as I sprayed.

I think I began to love Heidi that night in the dish room, but who is to say that I hadn't begun to love her the first time I met her? I sprayed her and sprayed her, and she turned over and over like a large beautiful dolphin, lolling about in the sun.

Heidi started sleeping at my place. Sometimes she slept on the floor; sometimes we slept sardinelike, my feet at her head, until she complained that my feet were "taunting" her. When we finally slept head to head, she said, "Much better." She was so close I could smell her toothpaste. "I like your hair," she told me, touching it through the darkness. "You should wear it out more often."

"White people always say that about black people's hair. The worse it looks, the more they say they like it."

I'd expected her to disagree, but she kept touching my hair, her hands passing through it till my scalp tingled. When she began to touch the hair around the edge of my face, I felt myself quake. Her fingertips stopped for a moment, as if checking my pulse, then resumed.

"I like how it feels right here. See, mine just starts with the same old texture as the rest of my hair." She found my hand under the blanket and brought it to her hairline. "See," she said.

It was dark. As I touched her hair, it seemed as though I could smell it, too. Not a shampoo smell. Something richer, murkier. A bit dead, but sweet, like the decaying wood of a ship. She guided my hand.

"I see," I said. The record she'd given me was playing in my mind, and I kept trying to shut it off. I could also hear my mother saying that this is what happens when you've been around white people: things get weird. So weird I could hear the stylus etching its way into the flat vinyl of the record. "Listen," I said finally, when the bass and saxes started up. I heard Heidi breathe deeply, but she said nothing.

We spent the winter and some of the spring in my room—never hers—missing tests, listening to music, looking out my window to comment on people who wouldn't have given us a second thought. We read books related to none of our classes. I got riled up by *The Autobiography of Malcolm X* and *The Chomsky Reader*; Heidi read aloud passages from *The Anxiety of Influence*. We guiltily read mysteries and *Clan of the Cave Bear*, then immediately threw them away. Once we looked up from our books at exactly the same moment, as though trapped at a dinner table with nothing to say. A pleasant trap of silence.

Then one weekend I went back to Baltimore and stayed with my father. He asked me how school was going, but besides that, we didn't talk much. He knew what I thought of him. I stopped by the Enoch Pratt Library, where my favorite librarian, Mrs. Ardelia, cornered me into giving a little talk to the after-school kids, telling them to stay in school. They just looked at me like I was crazy; they were only nine or ten, and it hadn't even occurred to them to bail.

When I returned to Yale—to a sleepy, tree-scented spring—a group of students were holding what was called "Coming Out Day." I watched it from my room.

The emcee was the sepia boy who'd given us the invitation months back. His speech was strident but still smooth and peppered with jokes. There was a speech about AIDS, with lots of statistics: nothing that seemed to make "coming out" worth it. Then the women spoke. One girl pronounced herself "out" as casually as if she'd announced the time. Another said nothing at all: she came to the microphone with a woman who began cutting off her waist-length, bleached-blond hair. The woman doing the cutting tossed the shorn hair in every direction as she cut. People were clapping and cheering and catching the locks of hair.

And then there was Heidi. She was proud that she liked girls, she said when she reached the microphone. She loved them, wanted to sleep with them. She was a dyke, she said repeatedly, stabbing her finger to her chest in case anyone was unsure to whom she was referring. She could not have seen me. I was across the street, three stories up. And yet, when everyone clapped for her, she seemed to be looking straight at me.

Heidi knocked. "Let me in."

It was like the first time I met her. The tears, the raw pink of her face.

We hadn't spoken in weeks. Outside, pink-and-white blossoms hung from the Old Campus trees. Students played Hacky Sack in T-shirts and shorts. Though I was the one who'd broken away after she went up to that podium, I still half expected her to poke her head out a window in Linsly-Chit, or tap on my back in Harkness, or even join me in the Commons dining hall, where I'd asked for my dish-room shift to be transferred. She did none of these.

"Well," I said, "what is it?"

She looked at me. "My mother," she said.

She continued to cry, but seemed to have grown so silent in my room I wondered if I could hear the numbers change on my digital clock.

"When my parents were getting divorced," she said, "my mom bought a car. A used one. An El Dorado. It was filthy. It looked like a huge crushed can coming up the street. She kept trying to clean it out. I mean—"

I nodded and tried to think what to say in the pause she left behind. Finally I said, "We had one of those," though I was sure ours was an Impala.

She looked at me, eyes steely from trying not to cry. "Anyway, she'd drive me around in it and although she didn't like me to eat in it, I always did. One day I was eating cantaloupe slices, spitting the seeds on the floor. Maybe a month later, I saw this little sprout, growing right up from the car floor. I just started laughing and she kept saying what, what? I was laughing and then I saw she was so—"

She didn't finish. So what? So sad? So awful? Heidi looked at me with what seemed to be a renewed vigor. "We could have gotten a better car, eh?"

"It's all right. It's not a big deal," I said.

Of course, that was the wrong thing to say. And I really didn't mean it to sound the way it had come out.

I told Dr. Raeburn about Heidi's mother having cancer and how I'd said it wasn't a big deal, though I'd wanted to say the opposite. I told Dr. Raeburn how I meant to tell Heidi that my mother had died, that I knew how one eventually accustoms oneself to the physical world's lack of sympathy: the buses that are still running late, the kids who still play in the street, the clocks that won't stop ticking for the person who's gone.

"You're pretending," Dr. Raeburn said, not sage or professional, but a little shocked by the discovery, as if I'd been trying to hide a pack of his cigarettes behind my back.

"I'm pretending?" I shook my head. "All those years of psych grad," I said. "And to tell me *that*?"

"What I mean is that you construct stories about yourself and dish them out—one for you, one for you—" Here he reenacted this process, showing me handing out lies as if they were apples.

"Pretending. I believe the professional name for it might be denial," I said. "Are you calling me gay?"

He pursed his lips noncommittally, then finally said, "No, Dina. I don't think you're gay."

I checked his eyes. I couldn't read them.

"No. Not at all," he said, sounding as if he were telling a subtle joke. "But maybe you'll finally understand."

"Understand what?"

"Oh, just that constantly saying what one doesn't mean accustoms the mouth to meaningless phrases." His eyes narrowed. "Maybe you'll understand that when you finally need to express something truly significant your mouth will revert to the insignificant nonsense it knows so well." He looked at me, his hands sputtering in the air in a gesture of defeat. "Who knows?" he asked with a glib, psychiatric smile I'd never seen before. "Maybe it's your survival mechanism. Black living in a white world."

I heard him, but only vaguely. I'd hooked on to that one word, pretending. Dr. Raeburn would never realize that "pretending" was what had got me this far. I remembered the morning of my mother's funeral. I'd been given milk to settle my stomach; I'd pretended it was coffee. I imagined I was drinking coffee elsewhere. Some Arabic-speaking country where the thick coffee served in little cups was so strong it could keep you awake for days.

Heidi wanted me to go with her to the funeral. She'd sent this message through the dean. "We'll pay for your ticket to Vancouver," the dean said.

These people wanted you to owe them for everything. "What about my return ticket?" I asked the dean. "Maybe the shrink will chip in for that."

The dean looked at me as though I were an insect she'd like to squash. "We'll pay for the whole thing. We might even pay for some lessons in manners."

So I packed my suitcase and walked from my suicide single dorm to Heidi's room. A thin wispy girl in ragged cutoffs and a shirt that read "LSBN!" answered the door. A group of short-haired girls in thick black leather jackets, bundled up despite the summer heat, encircled Heidi in a protective fairy ring. They looked at me critically, clearly wondering if Heidi was too fragile for my company.

"You've got our numbers," one said, holding on to Heidi's shoulder. "And Vancouver's got a great gay community."

"Oh, God," I said. "She's going to a funeral, not a Save the Dykes rally."

One of the girls stepped in front of me.

"It's OK, Cynthia," Heidi said. Then she ushered me into her bedroom and closed the door. A suitcase was on her bed, half packed.

"I could just uninvite you," Heidi said. "How about that? You want that?" She folded a polka-dotted T-shirt that was wrong for any occasion and put it in her suitcase. "Why haven't you talked to me?" she said, looking at the shirt instead of me. "Why haven't you talked to me in two months?"

"I don't know," I said.

"*You don't know,*" she said, each syllable steeped in sarcasm. "You don't know. Well, *I* know. You thought I was going to try to sleep with you."

"Try to? We slept together all winter!"

"If you call smelling your feet sleeping together, you've got a lot to learn." She seemed thinner and meaner; every line of her body held me at bay.

"So tell me," I said. "What can you show me that I need to learn?" But as soon as I said it I somehow knew she still hadn't slept with anyone. "Am I supposed to come over there and sweep your enraged self into my arms?" I said. "Like in the movies? Is this the part where we're both so mad we kiss each other?"

She shook her head and smiled weakly. "You don't get it," she said. "My mother is dead." She closed her suitcase, clicking shut the old-fashioned locks. "My mother is dead," she said again, this time reminding herself. She set her suitcase upright on the floor and sat on it. She looked like someone waiting for a train.

"Fine," I said. "And she's going to be dead for a long time." Though it sounded stupid, I felt good saying it. As though I had my own locks to click shut.

Heidi went to Vancouver for her mother's funeral. I didn't go with her. Instead, I went back to Baltimore and moved in with an aunt I barely knew. Every day was the same: I read and smoked outside my aunt's apartment, studying the row of hair salons across the street, where girls in denim cutoffs and tank tops would troop in and come out hours later, a flash of neon nails, coifs the color and sheen of patent leather. And every day I imagined Heidi's house in Vancouver. Her place would not be large, but it would be clean. Flowery shrubs would line the walks. The Canadian wind would whip us about like pennants. I'd be visiting her in some vague time in the future, deliberately vague, for people like me, who realign past events to suit themselves. In that future time, you always have a chance to catch the groceries before they fall; your words can always be rewound and erased, rewritten and revised.

Then I'd imagine Heidi visiting me. There are no psychiatrists or deans, no boys with nice shoes or flip cashiers. Just me in my single room. She knocks on the door and says, "Open up."

The Burning Heart
Louise Glück

> ". . . No sadness
> is greater than in misery to rehearse
> memories of joy. . . ."

Ask her if she regrets anything.

I was
promised to another—
I lived with someone.
You forget these things when you're touched.

Ask her how he touched her.

His gaze touched me
before his hands touched me.

Ask her how he touched her.

I didn't ask for anything;
everything was given.

Ask her what she remembers.

We were hauled into the underworld.

Louise Glück

I thought
we were not responsible
any more than we were responsible
for being alive. I was
a young girl, rarely subject to censure:
then a pariah. Did I change that much
from one day to the next?
If I didn't change, wasn't my action
in the character of that young girl?

Ask her what she remembers.

I noticed nothing. I noticed
I was trembling.

Ask her if the fire hurts.

I remember
we were together.
And gradually I understood
that though neither of us ever moved
we were not together but profoundly separate.

Ask her if the fire hurts.

You expect to live forever with your husband
in fire more durable than the world.
I suppose this wish was granted,
where we are now being both
fire and eternity.

Do you regret your life?

Even before I was touched, I belonged to you;
you had only to look at me.

Re-forming the Crystal
Adrienne Rich

I am trying to imagine
how it feels to you
to want a woman

trying to hallucinate
desire
centered in a cock
focused like a burning-glass

desire without discrimination:
to want a woman like a fix

Desire: yes: the sudden knowledge, like out of 'flu, that the body is sexual. Walking in the streets with that knowledge. That evening in the plane from Pittsburgh, fantasizing going to meet you. Walking through the airport blazing with energy and joy. But knowing all along that you were not the source of that energy and joy; you were a man, a stranger, a name, a voice on the telephone, a friend; this desire was mine, this energy was my energy; it could be used a hundred ways, and going to meet you could be one of them.

> Tonight is a different kind of night.
> I sit in the car, racing the engine,
> calculating the thinness of the ice.
> In my head I am already threading the beltways
> that rim this city,
> all the old roads that used to wander the country

> having been lost.
> Tonight I understand
> my photo on the license is not me,
> my
> name on the marriage-contract was not mine.
> If I remind you of my father's favorite daughter,
> look again. The woman
> I needed to call my mother
> was silenced before I was born.

Tonight if the battery charges I want to take the car out on sheet-ice; I want to understand my fear both of the machine and of the accidents of nature. My desire for you is not trivial; I can compare it with the greatest of those accidents. But the energy it draws on might lead to racing a cold engine, cracking the frozen spiderweb, parachuting into the field of a poem wired with danger, or to a trip through gorges and canyons, into the cratered night of female memory, where delicately and with intense care the chieftainess inscribes upon the ribs of the volcano the name of the one she has chosen.

Work

To what extent does gender affect work and creativity? The selections in this section explore how specifics of the workplace and variables of income can both foster and stifle creative acts. The featured writers approach questions of sexism, racism, poverty, child care, and the relationship between the intellectual and the physical to portray a wide range of work experiences.

The essay "Mind-Body Story," by **Nina Barrett** (1960–), is from her 1994 book *The Playgroup*, in which three women contend with the myths of motherhood. In this piece Barrett explores the tension between her intellectual professionalism and her female physicality, evidenced particularly in her own and others' reactions to her pregnancy.

In this selection from "One Out of Twelve: Writers Who Are Women in Our Century" (1972), an essay adapted from a 1971 speech, **Tillie Olsen** (1912–2007) offers thoughts on the disproportionate number of male writers in Western literature and the possible pragmatic reasons for this disparity.

"Baby Gotta Eat, Parts I–V," by Los Angeles–based poet **Kima Jones** (1982–), was published in 2014. In this piece Jones documents the financial travails of her career as a poet and her struggle to achieve both material and literary success.

In her poem "Lowering Your Standards for Food Stamps," published in 2014, **Sheryl Luna** (1965–) voices the frustration felt by a poet working long hours in a menial job. The lack of time to produce creatively is explored over the course of one shift, highlighting the financial necessities that can impede artistic output.

"Color Blind or Color Brave?," the TED talk delivered by **Mellody Hobson** (1969–) in 2014, has been viewed online over one million times. In this speech, investment expert Hobson relates her own experiences of racism in the workplace and encourages her audience to engage in an honest conversation about race.

The short story "Reeling for the Empire," by **Karen Russell** (1981–), was published in her collection *Vampires in the Lemon Grove* (2013). In this fantastical piece, women are contracted to work in an unusual factory far from home, with life-changing consequences for all involved.

Mind-Body Story
Nina Barrett

> For women who wish to live a quest plot, as men's stories allow, indeed, encourage, them to do, some event must be invented to transform their lives, all unconsciously, apparently "accidentally," from a conventional to an eccentric story.
>
> **Carolyn Heilbrun, *Writing a Woman's Life***

Every morning for the past fifteen years I have ringed my eyes with black eyeliner before facing the outside world. Otherwise, I'm not much of a makeup wearer, and actually used to be against it on feminist principle, until my freshman year of college. That fall I had a brief but emotionally intense involvement with a young man who did not approve of women wearing makeup on the grounds of its being fake. Which was of course one of the opinions for which I adored him, until he suddenly broke things off for reasons I did not entirely understand. Somehow, in my furious determination to prove both to myself and to him that I didn't need him anyway, I ended up at the makeup counter in Lord & Taylor outlining my eyes with kohl.

I am still against makeup on feminist principle, on the grounds that the industry makes a fortune convincing women that their natural faces are inherently flawed. On the other hand, I trace my own addiction to eyeliner not to a desire to attract a man but to a desire to rid my heart of one, and I still feel a little kick of resolution every time I apply it, as a smoker feels the little kick of nicotine on the initial drag.

I only mention this now to illustrate how complicated the definition of "feminism" has become for me—and many other women—these days. Is it about independence of individual action, in other words, personal choice? Or adherence to a preconceived set of political principles, in other words, political correctness? When I read the writings of the older generation of feminists, I'm often simultaneously impressed by my deep agreement with the essence of the arguments they make and by the ironic divergence of the actual choices I have made in my life; but then I think, one woman's conformity is another woman's rebellion, and every woman's quest begins with the collapse of her personal expectations.

I can remember the exact moment I fell out of my story. It happened one dreary mid-January day in 1987, in the career advisory office of the Medill School of Journalism, when I was seven months pregnant. I had just finished work on my master's degree in December, and I was there for a job interview with the *New York Times*.

"Now remember," joked a friend who was scheduled for the interview after mine, "he's not legally allowed to ask you if you're pregnant."

We both laughed. I had already put on thirty pounds and my gray wool maternity jumper stretched tight across the mountain of my belly; I looked as though I might be about to go into labor at any moment. I hadn't given this fact much thought in regard to the interview. In my last quarter at Medill, I'd been running all over the city of Chicago interviewing people for news stories and, far from being an obstacle, my belly had been functioning as a handy conversational icebreaker.

As I steered it into the interview room, however, it became almost immediately apparent that on this occasion my belly was going to be the iceberg that sunk the *Titanic*. After a fleeting expression of shock, the interviewer, a white man in his early fifties, composed his face and proceeded to address my stomach: "So, tell me why you are interested in working for the *Times*."

It was clear as I talked, however, that he wasn't remotely interested. He didn't ask any questions. He didn't meet my eyes. He did deliver a little lecture about what the *Times* expected from its young copy clerks, which, he kept reiterating, was very long hours and total commitment. His tone implied that I had probably misunderstood this, and that once he cleared up the misunderstanding, I'd get up and thank him and apologize for wasting his time. Instead I kept desperately asking him questions because it was the only way I could think of to insist that I was taking this seriously, and so should he. "Well, we'll let you know," he said finally, glancing at his watch and escorting me to the door, and I bit my lip to keep from saying, "I think you already have."

"They're famous for their arrogance," my friends consoled me afterward. But they had prescreened my résumé, so I know I couldn't have been utterly out of the ballpark. At least on paper. And I had spent most of my life getting into elite institutions, including Andover, Yale, and Medill, so I was positive, thinking it over, that it couldn't be a problem with what I looked like—on paper. As for what *I* looked like—well, I suddenly realized I thought of "I" primarily as being my mind. I had always measured myself by work, first in sixteen years of school, then in book publishing, then in journalism, so wasn't I actually an identity that existed most *really* on paper? I had spent so many years of my life in male institutions, playing male games by male rules, often dressed in male clothing, that I had forgotten that my mind was attached to a physical form that could betray me at any moment by sending out the signal that allowed men to ridicule or disqualify me: that I was, in fact, a woman.

In 1971, when I was eleven years old, my parents decided to take me out of the public school in the rural Connecticut town where we were living and enter me instead in private school. The private school was a boys' boarding school that had only recently begun taking in girls as day students. The year I started, there were 150 boys and 4 girls.

The school itself was lovely, a series of low white buildings sprawling off from the Main House, which had once been a private mansion. It was set in the rolling Connecticut countryside, with rich green playing fields stretched out to the woods in back and a running track that wrapped around a scenic tree-lined pond off to one side. It was affiliated with one of those somber New England Protestant sects and actively committed to instilling proper morality in its boys, who ranged from fifth graders up to ninth and seemed to be there mostly because of learning disabilities or mild behavioral problems, or because their wealthy parents had other priorities in life.

The attitude toward girls in the school community was markedly ambivalent. Although we were sent every Wednesday afternoon to the headmaster's mansion to drink tea and make polite chitchat in the solarium with the headmaster's wife, we were also expected to attend school assembly every morning and recite, along with the boys, the prayer that ended with a plea to God to help us become "more of a man each day." Neither the chitchat nor the prayer availed me socially. Skipped from fifth grade into seventh because of my test scores, I was a prepubescent brain adrift in a sea of raging male hormones, and I came unequipped with traditional female flotation devices. The other girls seemed to know instinctively how to flirt; I knew instinctively how to compete. I withdrew into myself and studied my way to the top of my classes. The boys sidled up to me in the hallways, sneering, "Hey, Nina, are we still lovers?" and "Hey, Nina, I like your booooobs." One boy followed me around asking lewd questions about the female anatomy, humiliating me into speechlessness, until one day when he wondered, in his leering southern drawl, if it was true that I wore "tamp-POONS." I stared at him a moment until I realized his mispronunciation was ignorant rather than malicious, and then dissolved into such gales of derisive laughter that he beat a confused retreat and thereafter left me alone.

I do not remember whether my parents were aware of how miserable I was during those two years; if they were, it must have seemed to them that I was getting something called an Education which would make all the misery ultimately worthwhile. I remember that my only source of hope and comfort at that time came not from home or from school but from a faraway world that existed only on television and in the books and magazines my mother read. In the great outer world, a feminist revolution was sweeping the country, addressing the problems women encountered in life simply because they were *female*. The Senate was passing the Equal Rights Amendment, which would prohibit discrimination against women; a new form of address and then a magazine—*Ms.*—were born, to insist that a woman's identity encompassed more than her marital status; Betty Friedan was a regular heroine of the media, proclaiming that now was the time that women would begin to make "policy, not coffee!"; and Billie Jean King was playing Bobby Riggs at tennis.

The battle of the sexes was my everyday element, and so I took Women's Lib immediately to heart, and used it as my inspiration and the key to my resistance. I began by refusing to say the last line of the daily prayer in assembly. The assistant headmaster noticed and gave me a disapproving look, but when nothing further happened, I began to boycott the entire prayer. After all, I reasoned, I wasn't just a libber, but an atheist libber.

One day my eighth-grade English teacher assigned a class debate on the topic "Men Are Superior to Women, or Vice Versa." We were allowed to choose sides, which instantly set me against eleven boys. One of the faculty wives, who did arts and crafts with the girls in the afternoons while the boys went off to sports, encouraged me to make the argument that all embryos start out anatomically as girls; she had just had a baby, so she had done some reading, and she assured me that the penis was a mere afterthought of fetal development.

That sounded fine to me, except that I didn't see how I could possibly get up in front of the eleven boys and say the word "penis." At the time, my impression of a penis was of a slimy, uncontrollable thing that made males deeply perverted (as it was clear, at that school at least, they were). As long as men walked around in their clothes, hiding it, it was possible to pretend that they didn't have it, and therefore that they were normal, decent human beings. But to say the word—to suggest that eleven penises actually lurked right there in my English class (twelve, counting Mr. Hunter's) underneath eleven innocent pairs of corduroy and khaki slacks—would have been outrageously rude, like pointing to a person in a wheelchair and screaming, "You are crippled!" Surely, after that, we could never return to the diagramming of sentences.

I no longer remember what argument I used, except that I spent hours in the library researching it. The boys' team, on the other hand, did no research at all. Research, they felt, would have demeaned them. It would have suggested that *evidence* of male superiority was required, when actually this fact was apparent, a priori, to all.

Nina Barrett

So I won the debate easily, at least according to the teacher. But about a week later Margaret Court played that first, highly publicized libber-versus-male-chauvinist-pig tennis match against Bobby Riggs, and lost. The boys in my English class were ebullient. Here it was, empirical proof! Her boobs had gotten in the way of her swing; it must have been "that time of the month"; and on and on. I sat in my seat, trying to make myself deaf. It didn't matter how much research I did; they outnumbered me, so they would always decide what constituted superiority, and what constituted proof. And it didn't matter how careful I was to respect the privacy of their embarrassing penises; they would always feel free to relentlessly ridicule my "boobs." Mr. Hunter, sitting on one corner of the desk with his arms crossed over his chest, made no attempt to control the class. When I looked at him, desperately, he gave me a little wink, as if to say, "Boys will be boys." He did call after me, though, as I got up and walked toward the door. He came out into the hall several times during the forty-minute period to try to get me to come back in, first by cajoling me, next by warning that I was about to flunk Conduct, and finally by threatening to send me to the headmaster. But I had already learned the lesson of the day. I knew I couldn't win, but I had nothing to gain by surrendering except collaboration in my own humiliation.

PENISES AND BOOBS

CHICAGO—Penises and boobs, penises and boobs. Underneath all the carefully crafted, passionless language of the feminist scholars who write about sexual harassment, this is what it boils down to. For a long time after women flooded the workplace in the 1970s, we worried about how they could Dress for Success, i.e., cover up the boobs as well as business suits have camouflaged the penis; perhaps we should have tried to reintroduce the codpiece, in variable sizing. But now, here I am at this job interview with this great undisguisable third boob, the Mother of All Boobs, and if the first two came stamped with a warning sticker (and what would the warning sticker say, anyway: "Handle with Care: This creature may be sexually active" or "Beware: This creature may remind you of your mother, about whom you have mixed feelings"?), this third one clearly comes with an equally severe deterrent: "Warning: This potential employee may have other priorities."

I left the little boys' school at the end of my eighth grade year in what seemed to me at the time to be triumph: clutching an engraved silver cup awarded for the top academic performance in the graduating class. Only a very long time afterward did I understand that the price of the triumph had been that the school had succeeded, despite my resistance, in Building my Character—that I had, in fact, become "more of a Man each day."

I went on as a day student to another nearby boys' prep school that had recently gone co-ed, where I was academically bored and still socially withdrawn and spent a great deal of my time reading my way through the library. I read eclectically. Having discovered the *Iliad* and the *Odyssey*, and stumbled on the dramatic story of how Heinrich Schliemann had actually gone and unearthed Troy exactly where the old stories said it would be, I had resolved to become an archaeologist, and was studying ancient Greek and Latin. I knew the history of every English monarch from the Plantagenets to James I, and the names of all six wives of Henry VIII in order, and in addition to the authorized Desmond Morris version of human evolution, which was assigned for freshman biology, I knew the feminist revisionist Elaine Morgan version, which was not. I discovered a series of Suburban Novels that offered intriguing clues about what might be going on beneath the surface of my own outwardly perfect but ominously muffled home life: *Mr. Bridge, Mrs. Bridge*, and *The Man in the Gray Flannel Suit* portrayed the emptiness and futility of the middle-class American Dream, where the man does something dull and demeaning so the wife can lead a dull and demeaning life among her high-status possessions, and their children, burning with genuine passion, grow up to hate them. And then there were the Women's Novels my mother read, a genre that continued to grow throughout the years in which I came of age, gaining momentum and credibility as the seventies rolled along: *Diary of a Mad Housewife, Memoirs of an Ex-Prom Queen, Fear of Flying, How to Save Your Own Life*, the resurrected nineteenth-century novel *The Awakening*, which

Nina Barrett

became a basic feminist text, and culminating, in 1977—the year I started college—in *The Women's Room.*

The Women's Novels created in my mind a strong impression of the shape of a woman's life that I carried with me all through my teens and twenties, and that was this: In the Old Days (the fifties, when most of the authors of the Women's Novels had come of age), there were Bad Girls and Good Girls. Bad Girls got their lives ruined because they gave in to male sexuality and lost their reputations and no good man would marry them, or they got pregnant and had to have the baby, or they got pregnant and died having a botched abortion. Good Girls got their lives ruined because they resisted boys' sexuality and therefore repressed their own, until they got married and got pregnant and frittered away all their energy and ambition and repressed sexuality trying to raise impossible, ungrateful, spoiled children, while their husbands went out and had affairs and ultimately abandoned them for younger women. The solution—which Liberation had achieved for us—was total independence, meaning that women fully expressed themselves sexually through premarital, extramarital, postmarital, or instead-of-marital affairs, fully expressed themselves intellectually through stimulating careers, and left or divorced their mates at any sign of resistance. The impossible, ungrateful, spoiled children pretty much disappeared from the equation, or at least no one seemed to worry about them, least of all me. I was one myself, and saw little charm in the idea of ruining my own life for the sake of producing more.

It would be hard to imagine a message more perfectly tailored to the needs of a thirteen-year-old girl who now believed that her body was the source of all humiliation and her brain the means of salvation. It left me free, as I plodded through the dull routine of my real life, to fantasize a future in which I would excavate lost palaces or observe primates in the bush or point telescopes at the stars. I didn't worry about the sexual repression part. There was an exquisite feeling I already knew about that could happen in my body when I was by myself, but I didn't associate that with sex, because I thought sex was something you had to have with a boy, and I frankly couldn't imagine meeting an actual boy I would want to have it with, or a desirable one who would actually want to have it with me.

So naturally I was not prepared when, in the spring of my first high school year, I inadvertently landed a very big catch. It seemed that way, anyway, since it was the guy my best friend had had a crush on from afar all year. I had spent a lot of time consoling her because he was so far out of our league, so cool, so nonintellectual, so arrogant, so . . . blond. I didn't especially like him. However, here he suddenly was, hovering around me in the library lounge, where the day students hung out, inviting me for long walks in the woods in back of the school, and, after weeks of the shiest, subtlest overtures, gently kissing me, his hand on the back of my neck, trembling. Just thinking about it the next day made something deep within my belly tighten with excitement.

He had his hand inside my bra by the time summer vacation cut short our exploration. How could I go the whole summer with my body extinguished, when I now understood it was meant to have this electrical current running through it, which was produced by the male? But he lived fairly far away and wouldn't be eligible for his driver's license until he turned sixteen in the fall; therefore, our parents would have to drive us back and forth, something we both instinctively wished to avoid. One day, he promised, he would get on his bike and make the very long ride over to my house, and we'd hang around at my swimming pool.

Oh God, he was going to see me in a *bathing suit*. That, I understood, would be a disaster. My body could not withstand that kind of exposure. My body did not look anything like what I understood a normal female teenage body to look like. I had the kind of body that would have made some hearty Ukrainian peasant man happy. It was a sturdy workhorse kind of body, not that high-strung thoroughbred kind of body I saw in women's magazines and in movies, with all the visible bone structure: the high cheekbones with hollows underneath, the protuberant collarbone, the slightly concave belly framed by two prominent hipbones, the minimalist breasts, no more than a pair of pointy nipples, that looked so good in the politically fashionable braless style, under clingy shirts.

Well, this, the magazines assured me, I could control. I would simply have to lose ten pounds, preferably twelve. I set about it in the same quiet, determined manner I had studied my way to the top of the class. I read my mother's diet books cover to cover and memorized the calorie charts in the back. I cut out pictures of the boniest models from the magazines and pasted them into a scrapbook for inspiration. Then I stopped eating.

And I discovered that I was good at it. In the diet books, there were lots of stories of backsliding and complaining, lots of exhortations to continue despite the fact that one would feel continually deprived and hungry. But that, I thought, was like how you had to work very hard in school if you weren't very gifted naturally. I was naturally gifted at dieting. I didn't feel deprived at all, I felt a great rush of energy and enthusiasm, a sense of being hugely challenged every day and hugely gratified when I met each challenge. I didn't feel hungry, in the sense of having an appetite, of interpreting the sensation of hunger as a cue to eat. To me, hunger became its own reward, the sign that my goal was coming quickly closer, a sign that my body was consuming itself: *Only with the removal of the flesh could my body become slender.*

At the same time, I became obsessed with food. Each night as I lay in bed, I planned the next day's minimal menu, going over it and over it, adding the calories, trying to engrave the total in my mind, brainwashing myself to ensure that my intake would be fully programmed and not subject in any way to whim or failure of will. I might also fantasize about something I was going to cook. The only books I read now, besides diet books, were cookbooks; it didn't cost, after all, to *look*. Sometimes I acted out my food fantasies, in the manner of a voyeur, producing elaborate linzer tortes and braided dinner rolls and three-cheese soufflés, which I would not touch myself but would set before the family. And it was not their pleasure that I relished, watching them eat, but their weakness, which only highlighted my own strength. I kept track of their intake as well as my own, calculations running constantly in my head, my calories subtracted from their calories, an exact arithmetic of my virtue and self-control, more absolute than any school report card.

When I had lost the twelve pounds, I felt ready to consummate the swimming date. But it was a week before my friend could come, and I was having trouble stopping the diet, so by then I had actually lost fifteen. I was trembling with excitement as I unveiled my bikini-clad form before him, but he did not seem to comprehend the momentousness of the occasion, and simply dived into the water. Later, we went into the crumbling barn behind the house and made out, but now his lips on mine seemed wet and rubbery, his tongue thrusting and invasive, his hands hot and clumsy on my body.

We did not speak to each other again that summer, or after school began again in the fall. I continued to lose weight; then I stopped menstruating. After school began, my friend who had originally had the crush on him reported, "He's worried that you're sick or something. He says you bent over to put some books away the other day and he could see the whole outline of your spinal cord through your shirt."

Well, it wasn't boniness, exactly, but surely a visible spinal cord was as sexy as protuberant hipbones. Why, then, wasn't he still hanging around? My friend reported a little later that *she* had heard from a friend of hers that he had felt I "wasn't coming along fast enough."

"You're kidding," I gasped. "You mean he actually thought I was going to *do it* with him? He thought a fourteen-year-old girl was going to *do it*?"

A month later, just before Thanksgiving, she reported further that the friend of hers who had passed this information along was now going out with him. And they were Doing It.

That night I couldn't sleep. I kept thinking about graham cracker pie crust. I had been planning to make a chocolate cream pie for Thanksgiving, mostly so I could scrape the chocolate and whipped cream off my piece and just eat the crust. I began to fantasize about that crust, how satisfying it would be in my mouth, how heavy and crumbly and sweet.

I slipped out of bed and crept quietly downstairs through the darkened house to the pantry. The store-bought pie crust was there in its pie pan, protected by a plastic sheath. I crouched down on the floor of the pantry in my nightgown, ripped off the plastic sheath, and began to cram greedy handfuls of pie crust into my mouth. It tasted rich and wonderful. I knew what I was doing was disgusting, but I couldn't stop myself: I was hungry. When I finally crawled back into bed, there was a slight hill between my hipbones, where I had so arduously carved a valley. I was full and drowsy. My parents had recently offered to send me to boarding school for the last two years before college, as they had sent my older sister to Exeter. I hadn't been sure, but now, as I drifted off to sleep, I suddenly knew: I wanted to go away, to somewhere I could start life over again, from scratch.

THE HUNGER

CHICAGO—Where did this pregnancy come from, anyway? Feminist Life Principle #1 is, Control your fertility. And anybody could tell you, the final six months of graduate school is not an optimal maternal moment for the ambitious, modern overachiever interested in prestigious job opportunities. But this was when I began to feel the hunger gnawing at my belly. I was married to a man I loved, a gentle, funny, warm man who felt like family, and suddenly for the first time in my life the women at the beach with two small kids made me more envious than the women with their lovers, and I felt somewhere deep inside me that it was time. So I surrendered control; I indulged the hunger of my body, and it filled and swelled, smothering my lovely hipbones, until it attained this grotesque shape of the third boob, which makes professionalism quite impossible, because professionalism equals control equals denial of hunger equals a woman's body stripped of its breasts and hips and belly and period and pared down to look as hard and streamlined and non-threatening as a man's body (as long as they smile benignly and pretend not to have penises).

At Andover from 1975 to 1977, I studied Virgil in the original Latin, read the major documents of American history in the original sources, won an English prize for an essay on *Hamlet*, took a course in the biology of cancer, and lived with my entire urban studies class in a Boston brownstone while I did an internship at the *Boston Globe*. I also learned to drink, to get stoned, to dump a boy before he could dump me, and to wear boys' clothing. This last was an expensive lesson, as my mother had taken me out shopping just before school started, outfitting me with a complete wardrobe of high-waisted, elephant-leg, bell-bottom blue jeans, floral blouses, shoes with fashionable clunky heels, and a new pocketbook. I understood that it wasn't just money my mother was spending on me, but love; I had heard often enough her stories of being young and poor and shabby, of how her parents had not considered her good appearance a valid expense.

But then I got up to school and noted immediately The Look. The ideal Andover girl, of whom there were actually an intimidating number, dressed in boys' straight-leg Levi's; boys' button-down Oxford shirts, with the tails hanging out; boys' cable-knit wool fishermen's sweaters, oversized; and big rugged hiking boots. She had medium-length brownish-blond hair that was not in any way fussed with, nor did she wear makeup, but her face was naturally beautiful, with high cheekbones, a small, tasteful nose, perfect skin, and blue eyes that were never soft and inviting, but rather cold and tough; and she rarely smiled. And, of course, she had a body that looked good in those clothes: minimal breasts, flat belly, long, lanky legs. It was a miracle of gender transubstantiation, this elite New England WASP sexual aesthetic: The more boyish she looked, the more "feminine" she was. *Write on the blackboard a thousand times: I will look like a boy, act like a boy, perform like a boy. And more of a man each day.* My second day in Andover, I went shopping for a new wardrobe that cost me half my first year's allowance, and hid the unworn clothes my mother had bought me at the bottom of my trunk.

That fall I was very homesick and often lingered on the streets of Andover at dusk, watching the lights come on in the big Victorian houses, dawdling to stare at the jack-o'-lanterns on the front porches and the childish crayon drawings in the windows, sniffing like a pauper at the aromas of pot roast and apple crisp and wood smoke that drifted outward on the frosty air and mixed with the rich scent of rotting leaves. There was something in those houses that I longed for desperately, but I sensed that it was too late for me now to get it back; it had outlived its usefulness for my survival. For this was about the time, I realize in retrospect, that my childhood ended, and my resumé began.

THE ABYSS

CHICAGO—Desperately, I find myself suggesting to the interviewer that the paper must have night and weekend shifts, which are unpopular with most people but would be perfect for me. I am imagining that I will care for the baby while Ellis is at work, and run out the door to a job of my own the moment he returns. Afterward, I am ashamed of myself; how I care for this baby is none of the interviewer's business. However, I am forced for the first time to recognize that I simply have not thought this question through. I have somehow assumed that feminists have worked this kind of thing out by now, as though they had discovered a cure for cancer. I know there is a solution known as Day Care, but it is not until this exact moment of being fully irrevocably imminently on the verge of giving birth that I have thought to face the reality: *What* day care? There is no money for a nanny. There is no willing aunt or grandmother in the wings. Ellis has not expressed any desire to become a homemaker, nor can we, at the moment, afford for him to work less than full-time, since any entry-level journalism job I get would pay less than half of what he already earns, and we can barely afford the rent on our run-down Chicago apartment.

But there is something else: I *want* to mother this baby—at least more than simply on evenings and weekends. And once I acknowledge this, I see a huge and terrifying abyss open up beneath my feet. I don't know how to see myself as female, without taunting myself with derogatory connotations; I don't know how to choose to do something "feminine" without immediately discounting it as worthless, a nonachievement. All those years spent trying to be a boy, trying so desperately to minimize the significance of having a female body; all those years spent identifying myself as a feminist, thinking that what that *meant* was trying to minimize the significance of having a female body; all those years of fierce insistence that this body must never be allowed to define Me. And though I am still sure that it doesn't, completely, here is my belly going before me like a megaphone, screaming something else to the world, the world of men—the only world whose standards I have ever used to measure myself—commanding it to draw its own conclusions.

One Out of Twelve: Writers Who Are Women in Our Century

Tillie Olsen

It is the women's movement, part of the other movements of our time for a fully human life, that has brought this forum into being; kindling a renewed, in most instances a first-time, interest in the writings and writers of our sex.

Linked with the old, resurrected classics on women, this movement in three years has accumulated a vast new mass of testimony, of new comprehensions as to what it is to be female. Inequities, restrictions, penalties, denials, leechings have been painstakingly and painfully documented; damaging differences in circumstances and treatment from that of males attested to; and limitations, harms, a sense of wrong, voiced.

It is in the light and dark of this testimony that I examine my subject today: the lives and work of writers, women, in our century (though I speak primarily of those writing in the English language—and in prose).[1]

Compared to the countless centuries of the silence of women, compared to the century preceding ours—the first in which women wrote in any noticeable numbers—ours has been a favorable one.

The road was cut many years ago, as Virginia Woolf reminds us:

> by Fanny Burney, by Aphra Behn, by Harriet Martineau, by Jane Austen, by George Eliot, many famous women and many more unknown and forgotten.... Thus, when I came to write ... writing was a reputable and harmless occupation.

---

1. This is the poorer for such limitation.

155

Predecessors, ancestors, a body of literature, an acceptance of the right to write: each in themselves an advantage.

In this second century we have access to areas of work and of life experience previously denied; higher education; longer, stronger lives; for the first time in human history, freedom from compulsory childbearing; freer bodies and attitudes toward sexuality; a beginning of technological easing of household tasks; and—of the greatest importance to those like myself who come from generations of illiterate women—increasing literacy, and higher degrees of it. *Each one of these a vast gain.*[2]

And the results?

Productivity: books of all manner and kind. My own crude sampling, having to be made without benefit of research assistants, secretary, studies (nobody's made them), or computer (to feed the entire *Books in Print* and *Contemporary Authors* into, for instance) indicates that at present four to five books are published by men to every one by a woman.[3]

Comparative earnings: no authoritative figures available.

Achievement: as gauged by what supposedly designates it: appearance in twentieth-century literature courses, required reading lists, textbooks, quality anthologies, the year's best, the decade's best, the fifty years' best, consideration by critics or in current reviews—*one woman writer for every twelve men* (8 percent women, 92 percent men). For a week or two, make your own survey whenever you pick up an anthology, course bibliography, quality magazine or quarterly, book review section, book of criticism.

What weights my figures so heavily toward the one-out-of-twelve ratio are twentieth-century literature course offerings, and writers decreed worthy of critical attention in books and articles. Otherwise my percentage figures would have come closer to one out of seven.

---

2. These are measured phrases, enormously compressed. Each asks an entire book or books, to indicate its enabling relationship to literature written by women in this century—including the very numbers of women enabled to write.
3. Richard Altick in his "Sociology of Authorship" found the proportion of women writers to men writers in Britain a fairly constant one for the years 1800 to 1935: 20 percent. This was based on books published, not on recognized achievement.

> *But it would not matter if the ratio had been one out of six or five. Any figure but one to one would insist on query: Why? What, not true for men but* only *for women, makes this enormous difference? (Thus, class—economic circumstance—and color, those other traditional silencers of humanity, can be relevant only in the special ways that they affect the half of their numbers who are women.)*
>
> *Why are so many more women silenced than men? Why, when women do write (one out of four or five works published) is so little of their writing known, taught, accorded recognition? What is the nature of the critical judgments made throughout that (along with the factors different in women's lives) steadily reduce the ratio from one out of three in anthologies of student work, to one out of seventeen in course offerings.*
>
> *This talk, originally intended to center on the writing, the achievement of women writers in our century, became instead these queryings. Yet—in a way sadder, angrier, prouder—it still centers on the writing, the achievement.*[4]

One woman writer of achievement for every twelve men writers so ranked. Is this proof again—and in this so much more favorable century—of women's innately inferior capacity for creative achievement?

Only a few months ago (June 1971), during a Radcliffe-sponsored panel on "Women's Liberation, Myth or Reality," Diana Trilling, asking why it is that women

> have not made even a fraction of the intellectual, scientific, or artistic-cultural contributions which men have made

came again to the traditional conclusion that

> it is not enough to blame women's place in culture or culture itself, because that leaves certain fundamental questions unanswered... necessarily raises the question of the biological aspects of the problem.

---

4. Added to text, 1976.

Biology: that difference.[5] Evidently unknown to or dismissed by her and the others who share her conclusion are the centuries of prehistory during which biology did not deny equal contribution; and *the other determining difference—not* biology—between male and female in the centuries after; the *differing past of women—* that should be part of every human consciousness, certainly every woman's consciousness (in the way that the 400 years of bondage, colonialism, the slave passage, are to black humans).

Work first:

> Within our bodies we bore the race. Through us it was shaped, fed and clothed. . . . Labour more toilsome and unending than that of man was ours. . . . No work was too hard, no labour too strenuous to exclude us.[6]

True for most women in most of the world still.

Unclean; taboo. The Devil's Gateway. The three steps behind; the girl babies drowned in the river; the baby strapped to the back. Buried alive with the lord, burned alive on the funeral pyre, burned as witch at the stake. Stoned to death for adultery. Beaten, raped. Bartered. Bought and sold. Concubinage, prostitution, white slavery. The hunt, the sexual prey, "I am a lost creature, O the poor Clarissa." Purdah, the veil of Islam, domestic confinement. Illiterate. Denied vision. Excluded, excluded, excluded from council, ritual, activity, learning, language, when there was neither biological nor economic reason to be excluded.

Religion, when all believed. In sorrow shalt thou bring forth children. May thy wife's womb never cease from bearing. Neither was the man created for the woman but the woman for the man. Let the woman learn in silence and in all subjection. Contrary to biological birth fact: Adam's rib. The Jewish male morning prayer: thank God I was not born a woman. Silence in holy places, seated apart, or not

---

5. Biologically, too, the change for women now is enormous: life expectancy (USA) seventy-eight years—as contrasted with forty-eight years in 1900. Near forty-eight years of life before and after one is "a woman," that is: "capable of conceiving and bearing young." (And childbearing more and more voluntary.)
6. Olive Schreiner. *Women and Labour.*

permitted entrance at all; castration of boys because women too profane to sing in church.

And for the comparative handful of women born into the privileged class; being, not doing; man does, woman is; to you the world says work, to us it says seem. God is thy law, thou mine. Isolated. Cabin'd, cribb'd, confin'd; the private sphere. Bound feet: corseted, cosseted, bedecked; denied one's body. Powerlessness. Fear of rape, male strength. Fear of aging. Subject to. Fear of expressing capacities. Soft attractive graces; the mirror to magnify man. Marriage as property arrangement. The vices of slaves:[7] dissembling, flattering, manipulating, appeasing.

Bolstering. Vicarious living, infantilization, trivialization. Parasitism, individualism, madness. Shut up, you're only a girl. O Elizabeth, why couldn't you have been born a boy? For twentieth-century woman: roles, discontinuities, part-self, part-time; conflict; imposed "guilt"; "a man can give full energy to his profession, a woman cannot."

> How is it that women have not made a fraction of the intellectual, scientific, or artistic-cultural contributions that men have made?

Only in the context of this punitive difference in circumstance, in history, between the sexes; this past, hidden or evident, that (though objectively obsolete—yes, even the toil and the compulsory childbearing obsolete) continues so terribly, so determiningly to live on, only in this context can the question be answered or my subject here today—the woman writers in our century: one out of twelve—be understood.

How much it takes to become a writer. Bent (far more common than we assume), circumstances, time, development of craft—but beyond that: how much conviction as to the importance of what one has to say, one's right to say it. And the will, the measureless store of belief

---

7. Elizabeth Barrett Browning's phrase; other phrases throughout from the Bible, John Milton, Richardson's *Clarissa*, Matthew Arnold, Elizabeth Cady Stanton, Virginia Woolf, Viola Klein, Mountain Wolf Woman.

in oneself to be able to come to, cleave to, find the form for one's own life comprehensions. Difficult for any male not born into a class that breeds such confidence. Almost impossible for a girl, a woman.

The leeching of belief, of will, the damaging of capacity begins so early. Sparse indeed is the literature on the way of denial to small girl children of the development of their endowment as born human: active, vigorous bodies; exercise of the power to do, to make, to investigate, to invent, to conquer obstacles, to resist violations of the self; to think, create, choose; to attain community, confidence in self. Little has been written on the harms of instilling constant concern with appearance; the need to please, to support; the training in acceptance, deferring. Little has been added in our century to George Eliot's *The Mill on the Floss* on the effect of the differing treatment—"climate of expectation"—for boys and for girls.

But it is there if one knows how to read for it, and indelibly there in the resulting damage. One—out of twelve.

In the vulnerable girl years, unlike their sisters in the previous century, women writers go to college.[8] The kind of experience it may be for them is stunningly documented in Elaine Showalter's pioneering "Women and the Literary Curriculum."[9] Freshman texts in which women have little place, if at all; language itself, all achievement, anything to do with the human in male terms—*Man in Crises, The Individual and His World*. Three hundred thirteen male writers taught; seventeen women writers: that classic of adolescent rebellion, *A Portrait of the Artist as a Young Man*; and sagas (male) of the quest for identity (but then Erikson, the father of the concept, propounds that identity concerns girls only insofar as making themselves into

---

8. True almost without exception among the writers who are women in *Twentieth Century Authors* and *Contemporary Authors*.
9. *College English*, May 1971. A year later (October 1972), *College English* published an extensive report, "Freshman Textbooks," by Jean Mullens. In the 112 most used texts, she found 92.47 percent (5,795) of the selections were by men; 7.53 percent (472) by women (One Out of Twelve). Mullens deepened Showalter's insights as to the subtly undermining effect on freshman students of the texts' contents and language, as well as the miniscule proportion of women writers.

attractive beings for the right kind of man).[10] Most, *not all*, of the predominantly male literature studied, written by men whose understandings are not universal, but restrictively male (as Mary Ellmann, Kate Millett, and Dolores Schmidt have pointed out); in our time more and more surface, hostile, one-dimensional in portraying women.

In a writer's young years, susceptibility to the vision and style of the great is extreme. Add the aspiration-denying implication, consciously felt or not (although reinforced daily by one's professors and reading) that (as Virginia Woolf noted years ago) women writers, women's experience, and literature written by women are by definition minor. (Mailer will not grant even the minor: "the one thing a writer has to have is balls.") No wonder that Showalter observes:

> Women [students] are estranged from their own experience and unable to perceive its shape and authenticity, in part because they do not see it mirrored and given resonance in literature. . . . They are expected to identify with masculine experience, which is presented as the human one, and have no faith in the validity of their own perceptions and experiences, rarely seeing them confirmed in literature, or accepted in criticism . . . [They] notoriously lack the happy confidence, the exuberant sense of the value of their individual observations which enables young men to risk making fools of themselves for the sake of an idea.

Harms difficult to work through. Nevertheless, some young women (others are already lost) maintain their ardent intention to write—fed indeed by the very glories of some of this literature that puts them down.

But other invisible worms are finding out the bed of crimson joy.[11] Self-doubt; seriousness, also questioned by the hours agonizing over

---

10. In keeping with his 1950s–60s thesis of a distinctly female "biological, evolutionary need to fulfill self through serving others."
11. O Rose thou art sick/The invisible worm,
    That flies in the night/In the howling storm:

    Has found out thy bed/Of crimson joy:
    And his dark secret love/Does thy life destroy.
    —William Blake

appearance; concentration shredded into attracting, being attractive; the absorbing real need and love for working with words felt as hypocritical self-delusion ("I'm not truly dedicated"), for what seems (and is) esteemed is being attractive to men. High aim, and accomplishment toward it, discounted by the prevalent attitude that, as girls will probably marry (attitudes not applied to boys who will probably marry), writing is no more than an attainment of a dowry to be spent later according to the needs and circumstances within the true vocation: husband and family. The growing acceptance that going on will threaten other needs, to love and be loved; ("a woman has to sacrifice all claims to femininity and family to be a writer").[12]

And the agony—peculiarly mid-century, escaped by their sisters of pre-Freudian, pre-Jungian times—that "creation and femininity are incompatible."[13] Anaïs Nin's words.

> The aggressive act of creation; the guilt for creating. I did not want to rival man; to steal man's creation, his thunder. I must protect them, not outshine them.[14]

The acceptance—against one's experienced reality—of the sexist notion that the act of creation is not as inherently natural to a woman as to a man, but rooted instead in unnatural aggression, rivalry, envy, or thwarted sexuality.

And in all the usual college teaching—the English, history, psychology, sociology courses—little to help that young women understand the source or nature of this inexplicable draining self-doubt, loss of aspiration, of confidence.

It is all there in the extreme in Plath's *Bell Jar*—that (inadequate)[15] portrait of the artist as a young woman (significantly, one of the few that we have)—from the precarious sense of vocation to the paralyzing conviction that (in a sense different from what she wrote years later):

---

12. Plath. A letter when a graduate student.
13. *The Diary of Anaïs Nin*, Vol. III, 1939-1944.
14. A statement that would have baffled Austen, the Brontës, Mrs. Gaskell, Eliot, Stowe, Alcott, etc. The strictures were felt by them in other ways.
15. Inadequate, for the writer-being ("muteness is sickness for me") is not portrayed. By contrast, how present she is in Plath's own *Letters Home*.

> Perfection is terrible. It cannot have children. It tamps
> the womb.

And indeed, in our century as in the last, until very recently almost all distinguished achievement has come from childless women: Willa Cather, Ellen Glasgow, Gertrude Stein, Edith Wharton, Virginia Woolf, Elizabeth Bowen, Katherine Mansfield, Isak Dinesen, Katherine Anne Porter, Dorothy Richardson, Henry Handel Richardson, Susan Glaspell, Dorothy Parker, Lillian Hellman, Eudora Welty, Djuna Barnes, Anaïs Nin, Ivy Compton-Burnett, Zora Neale Hurston, Elizabeth Madox Roberts, Christina Stead, Carson McCullers, Flannery O'Connor, Jean Stafford, May Sarton, Josephine Herbst, Jessamyn West, Janet Frame, Lillian Smith, Iris Murdoch, Joyce Carol Oates, Hannah Green, Lorraine Hansberry.

Most never questioned, or at least accepted (a few sanctified) this different condition for achievement, not imposed on men writers. Few asked the fundamental human equality question regarding it that Elizabeth Mann Borghese, Thomas Mann's daughter, asked when she was eighteen and sent to a psychiatrist for help in getting over an unhappy love affair (revealing also a working ambition to become a great musician although "women cannot be great musicians"). "You must choose between your art and fulfillment as a woman," the analyst told her, "between music and family life." "Why?" she asked. "Why must I choose? No one said to Toscanini or to Bach or my father that they must choose between their art and personal, family life; fulfillment as a man. . . . Injustice everywhere." Not where it is free choice. But where it is forced because of the circumstances for the sex into which one is born—a choice men of the same class do not have to make in order to do their work—that is not choice, that is a coercive working of sexist oppression.[16]

What possible difference, you may ask, does it make to literature whether or not a woman writer remains childless—free choice or

---

16. "Them lady poets must not marry, pal," is how John Berryman, poet (himself oft married) expressed it. The old patriarchal injunction: "Woman, this is man's realm. If you insist on invading it, unsex yourself—and expect the road to be made difficult." Furthermore, this very unmarriedness and childlessness has been used to discredit women as unfulfilled, inadequate, somehow abnormal.

not—especially in view of the marvels these childless women have created.

Might there not have been other marvels as well, or other dimensions to these marvels? Might there not have been present profound aspects and understandings of human life as yet largely absent in literature?

More and more women writers in our century, primarily in the last two decades, are assuming as their right fullness of work *and* family life.[17] Their emergence is evidence of changing circumstances making possible for them what (with rarest exception) was not possible in the generations of women before. I hope and I fear for what will result. I hope (and believe) that complex new richness will come into literature; I fear because almost certainly their work will be impeded, lessened, partial. For the fundamental situation remains unchanged. Unlike men writers who marry, most will not have the societal equivalent of a wife—nor (in a society hostile to growing life) anyone but themselves to mother their children. Even those who can afford help, good schools, summer camps, may *(may)* suffer what seventy years ago W. E. B. Du Bois called "The Damnation of Women": "that only at the sacrifice of the chance to do their best work can women bear and rear children."[18]

---

17. Among those with children: Harriette Arnow, Mary Lavin, Mary McCarthy, Tess Slesinger, Eleanor Clark, Nancy Hale, Storm Jameson, Janet Lewis, Jean Rhys, Kay Boyle, Ann Petry, Dawn Powell, Meridel LeSueur, Evelyn Eaton, Dorothy Canfield Fisher, Pearl Buck, Josephine Johnson, Caroline Gordon, Shirley Jackson; and a sampling in the unparalleled last two decades: Doris Lessing, Nadine Gordimer, Margaret Laurence, Grace Paley, Hortense Calisher, Edna O'Brien, Sylvia Aston-Warner, Pauli Murray, Françoise Mallet-Joris, Cynthia Ozick, Joanne Greenberg, Joan Didion, Penelope Mortimer, Alison Lurie, Hope Hale Davis, Doris Betts, Muriel Spark, Adele Wiseman, Lael Wertenbaker, Shirley Ann Grau, Maxine Kumin, Margaret Walker, Gina Barriault, Mary Gray Hughes, Maureen Howard, Norma Rosen, Lore Segal, Alice Walker, Nancy Willard, Charlotte Painter, Sallie Bingham. (I would now add Clarice Lispector, Ruth Prawer Jhabvala, June Arnold, Ursula Le Guin, Diane Johnson, Alice Munro, Helen Yglesias, Susan Cahill, Rosellen Brown, Alta, and Susan Griffin.) Some wrote before children, some only in the middle or later years. Not many have directly used the material open to them out of motherhood as central source for their work.
18. *Darkwater: Voices from Within the Veil.*

> Substantial creative achievement demands time . . . and with rare exceptions only full-time workers have created it.[19]

I am quoting myself from "Silences," a talk nine years ago. In motherhood, as it is structured,

> circumstances for sustained creation are almost impossible. Not because the capacities to create no longer exist, or the need (though for a while as in any fullness of life the need may be obscured), but . . . the need cannot be first. It can have at best only part self, part time . . . Motherhood means being instantly interruptible, responsive, responsible. Children need one *now* (and remember, in our society, the family must often try to be the center for love and health the outside world is not). The very fact that these are needs of love, not duty, that one feels them as one's self; *that there is no one else to be responsible for these needs*, gives them primacy. It is distraction, not mediation, that becomes habitual; interruption, not continuity; spasmodic, not constant, toil. Work interrupted, deferred, postponed makes blockage—at best, lesser accomplishment. Unused capacities atrophy, cease to be.

There are other vulnerabilities to loss, diminishment. Most women writers (being women) have had bred into them the "infinite capacity"; what Virginia Woolf named (after the heroine of a famous Victorian poem) *The Angel in the House*, who "must charm . . . sympathize . . . flatter . . . conciliate . . . be extremely sensitive to the needs and moods and wishes of others before her own . . . excel in the difficult arts of family life . . ."

---

19. This does not mean that these full-time writers were hermetic or denied themselves social or personal life (think of James, Turgenev, Tolstoy, Balzac, Joyce, Gide, Colette, Yeats, Woolf, etc., etc.); nor did they, except perhaps at the flood, put in as many hours daily as those doing more usual kinds of work. Three to six hours daily have been the norm ("the quiet, patient, generous mornings will bring it"). Zola and Trollope are famous last-century examples of the four hours; the *Paris Review* interviews disclose many contemporary ones.

  Full-timeness consists not in the actual number of hours at one's desk, but in that writing is one's major profession, practiced habitually, in freed, protected, undistracted time as needed, when it is needed.

> It was she who used to come between me and my paper... who bothered me and wasted my time and so tormented me that at last I killed her... or she would have plucked out my heart as a writer.[20]

There is another angel, so lowly as to be invisible, although without her no art, or any human endeavor, could be carried on for even one day—the essential angel, with whom Virginia Woolf (and most women writers, still in the privileged class) did not have to contend—the angel who must assume the physical responsibilities for daily living, for the maintenance of life.

Almost always in one form or another (usually in the wife, two-angel form) she has dwelt in the house of men. She it was who made it possible for Joseph Conrad to "wrestle with the Lord for his creation":

> Mind and will and conscience engaged to the full, hour after hour, day after day... never aware of even flow of daily life made easy and noiseless for me by a silent, watchful, tireless affection.

The angel who was "essential" to Rilke's "great task":

> like a sister who would run the house like a friendly climate, there or not there as one wished... and would ask for nothing except just to be there working and warding at the frontiers of the invisible.

Men (even part-time writers who must carry on work other than writing[21]) have had and have this inestimable advantage toward productivity. I cannot help but notice how curiously absent both of these angels, these watchers and warders at the frontiers of the invisible, are from the actual contents of most men's books, except perhaps on the dedication page:

To my wife, without whom...

I digress, and yet I do not; the disregard for the essential angel, the large absence of any sense of her in literature or elsewhere, has

---

20. *Professions for Women.*
21. As must many women writers.

not only cost literature great contributions from those so occupied or partially occupied, but by failing to help create an arousing awareness (as literature has done in other realms) has contributed to the agonizingly slow elimination of this technologically and socially obsolete, human-wasting drudgery: Virginia Woolf's dream of a long since possible "economical, powerful, and efficient future when houses will be cleaned by a puff of hot wind."

Sometimes the essential angel is present in women's books,[22] though still most "heroines are in white dresses that never need washing" (Rebecca Harding Davis's phrase of a hundred years ago). Some poets admit her as occasional domestic image; a few preen her as femininity; Sylvia Plath could escape her only by suicide:

> ... flying ...
> Over the engine that killed her—
> The mausoleum, the wax house.

For the first time in literary history, a woman poet of stature, accustomed through years to the habits of creation, began to live the life of most of her sex: the honey drudgers: the winged unmiraculous two-angel, whirled mother-maintenance life, that most women, not privileged, know. A situation without help or husband and with twenty-four hours' responsibility for two small human lives whom she adored and at their most fascinating and demanding. The world was blood-hot and personal. Creation's needs at its height. She had to get up at

> four in the morning, that still blue almost eternal hour before the baby's cry

to write at all.[23] After the long expending day, tending, caring, cleaning, enjoying, laundering, feeding, marketing, delighting, outing; being:

---

22. Among them: Harriette Arnow, Willa Cather, Dorothy Canfield Fisher, H. H. Richardson (of *Ultima Thule*), Ruth Suckow, Elizabeth Madox Roberts, Sarah Wright, Agnes Smedley; Emily Dickinson, pre-eminently; Sylvia Plath, sometimes Christina Stead, Doris Lessing. (I would now add Edith Summers Kelley [*Weeds* and *The Devil's Hand*], the Marge Piercy of *Small Changes*, and my own fiction.)
23. In the long tradition of early rising, an hour here and there, or late-night mother-writers from Mrs. Trollope to Harriette Arnow to this very twenty-four hours—necessarily fitting in writing time in accordance with maintenance of life, and children's, needs.

> a very efficient tool or weapon, used and in demand from moment to moment. . . . Nights [were] no good [for writing]. I'm so flat by then that all I can cope with is music and brandy and water.

The smog of cooking, the smog of hell floated in her head. The smile of the icebox annihilated. There was a stink of fat and baby crap; viciousness in the kitchen! And the blood jet poetry (for which there was never time and self except in that still blue hour before the baby's cry) there was no stopping it:[24]

> It is not a question in these last weeks of the conflict in a woman's life between the claims of the feminine and the agonized work of art.

Elizabeth Hardwick, a woman, can say of Sylvia Plath's suicide,

> Every artist is either a man or woman, and the struggle is pretty much the same for both.

A comment as insensible of the two-angel realities ("so lowly as to be invisible") as are the oblivious masculine assumptions, either that the suicide was because of Daddy's death twenty-three years before, revived and compounded by her husband's desertion; or else a real-life *Story of O* (that elegant pornography) sacramental culmination of being used up by ecstasy (poetry in place of sex this time):

> the pride of an utter and ultimate surrender, like the pride of O, naked and chained in her owl mask as she asks Sir Stephen for death. . . .[25]

If in such an examined extremity, the profound realities of woman's situation are ignored, how much less likely are they—particularly the subtler ones—to be seen, comprehended, taken into account, as they affect lesser-known women writers in more usual circumstances.

* * *

---

24. Phrases, lines, throughout from Plath's *Ariel*, letters, BBC broadcasts.
25. Richard Howard, in *The Art of Sylvia Plath*, edited by Charles Newman.

In younger years, confidence and vision leeched, aspiration reduced. In adult years, sporadic effort and unfinished work; women made "mediocre caretakers of their talent": that is, writing is not first. The angel in the house situation; probably also the essential angel, maintenance-of-life necessity; increasingly in our century, work on a paid job as well; and for more and more women writers, the whirled expending motherhood years. Is it so difficult to account for the many occasional-fine-story or one-book writers; the distinguished but limited production of others (Janet Lewis, Ann Petry, for example); the years and years in getting one book done (thirty years for Margaret Walker's *Jubilee*, twenty for Marguerite Young's *Miss Macintosh My Darling*); the slowly increasing numbers of women who not until their forties, fifties, sixties, publish for the first time (Dorothy Richardson, Hortense Calisher, Theodora Kroeber, Linda Hoyer—John Updike's mother); the women who start with children's, girls' books (Maxine Kumin), some like Cid Ricketts Sumner (*Tammy*) seldom or never getting to adult fiction that would encompass their wisdom for adults; and most of all, the unsatisfactory quality of book after book that evidence the marks of part-time, part-self authorship, and to whose authors Sarah Orne Jewett's words to the part-time, part-self young Willa Cather still apply, seventy years after:

> If you don't keep and mature your force and above all have time and quiet to perfect your work, you will be writing things not much better than you did five years ago.... Otherwise, what might be strength is only crudeness, and what might be insight is only observation. You will write about life, but never life itself.[26]

Yes, the loss in quality, the minor work, the hidden silences, are there in woman after woman writer in our century.[27] We will never

---

26. *Letters of Sarah Orne Jewett*, edited by Annie Fields.
27. Compared to men writers of like distinction and years of life, few women writers have had lives of unbroken productivity, or leave behind a "body of work." Early beginnings, then silence; or clogged late ones (foreground silences); long periods between books (hidden silences); characterize most of us. A Colette, Wharton, Glasgow, Millay, Lessing, Oates, are the exceptions.

have the body of work that we were capable of producing. Blight, said Blake, never does good to a tree:

> And if a blight kill not a tree but it still bear fruit, let none say that the fruit was in consequence of the blight.

As for myself, who did not publish a book until I was fifty, who raised children without household help or the help of the "technological sublime" (the atom bomb was in manufacture before the first automatic washing machine); who worked outside the house on everyday jobs as well (as nearly half of all women do now, though a woman with a paid job, except as a maid or prostitute, is still rarest of any in literature); who could not kill the essential angel (there was no one else to do her work); would not—if I could—have killed the caring part of the Woolf angel, as distant from the world of literature most of my life as literature is distant (in content too) from my world:

The years when I should have been writing, my hands and being were at other (inescapable) tasks. Now, lightened as they are, when I must do those tasks into which most of my life went, like the old mother, grandmother in my *Tell Me a Riddle* who could not make herself touch a baby, I pay a psychic cost: "the sweat beads, the long shudder begins." The habits of a lifetime when everything else had to come before writing are not easily broken, even when circumstances now often make it possible for writing to be first; habits of years—response to others, distractibility, responsibility for daily matters—stay with you, mark you, become you. The cost of "discontinuity" (that pattern still imposed on women) is such a weight of things unsaid, an accumulation of material so great, that everything starts up something else in me; what should take weeks, takes me sometimes months to write; what should take months, takes years.

I speak of myself to bring here the sense of those others to whom this is in the process of happening (unnecessarily happening, for it need not, must not continue to be) and to remind us of those (I so nearly was one) who never come to writing at all.

We must not speak of women writers in our century (as we cannot speak of women in any area of recognized human achievement) without speaking also of the invisible, the as-innately-capable: the born to the wrong circumstances—diminished, excluded, foundered, silenced.

We who write are survivors, *"only's."*[28] *One-out-of-twelve.*

---

28. For myself, "survivor" contains its other meaning: one who must bear witness for those who foundered; try to tell how and why it was that they, also worthy of life, did *not* survive. And pass on ways of surviving; and tell our chancy luck, our special circumstances.

    "Only's" is an expression out of the 1950s Civil Rights time: the young Ralph Abernathy reporting to his Birmingham Church congregation on his trip up north for support:

    > I go to Seattle and they tell me, "Brother, you got to meet so and so, why he's the only Negro Federal Circuit Judge in the Northwest"; I go to Chicago and they tell me, "Brother, you've got to meet so and so, why he's the only full black professor of Sociology there is"; I go to Albany and they tell me, "Brother, you *got* to meet so and so, why he's the only black senator in the state legislature . . ." [long dramatic pause] . . . WE DON'T WANT NO ONLY'S.

    Only's are used to rebuke ("to be models"); to imply the unrealistic, "see, it can be done, all you need is capacity and will." Accepting a situation of "only's" means: "let inequality of circumstance continue to prevail."

Baby Gotta Eat, Parts I–V

Kima Jones

I. For Further Consideration

Writer's block is a symptom of capitalism. The
more efficient we become the more brutal and in
that brutality the space for creativity diminishes.
We must all remain vigilant to the creative
viability in everything around us at all times.
As the great American poet Alice Notley says,
'Poetry's so common hardly anyone can find it.'
CAConrad, as shared on Gabrielle Calvocoressi's
Facebook page, April 2014

There are days when I cannot write down a word because I am making another list of my bills for the umpteenth time and calculating minimum payments, as if the numbers will change.

2 + 2 = 4, and I know that like I know my first and last name. My bills are due every month no matter what, so I have come to depend on them because they are as much a symbol of my financial burdens as they are a testament to my independence and will to choose.

I chose Los Angeles for myself and with it I chose my rent, which increases 4 percent annually. My lights, which must stay on. My internet, which is how I eat. My gas and sanitation bill because they came with the apartment. My cell phone bill because it keeps me connected. My student loan bill because one day I want to go back. Groceries because I choose what to put in this body now, to grow it and nourish it and water it. The bills that say, "This is my little bungalow in Silver Lake, I am the only person with a key to its door, I don't answer to anyone here or take care of anyone here. This is my home, all for me." My only companion is a dying orchid and that, too, is a choice.

Mostly my lists look like this: a list of my dream items, a list of my outstanding debts, a list of my recurring bills, a list of household items to buy, a list of groceries. I feel like an adult and responsible and on top of things when I cross items off of my list, but the crossing is slow. There are things I won't spend money on anymore—namely, manicures, pedicures, or the salon. Luxuries have long gone out of the window. Instead, I remember having health insurance is a luxury, being employed is a luxury, having an apartment that is mine all mine and being able to keep the rest of the world out is a luxury. There are days when I come in this house and take a nap because I don't have the answers or the funds or the energy to think about it anymore.

There are days when Editor X emails and says, "I would like for you to write for me for this amount _____," and there are times when I agree to write something just because I am being paid for it and extra money comes in handy and when is any money ever extra?

There are days when I think of my novel sitting in the corner room of my mind and of all of the research and travel and drafting I will do once I finish these other assignments that I don't want to do. I write stories and poems and essays but my novel won't budge until I have real time, and I don't have any time because I work seven days a week and when I get home I write for other people because they have money to pay me.

On my lunch break, I jot down little ideas about my novel in a yellow notebook. I have a protagonist and a premise and a setting. It feels rich. I think of the residencies I will attend to finish my novel. I think of the barns or lofts or studios or small apartments. I think about the little lamps there and the meals I will eat. I promise my protagonist tomorrow. I tell her, *When there is more time*. I am trying to make time for everything, but time is getting away from me.

I have always worked two jobs, my whole life. Two jobs and school. Two jobs and relationships. Two jobs and family. At the end of the summer I am leaving my second job so that I can write more and read more and sleep. I will make less money, but I will have more time for me. I think, *Am I worth it?* Am I worth it? Is my work worth my own time?

I want to feel awake and alive in the morning. I want to feel a new day arriving and know that it's for me. My day is somebody else's time because I am always working against time because somebody is always emailing me about a fucking deadline. I want the hours that I am up early to catch the metro, the hours I am waiting for the metro, the hours that I am on the metro.

I call my commute "Reading Time." It is the only way I can justify the hour it takes me to get everywhere. It is the way I justify waking up two and half hours before I need to be to work. A car is quick but a car is another bill, so I take the metro, slow as it is, around Los Angeles. The metro eats up all of my time: me and the other workers and the drifters and the aspiring and the homeless. Time is taking what it wants from us.

Poor people can't even have their days.

II. Considerations

> Poetry paid the poets in poems and the poems paid the poets in publications and the publications paid the poets with a press and the press paid the poets with titles and the titles paid the reviewer with an advanced copy and the advanced copy paid the reputation of the book and the reputation of the book paid its own spine because spines love prizes and the prizes paid the contest judges with ribboned name tags and dinner and dinner rhymes with winner and the winner was given a clear, plastic jacket and paid in a dusty library on the eve of a nasty, syllabic recount election.
>
> **Thomas Sayers Ellis, as shared on his Facebook page, May 2014**

I have never been paid for a poem. Poetry is the hardest thing to write and makes me feel the smallest and most afraid. My poems are not short or lyrical and people love short, lyrical, ethereal poems. I am scared that I will never be published or reviewed or have a reputation because no one cares about confessional poetry or persona poems or experimental poems or epics or narrative poems the way they care about short, lyrical poems, especially those that end in rhetorical questions. I don't write poems that end in rhetorical questions. I don't get it.

I don't write as much poetry because people pay me to write other things.

I write one poem every few months. They come slow and burn slower. I do not complain because I want poems that will keep me in love and stay with me. My poems will not put food on the table. These are not bread-and-butter poems. My poems are their own people.

Poetry is my whole life, and everything else—rice, meat, potatoes—is ruining it. Poetry is my whole life, and everything else—rent, lights, student loans—is ruining it. Poetry is my whole life, and if I am not careful I will ruin it.

III. The Real Question

What's wrong with liking poetry and money?
J. Bradley (@iheartfailure), Twitter, May 9, 2014

The following one-question interview was conducted on June 11, 2014, with twenty-nine poets:

Q: What did your mother teach you to always have in the house in case of hunger and no money?

1. Jonterri Gadson: Beans and cornbread.

2. Tricia Lockwood: Day-old bread from the day-old-bread store!

3. Joseph Delgado: My mother instilled the importance of flour. From flour, I can abate hunger, bread, crumbs. Nourishment.

4. Bettina Judd: My mother told me to always have canned goods, but especially canned fish. Tuna, sardines, anchovies, salmon. Tuna salad and fish cakes.

5. Afaa M. Weaver: Cheese, eggs, bread, bologna, and Kool-Aid. She told me to stay out of debt, too.

6. Jericho Brown: She didn't.

7. Tarfia Faizullah: Rice.

8. Lenelle Moïse: Cassava bread, peanut butter for spreading, and pickled peppers with cabbage ("pikliz") for spice.

9. Khadijah Queen: Chicken soup in the can.

10. Harryette Mullen: Like my mother, I try to keep my pantry stocked with staples such as dried beans, rice, pasta, canned tomatoes, corn meal, flour, and powdered milk—all useful for lean times between paychecks, or even to get by for a few days when I'm too busy to go shopping. My sister and I thought it was a treat to have pancakes for dinner, not realizing at the time that our mother was stretching until the next payday.

11. C. L. McFadyen: Bread, butter, white rice, any kind of soup.

12. Elisa Gabbert: This isn't something my mother taught me explicitly, but: I always have eggs in the house. I know this is what we both eat when we're too tired and broke to shop for "real" food. My mom supplements with saltines; I supplement with tortilla chips.

13. Sofia Samatar: Lentils.

14. Noni Limar: Potatoes, spaghetti sauce and noodles, rice, beans, eggs.

15. Rigoberto González: Sugar cubes. We knew that hunger; it wasn't hypothetical.

16. Brandon Amico: She always suggested stocking up on pasta, since it's cheap and lasts a while.

17. Brian Spears: Rice. It doesn't rot, and you can eat it by itself.

18. R. A. Villanueva: My mother never expressly said, "Here is what you must always have on hand," but I am fairly certain that our cupboards at home are right now stocked with: Cup Noodles, Campbell's Chunky Soup (New England Clam Chowder), and white—or jasmine—rice. The canned goods are likely the same provisions that were there when I was growing up; rice is bought each week and the kind of rice depends on what's on sale at the supermarket. There is always longganisa (Filipino sausage) and smoked fish in the freezer just in case. Always.

19. Matthew Nienow: My mother tried to offer us faith for hard times, and though I am no longer religious, a certain faith in the long road has carried me through some pretty rough financial hardships.

20. Ashaki Jackson: A phone to call her or my dad to rescue me.

21. Kyle G. Dargan: Savings. You can always turn that into food.

22. Metta Sáma: My mother never had end-of-the-world advice, just "always wear clean panties—you never know when you might have an accident."

23. avery r. young: Beans. Grow greens.

24. Michelle Meyering: Rice. At night, she'd make a pot of it. We'd eat some with our dinner and the rest the next morning with milk and sugar.

25. Sally Wen Mao: Oatmeal, soup, roasted seaweed laver, rice, wheat soba noodles.

26. Nichole Perkins: Mama always made sure we had peanut butter and (saltine) crackers during lean times. You can eat them separately or together and get satisfied pretty quickly. A spoonful of peanut butter goes a long way.

27. Abbie Leavens: My mother never directly told me what to keep around because even at our poorest we pretended like we weren't, but there was *always* a box of rice in the cupboard.

28. k. l. moore: Pasta, sauce. Should always be *some* meat in the freezer. But yeah, starches were on deck.

29. Annie Branigan: My mom's short answer: a karaoke machine. The long answer is that, growing up in the Philippines, I was surrounded by a lot of family. In a country where one in five people live below the poverty line, the idea of being "without money" means something different there than it does in the States. "Without money" happens frequently and isn't a cause for despair, mostly because there's the expectation that your family, your community, or your God will take care of you (the order may differ, depending on the person).

And, provided your family is there, "without food" simply is not an option. A Filipino will shoot his neighbor over a game of cards, but he won't let his neighbor starve. They feel hunger, I'm sure. But I've yet to know one, in his native land, who has gone hungry. So, as a child, I had no context for either being a possibility.

And so, she added, "for a Filipino family, a karaoke machine. They will sing even when they can't. They will bury their sorrow by belting out their favorite tunes: 'I Will Survive,' by Donna Summer, and the most popular requested karaoke song, 'My Way,' by Frank Sinatra."

I'll admit. As an American, I don't understand, and I'm still a bit embarrassed. What good is a karaoke machine when the lights are out and you haven't a single slice of bread?

But my mom doesn't see it that way.

IV. The Sum

Wrath of the Math.
Kyle Dargan (@Free_KGD), Twitter, June 4, 2014

cabbage makes its own water so oil and salt is enough
and one part rice is two parts water so watch it does not boil over

cabbage (about .33/lb but never more than .67/lb)
a bag of rice (bulk, kept cool and in the dark, no reason to ever
    run out)

There is a meal.

chicken legs or chicken leg quarters (with
all fat and skin and bones attached at .69/lb and never pay more
    than that.)

A gallon of vinegar always to clean the parts
or lemon juice or limes or whatever you can get

There is a meal.

Forget the fancy grocer
Try the bodega and wink at the fruit man

Learn the name of the boy who sweeps the door front

Smile at the bruised fruit he offers for free and take it.

In the sink wash its brown spots and soft spots
press your thumb against its fruit body and feel for its

browning and cut it clean away with your best knife.
Close your eyes and listen to the beef bones boil for the beans

Eat your fruit as if it is still hanging from its tree
Eat your fruit often and to the pit.

V. Where the Cash At? / Where the Stash At?

2012 Writing Expenses

EXPENSE	COST	NOTES
Cave Canem application fee	$10	Least amount of money I've ever paid to apply for anything.
VONA application fee	$20	
Lambda Literary application fee	$20	Not worth the price of the ticket.
Business cards	$20.49	Seemed really (1) important, (2) respectable, and (3) necessary at the time. I'm sure people threw them away, like I always do.
Website	$25	DIY Wordpress gets the job done.
VONA deposit	$100	
VONA payment	$500	Check from my second job.
VONA payment	$750	This is called increments or installments or deposits or "throwing a lil something on it," as my old aunties would say.

EXPENSE	COST	NOTES
OAK flight	$259.60	I have never purchased a round-trip ticket because I can't afford to spend the money all at once. I have to buy a one-way and then wait and save and buy the return fare.
LAMBDA deposit	$110	
OAK flight	$10	Southwest Airlines bullshit so that I can board before the zombie apocalypse gets on the plane.
LAX flight	$100	
Tennessee Williams/ New Orleans Literary Festival application fee	$20	I ended up a finalist, so yay!
PEN Center USA Emerging Voices application fee	$10	I won this fellowship, so the best $10 my black ass has ever spent.
PEN/USA application photocopy	$32	This is called not having a job or a printer, so walking to the local copyshop and paying some stupid rate for five copies of your application materials.
PEN/USA mailing at post office	$5.15	
Business card re-order	$25.49	Again, I thought I needed them.
LAX flight	$173.80	
NYC flight	$175.60	
Stegner Fellowship application fee	$75	What was I thinking? What unemployed person spends $75 on an application? Also, I didn't stand a chance.

EXPENSE	COST	NOTES
FAWC application fee and mailing	$51	Didn't get this shit either.
LAX flight	$249.10	I was convinced that, in order to change the course of my life, I had to go to California, and I was right.
Total	**$2,742.23**	Complete financial cost of pursuing my writing dream in 2012. This total is reflective of quitting both of my jobs in June (after having my vacation rejected).
		I needed the vacation time to be able to attend the workshops, so I made the decision to go anyway.
		I applied for unemployment and received $266 a week and rented a room in LA for $500 a month until I found a job and could afford my own apartment.

2013 Writing Expenses

EXPENSE	COST	NOTES
Hedgebrook application fee	$30	A lot of money for something I did not get.
Copyediting services	$100	When your short story is being anthologized, you find some thrifty copyediting in a jiff.
Website domain	$26	Annually recurring necessary fee. My website has funneled more work my way than anything else.
AWP hotel payment 1	$100	Praise God for credit cards.

EXPENSE	COST	NOTES
AWP registration	$45	Student registration. Praise God for classes at community colleges.
LAX to SEA flight	$78.90	Shout out to Alaska Airlines.
SEA to LAX flight	$108.90	Shout out to Virgin Airlines.
Google Chromebook, purchased 7/2013	$300	My Chromebook was stolen in a home burglary in October. No renter's insurance, and I cried and cried and cried. A friend bought me a new and real computer.
Total	**$788.80**	This total reflects less than a third of what I spent the year before because I elected not to attend any workshops or retreats after concluding my fellowship with PEN Center USA. I was also looking for a 32-hr/week job that would give me benefits but allow me to write.
		My unemployment was cut down to $166 a week in January 2013 and ended in June 2013. I found a job in July and started in August. A full year and a half of unemployment.
		In the time I was unemployed, I earned $11,232.
		$9,000 of that went to pay the rent for my room.

2014 Writing Expenses

EXPENSE	COST	NOTES
MacDowell Colony application fee	$30	Very pricey application, but worth the price of the ticket if accepted, and I got accepted.
Bread Loaf application fee	$15	
AWP application fee	$10	Scholarship application that would have offset the price of one workshop by $500, but I did not win.
LongHidden DJ	$100	Organizing a community literary event with no grant funding means a lot of out-of-pocket expenses; for example, the DJ.
LongHidden photographer	$100	And the photographer.
LongHidden snacks	$100	And the coffee, tea, and snacks for your readers.
Airfare, Kimbilio Center for African American Fiction retreat	$312	Round-trip airfare to New Mexico. I can afford a round trip this time. The great thing about this workshop is that I don't have to pay tuition, only housing.
Kimbilio housing	$525	The cost of a private studio. $175 more than a shared room, but I had to.
AWP hotel balance	$350	This is called paying off the credit card.
MacDowell airfare	$500	I'll be flying into Boston round-trip. No idea how much the shuttle from the airport will be yet. I applied for a travel stipend, so hopefully some of this will be reimbursed.

EXPENSE	COST	NOTES
LA City College class	$150	I took a three-credit course at a community college to circumvent the full registration fee at AWP but also for a refresher.
Google Chromebook	$325.91	Mama had to do it. Mama being me. Having the Chromebook to travel to workshops and coffee houses and retreats and fellowships with means (1) ease of transportation and (2) not schlepping my main and only computer all over the US because I can't afford to replace it. (3) I don't want back or shoulder problems later in life. (4) I travel too much not to have a tiny, convenient, light machine. I would LOVE a MacBook Air, but I can't afford it right now.
Total	**$2,517.91**	As of June 2014, I have two jobs, a FT job and PT job on the weekends. I make enough money now to finally leave my PT job at the end of the summer.
		A grand total of $5,988 invested into my career as a writer as of June 2014. That is a lot of money, but it is an investment in myself.
		I have made $1,925, as a writer, as of June 2014.

Notes

"Baby Gotta Eat" is a borrowed lyric from Outkast's "Slump," from the album *Aquemini*.

"Wrath of the Math" makes reference to the title of Jeru the Damaja's second album.

"Where the Cash At?/Where the Stash At?" is a borrowed lyric from The Notorious B.I.G.'s "Gimme the Loot," from the album *Ready to Die*.

Lowering Your Standards for Food Stamps

Sheryl Luna

Words fall out of my coat pocket,
soak in bleach water. I touch everyone's
dirty dollars. Maslow's got everything on me.
Fourteen hours on my feet. No breaks.
No smokes or lunch. Blank-eyed movements:
trash bags, coffee burner, fingers numb.
I am hourly protestations and false smiles.
The clock clicks its slow slowing.
Faces blur in a stream of hurried soccer games,
sunlight, and church certainty. I have no
poem to carry, no material illusions.
Cola spilled on hands, so sticky fingered,
I'm far from poems. I'd write of politicians,
refineries, and a border's barbed wire,
but I am unlearning America's languages
with a mop. In a summer-hot red
polyester top, I sell lotto tickets. Cars wait for gas
billowing black. Killing time has new meaning.
A jackhammer breaks apart a life. The slow globe
spirals, and at night black space has me dizzy.
Visionaries off their meds and wacked out
meth heads sing to me. A panicky fear of robbery
and humiliation drips with my sweat.
Words some say are weeping twilight and sunrise.

Sheryl Luna

I am drawn to dramas, the couple arguing, the man
headbutting his wife in the parking lot.
911: no metered aubade, and nobody but
myself to blame.

Color Blind or Color Brave?
Mellody Hobson

So it's 2006. My friend Harold Ford calls me. He's running for U.S. Senate in Tennessee, and he says, "Mellody, I desperately need some national press. Do you have any ideas?" So I had an idea. I called a friend who was in New York at one of the most successful media companies in the world, and she said, "Why don't we host an editorial board lunch for Harold? You come with him."

Harold and I arrive in New York. We are in our best suits. We look like shiny new pennies. And we get to the receptionist, and we say, "We're here for the lunch." She motions for us to follow her. We walk through a series of corridors, and all of a sudden we find ourselves in a stark room, at which point she looks at us and she says, "Where are your uniforms?"

Just as this happens, my friend rushes in. The blood drains from her face. There are literally no words, right? And I look at her, and I say, "Now, don't you think we need more than one black person in the U.S. Senate?"

Now Harold and I, we still laugh about that story, and in many ways, the moment caught me off guard, but deep, deep down inside, I actually wasn't surprised. And I wasn't surprised because of something my mother taught me about thirty years before. You see, my mother was ruthlessly realistic. I remember one day coming home from a birthday party where I was the only black kid invited, and instead of asking me the normal motherly questions like, "Did you have fun?" or "How was the cake?" my mother looked at me and she said, "How did they treat you?" I was seven. I did not understand. I mean, why would anyone treat me differently? But she knew. And she looked me right in the eye and she said, "They will not always treat you well."

Now, race is one of those topics in America that makes people extraordinarily uncomfortable. You bring it up at a dinner party or in a workplace environment, [and] it is literally the conversational equivalent of touching the third rail. There is shock, followed by a long silence. And even coming here today, I told some friends and colleagues that I planned to talk about race, and they warned me, they told me, don't do it, that there'd be huge risks in me talking about this topic, that people might think I'm a militant black woman and I would ruin my career. And I have to tell you, I actually for a moment was a bit afraid. Then I realized, the first step to solving any problem is to not hide from it, and the first step to any form of action is awareness. And so I decided to actually talk about race. And I decided that if I came here and shared with you some of my experiences, that maybe we could all be a little less anxious and a little more bold in our conversations about race.

Now I know there are people out there who will say that the election of Barack Obama meant that it was the end of racial discrimination for all eternity, right? But I work in the investment business, and we have a saying: The numbers do not lie. And here, there are significant, quantifiable racial disparities that cannot be ignored, in household wealth, household income, job opportunities, health care. One example from corporate America: Even though white men make up just 30 percent of the U.S. population, they hold 70 percent of all corporate board seats. Of the Fortune 250, there are only seven CEOs that are minorities, and of the thousands of publicly traded companies today, *thousands*, only two are chaired by black women, and you're looking at one of them—the same one who, not too long ago, was nearly mistaken for kitchen help. So that is a fact. Now I have this thought experiment that I play with myself, when I say, imagine if I walked you into a room and it was of a major corporation, like ExxonMobil, and every single person around the boardroom were black, you would think that [was] weird. But if I walked you into a Fortune 500 company, and everyone around the table were a white male, when will it be that we think that's weird too?

And I know how we got here. You know, there was institutionalized, at one time legalized, discrimination in our country. There's no question about it. But still, as I grapple with this issue, my mother's question hangs in the air for me: How did they treat you?

Now, I do not raise this issue to complain or in any way to elicit any kind of sympathy. I have succeeded in my life beyond my wildest expectations, and I have been treated well by people of all races more often than I have not. I tell the uniform story because it happened. I cite those statistics around corporate board diversity because they are real. And I stand here today talking about this issue of racial discrimination because I believe it threatens to rob another generation of all the opportunities that all of us want for our children, no matter what their color or where they are from. And I think it also threatens to hold back businesses.

You see, researchers have coined this term "color blindness" to describe a learned behavior where we pretend that we don't notice race. If you happen to be surrounded by a bunch of people who look like you, that's purely accidental. Now, color blindness, in my view, doesn't mean that there's no racial discrimination, and there's fairness. It doesn't mean that at all. It doesn't ensure it. In my view, color blindness is very dangerous because it means we're ignoring the problem. There was a corporate study that said that, instead of avoiding race, the really smart corporations actually deal with it head on. They actually recognize that embracing diversity means recognizing all races, including the majority one. But I'll be the first to tell you, this subject matter can be hard, awkward, uncomfortable—but that's kind of the point.

In the spirit of debunking racial stereotypes, the one that black people don't like to swim, I'm going to tell you how much I love to swim. I love to swim so much that as an adult, I swim with a coach. And one day my coach had me do a drill where I had to swim to one end of a 25-meter pool without taking a breath. And every single time I failed, I had to start over. And I failed a lot. By the end, I got it, but when I got out of the pool, I was exasperated and tired and annoyed, and I said, "Why are we doing breath-holding exercises?" And my coach looked at me, and he said, "Mellody, that was not a breath-holding exercise. That drill was to make you comfortable being uncomfortable, because that's how most of us spend our days." If we can learn to deal with our discomfort, and just relax into it, we'll have a better life.

So I think it's time for us to be comfortable with the uncomfortable conversation about race: black, white, Asian, Hispanic, male, female, all of us, if we truly believe in equal rights and equal opportunity in America, I think we have to have real conversations about this issue. We cannot afford to be color blind. We have to be color brave. We have to be willing, as teachers and parents and entrepreneurs and scientists, we have to be willing to have proactive conversations about race with honesty and understanding and courage, not because it's the right thing to do, but because it's the smart thing to do, because our businesses and our products and our science, our research, all of that will be better with greater diversity.

Now, my favorite example of color bravery is a guy named John Skipper. He runs ESPN. He's a North Carolina native, quintessential Southern gentleman, white. He joined ESPN, which already had a culture of inclusion and diversity, but he took it up a notch. He demanded that every open position have a diverse slate of candidates. Now he says the senior people in the beginning bristled, and they would come to him and say, "Do you want me to hire the minority, or do you want me to hire the best person for the job?" And Skipper says his answers were always the same: "Yes." And by saying yes to diversity, I honestly believe ESPN is the most valuable cable franchise in the world. I think that's a part of the secret sauce.

Now I can tell you, in my own industry, at Ariel Investments, we actually view our diversity as a competitive advantage, and that advantage can extend way beyond business. There's a guy named Scott Page at the University of Michigan. He is the first person to develop a mathematical calculation for diversity. He says, if you're trying to solve a really hard problem, really hard, that you should have a diverse group of people, including those with diverse intellects. The example that he gives is the smallpox epidemic. When it was ravaging Europe, they brought together all these scientists, and they were stumped. And the beginnings of the cure to the disease came from the most unlikely source, a dairy farmer who noticed that the milkmaids were not getting smallpox. And the smallpox vaccination is bovine-based because of that dairy farmer.

Now I'm sure you're sitting here and you're saying, I don't run a cable company, I don't run an investment firm, I am not a dairy farmer. What can I do? And I'm telling you, you can be color brave. If you're part of a hiring process or admissions process, you can be color brave. If you are trying to solve a really hard problem, you can speak up and be color brave. Now I know people will say, but that doesn't add up to a lot, but I'm actually asking you to do something really simple: Observe your environment, at work, at school, at home. I'm asking you to look at the people around you purposefully and intentionally. Invite people into your life who don't look like you, don't think like you, don't act like you, don't come from where you come from, and you might find that they will challenge your assumptions and make you grow as a person. You might get powerful new insights from these individuals, or, like my husband, who happens to be white, you might learn that black people—men, women, children—we use body lotion every single day.

Now, I also think that this is very important so that the next generation really understands that this progress will help them, because they're expecting us to be great role models.

Now, I told you, my mother, she was ruthlessly realistic. She was an unbelievable role model. She was the kind of person who got to be the way she was because she was a single mom with six kids in Chicago. She was in the real estate business, where she worked extraordinarily hard but oftentimes had a hard time making ends meet. And that meant sometimes we got our phone disconnected, or our lights turned off, or we got evicted. When we got evicted, sometimes we lived in these small apartments that she owned, sometimes in only one or two rooms, because they weren't completed, and we would heat our bath water on hot plates. But she never gave up hope, ever, and she never allowed us to give up hope either. This brutal pragmatism that she had—I mean, I was four and she told me, "Mommy is Santa." She was this brutal pragmatist. She taught me so many lessons, but the most important lesson was that every single day she told me, "Mellody, you can be anything." And because of those words, I would wake up at the crack of dawn, and because of those words, I would love school more than anything, and because of those words, when I was on a bus going to school, I dreamed the biggest dreams. And it's because of those words that I stand here right now full of passion, asking you to be brave for the kids who are dreaming those dreams today.

You see, I want them to look at a CEO on television and say, "I can be like her," or, "He looks like me." And I want them to know that anything is possible, that they can achieve the highest level that they ever imagined, that they will be welcome in any corporate boardroom, or they can lead any company. You see, this idea of being the land of the free and the home of the brave, it's woven into the fabric of America. America, when we have a challenge, we take it head on, we don't shrink away from it. We take a stand. We show courage. So right now, what I'm asking you to do, I'm asking you to show courage. I'm asking you to be bold. As business leaders, I'm asking you not to leave anything on the table. As citizens, I'm asking you not to leave any child behind. I'm asking you not to be color blind, but to be color brave, so that every child knows that their future matters and their dreams are possible.

Reeling for the Empire
Karen Russell

Several of us claim to have been the daughters of samurai, but of course there is no way for anyone to verify that now. It's a relief, in its way, the new anonymity. We come here tall and thin, noblewomen from Yamaguchi, graceful as calligraphy; short and poor, Hida girls with bloody feet, crow-voiced and vulgar; entrusted to the Model Mill by our teary mothers; rented out by our destitute uncles—but within a day or two the drink the Recruitment Agent gave us begins to take effect. And the more our *kaiko*-bodies begin to resemble one another, the more frantically each factory girl works to reinvent her past. One of the consequences of our captivity here in Nowhere Mill, and of the darkness that pools on the factory floor, and of the polar fur that covers our faces, blanking us all into sisters, is that anybody can be anyone she likes in the past. Some of our lies are quite bold: Yuna says that her great-uncle has a scrap of sailcloth from the Black Ships. Dai claims that she knelt alongside her samurai father at the Battle of Shiroyama. Nishi fibs that she once stowed away in the imperial caboose from Shimbashi Station to Yokohama, and saw Emperor Meiji eating pink cake. Back in Gifu I had tangly hair like a donkey's tail, a mouth like a small red bean, but I tell the others that I was very beautiful.

"Where are you from?" they ask me.

"The castle in Gifu, perhaps you know it from the famous woodblocks? My great-grandfather was a warrior."

"Oh! But Kitsune, we thought you said your father was the one who printed the woodblocks? The famous *ukiyo-e* artist, Utagawa Kuniyoshi . . ."

"Yes. He was, yesterday."

I'll put it bluntly: we are all becoming reelers. Some kind of hybrid creature, part *kaiko*, silkworm caterpillar, and part human female. Some of the older workers' faces are already quite covered with a coarse white fur, but my face and thighs stayed smooth for twenty days. In fact I've only just begun to grow the white hair on my belly. During my first nights and days in the silk-reeling factory I was always shaking. I have never been a hysterical person, and so at first I misread these tremors as mere mood; I was in the clutches of a giddy sort of terror, I thought. Then the roiling feeling became solid. It was the thread: a color purling invisibly in my belly. Silk. Yards and yards of thin color would soon be extracted from me by the Machine.

Today, the Agent drops off two new recruits, sisters from the Yamagata Prefecture, a blue village called Sakegawa, which none of us have visited. They are the daughters of a salmon fisherman and their names are Tooka and Etsuyo. They are twelve and nineteen. Tooka has a waist-length braid and baby fat; Etsuyo looks like a forest doe, with her long neck and watchful brown eyes. We step into the light and Etsuyo swallows her scream. Tooka starts wailing—"Who are you? What's happened to you? What is this place?"

Dai crosses the room to them, and despite their terror the Sakegawa sisters are too sleepy and too shocked to recoil from her embrace. They appear to have drunk the tea very recently, because they're quaking on their feet. Etsuyo's eyes cross as if she is about to faint. Dai unrolls two tatami mats in a dark corner, helps them to stretch out. "Sleep a little," she whispers. "Dream."

"Is this the silk-reeling factory?" slurs Tooka, half-conscious on her bedroll.

"Oh, yes," Dai says. Her furry face hovers like a moon above them.

Tooka nods, satisfied, as if willing to dismiss all of her terror to continue believing in the Agent's promises, and shuts her eyes.

Sometimes when the new recruits confide the hopes that brought them to our factory, I have to suppress a bitter laugh. Long before the *kaiko* change turned us into mirror images of one another, we were sisters already, spinning identical dreams in beds thousands of miles apart, fantasizing about gold silks and an "imperial vocation." We envisioned our future dowries, our families' miraculous freedom from debt. We thrilled to the same tales of women working in the grand textile mills, where steel machines from Europe gleamed in the light of the Meiji sunrise. Our world had changed so rapidly in the wake of the Black Ships that the poets could barely keep pace with the scenes outside their own windows. Industry, trade, unstoppable growth: years before the Agent came to find us, our dreams anticipated his promises.

Since my arrival here, my own fantasies have grown as dark as the room. In them I snip a new girl's thread midair, or yank all the silk out of her at once, so that she falls lifelessly forward like a *Bunraku* puppet. I haven't been able to cry since my first night here—but often I feel a water pushing at my skull. "Can the thread migrate to your brain?" I've asked Dai nervously. Silk starts as a liquid. Right now I can feel it traveling below my navel, my thread. Foaming icily along the lining of my stomach. Under the blankets I watch it rise in a hard lump. There are twenty workers sleeping on twelve tatami, two rows of us, our heads ten centimeters apart, our earlobes curled like snails on adjacent leaves, and though we are always hungry, every one of us has a round belly. Most nights I can barely sleep, moaning for dawn and the Machine.

Every aspect of our new lives, from working to sleeping, eating and shitting, bathing when we can get wastewater from the Machine, is conducted in one brick room. The far wall has a single oval window, set high in its center. Too high for us to see much besides scraps of cloud and a woodpecker that is like a celebrity to us, provoking gasps and applause every time he appears. *Kaiko-joko*, we call ourselves. Silkworm-workers. Unlike regular *joko*, we have no foreman or men. We are all alone in the box of this room. Dai says that she's the dormitory supervisor, but that's Dai's game.

We were all brought here by the same man, the factory Recruitment Agent. A representative, endorsed by Emperor Meiji himself, from the new Ministry for the Promotion of Industry.

We were all told slightly different versions of the same story.

Our fathers or guardians signed contracts that varied only slightly in their terms, most promising a five-yen advance for one year of our lives.

The Recruitment Agent travels the countryside to recruit female workers willing to travel far from their home prefectures to a new European-style silk-reeling mill. Presumably, he is out recruiting now. He makes his pitch not to the woman herself but to her father or guardian, or in some few cases, where single women cannot be procured, her husband. I am here on behalf of the nation, he begins. In the spirit of *Shokusan-Kōgyō. Increase production, encourage industry.* We are recruiting only the most skillful and loyal mill workers, he continues. Not just peasant girls—like your offspring, he might say with his silver tongue to men in Gifu and Mie prefectures—but the well-bred daughters of noblemen. Samurai and aristocrats. City-born governors have begged me to train their daughters on the Western technologies. Last week, the Medical General of the Imperial Army sent his nineteen-year-old twins, by train! Sometimes there is resistance from the father or guardian, especially among the hicks, those stony-faced men from distant centuries who still make bean paste, wade into rice paddies, brew sake using thousand-year-old methods; but the Agent waves all qualms away—Ah, you've heard about x-Mill or y-Factory? No, the French *yatoi* engineers don't drink girls' blood, haha, that is what they call *red wine*. Yes, there *was* a fire at Aichi Factory, a little trouble with tuberculosis in Suwa. But our factory is quite different—it is a national secret. Yes, a place that makes even the French filature in the backwoods of Gunma, with its brick walls and steam engines, look antiquated! This phantom factory he presents to her father or guardian with great cheerfulness and urgency, for he says we have awoken to dawn, the Enlightened Era of the Meiji, and we must all play our role now. Japan's silk is her world export. The Blight in Europe, the pébrine virus, has killed every silkworm, forever halted the Westerners' cocoon production. The demand is as vast as the ocean. This is the moment to seize. Silk reeling is a sacred vocation—she will be reeling for the empire.

The fathers and guardians nearly always sign the contract. Publicly, the *joko*'s family will share a cup of hot tea with the Agent.

They celebrate her new career and the five-yen advance against her legally mortgaged future. Privately, an hour or so later, the Agent will share a special toast with the girl herself. The Agent improvises his tearooms: an attic in a forest inn or a locked changing room in a bathhouse or, in the case of Iku, an abandoned cowshed.

After sunset, the old blind woman arrives. "The zookeeper," we call her. She hauls our food to the grated door, unbars the lower panel. We pass her that day's skeins of reeled silk, and she pushes two sacks of mulberry leaves through the panel with a long stick. The woman never speaks to us, no matter what questions we shout at her. She simply waits, patiently, for our skeins, and so long as they are acceptable in quality and weight, she slides in our leaves. Tonight she has also slid in a tray of steaming human food for the new recruits. Tooka and Etsuyo get cups of rice and miso soup with floating carrots. Hunks of real ginger are unraveling in the broth, like hair. We all sit on the opposite side of the room and watch them chew with a dewy nostalgia that disgusts me even as I find myself ogling their long white fingers on their chopsticks, the balls of rice. The salt and fat smells of their food make my eyes ache. When we eat the mulberry leaves, we lower our new faces to the floor.

They drink down the soup in silence. "Are we dreaming?" I hear one whisper.

"The tea drugged us!" the younger sister, Tooka, cries at last. Her gaze darts here and there, as if she's hoping to be contradicted. They traveled nine days by riverboat and oxcart, Etsuyo tells us, wearing blindfolds the entire time. So we could be that far north of Yamagata, or west. Or east, the younger sister says. We collect facts from every new *kaiko-joko* and use them to draw thread maps of Japan on the factory floor. But not even Tsuki the Apt can guess our whereabouts.

Nowhere Mill, we call this place.

Dai crosses the room and speaks soothingly to the sisters; then she leads them right to me. Oh, happy day. I glare at her through an unchewed mouthful of leaves.

"Kitsune is quite a veteran now," says smiling Dai, leading the fishy sisters to me, "she will show you around—"

Karen Russell

I hate this part. But you have to tell the new ones what's in store for them. Minds have been spoiled by the surprise.

"Will the manager of this factory be coming soon?" Etsuyo asks, in a grave voice. "I think there has been a mistake."

"We don't belong here!" Tooka breathes.

There's nowhere else for you now, I say, staring at the floor. That tea he poured into you back in Sakegawa? The Agent's drink is remaking your insides. Your intestines, your secret organs. Soon your stomachs will bloat. You will manufacture silk in your gut with the same helpless skill that you digest food, exhale. The *kaiko*-change, he calls it. A revolutionary process. Not even Chiyo, who knows sericulture, has ever heard of a tea that turns girls into silkworms. We think the tea may have been created abroad, by French chemists or British engineers. *Yatoi*-tea. Unless it's the Agent's own technology.

I try to smile at them now.

In the cup it was so lovely to look at, wasn't it? An orange hue, like something out of the princess's floating world woodblocks.

Etsuyo is shaking. "But we can't undo it? Surely there's a cure. A way to reverse it, before it's . . . too late."

Before we look like you, she means.

"The only cure is a temporary one, and it comes from the Machine. When your thread begins, you'll understand . . ."

It takes thirteen to fourteen hours for the Machine to empty a *kaiko-joko* of her thread. The relief of being rid of it is indescribable.

These seashore girls know next to nothing about silkworm cultivation. In the mountains of Chichibu, Chiyo tells them, everyone in her village was involved. Seventy families worked together in a web: planting and watering the mulberry trees, raising the *kaiko* eggs to pupa, feeding the silkworm caterpillars. The art of silk production was very, very inefficient, I tell the sisters. Slow and costly. Until us.

I try to weed the pride from my voice, but it's difficult. In spite of everything, I can't help but admire the quantity of silk that we *kaiko-joko* can produce in a single day. The Agent boasts that he has made us the most productive machines in the empire, surpassing even those steel zithers and cast-iron belchers at Tomioka Model Mill.

Eliminated: mechanical famine. Supply problems caused by the cocoons' tiny size and irregular quality.

Eliminated: waste silk.

Eliminated: the cultivation of the *kaiko*. The harvesting of their eggs. The laborious collection and separation of the silk cocoons. We silkworm-girls combine all these processes in the single factory of our bodies. Ceaselessly, even while we dream, we are generating thread. Every droplet of our energy, every moment of our time flows into the silk.

I guide the sisters to the first of three workbenches. "Here are the basins," I say, "steam heated, quite modern, eh, where we boil the water."

I plunge my left hand under the boiling water for as long as I can bear it. Soon the skin of my fingertips softens and bursts, and fine waggling fibers rise from them. Green thread lifts right out of my veins. With my right hand I pluck up the thread from my left fingertips and wrist.

"See? Easy."

A single strand is too fine to reel. So you have to draw several out, wind six or eight around your finger, rub them together, to get the right denier; when they are thick enough, you feed them to the Machine.

Dai is drawing red thread onto her reeler, watching me approvingly.

"Are we monsters now?" Tooka wants to know.

I give Dai a helpless look; that's a question I won't answer.

Dai considers.

In the end she tells the new reelers about the *juhyou*, the "snow monsters," snow-and-ice-covered trees in Zao Onsen, her home. "The snow monsters"—Dai smiles, brushing her white whiskers—"are very beautiful. Their disguises make them beautiful. But they are still trees, you see, under all that frost."

While the sisters drink in this news, I steer them to the Machine.

The Machine looks like a great steel-and-wood beast with a dozen rotating eyes and steaming mouths—it's twenty meters long and takes up nearly half the room. The central reeler is a huge and ever-spinning *O*, capped with rows of flashing metal teeth. Pulleys swing our damp thread left to right across it, refining it into finished silk. Tooka shivers and says it looks as if the Machine is smiling at us. *Kaiko-joko* sit at the workbenches that face the giant wheel, pulling glowing threads from their own fingers, stretching threads across their reeling frames like zither strings. A stinging music.

No *tebiki* cranks to turn, I show them. Steam power has freed both our hands,

" 'Freed,' I suppose, isn't quite the right word, is it?" says Iku drily. Lotus-colored thread is flooding out of her left palm and reeling around her dowel. With her right hand she adjusts the outflow.

Here is the final miracle, I say: our silk comes out of us in colors. There is no longer any need to dye it. There is no other silk like it on the world market, boasts the Agent. If you look at it from the right angle, a pollen seems to rise up and swirl into your eyes. Words can't exaggerate the joy of this effect.

Nobody has ever guessed her own color correctly—Hoshi predicted hers would be peach and it was blue; Nishi thought pink, got hazel. I would have bet my entire five-yen advance that mine would be light gray, like my cat's fur. But then I woke and pushed the swollen webbing of my thumb and a sprig of green came out. On my day zero, in the middle of my terror, I was surprised into a laugh: here was a translucent green I swore I'd never seen before anywhere in nature, and yet I knew it as my own on sight.

"It's as if the surface is charged with our aura," says Hoshi, counting syllables on her knuckles for her next haiku.

About this I don't tease her. I'm no poet, but I'd swear to the silks' strange glow. The sisters seem to agree with me; one looks like she's about to faint.

"Courage, sisters!" sings Hoshi. Hoshi is our haiku laureate. She came from a school for young noblewomen and pretends to have read every book in the world. We all agree that she is generally insufferable.

"Our silks are sold in Paris and America—they are worn by Emperor Meiji himself. The Agent tells me we are the treasures of the realm." Hoshi's white whiskers extend nearly to her ears now. Hoshi's optimism is indefatigable.

"That girl was hairy when she got here," I whisper to the sisters, "if you want to know the truth."

The old blind woman comes again, takes our silks, pushes the leaves in with a stick, and we fall upon them. If you think we *kaiko-joko* leave even one trampled stem behind, you underestimate the deep, death-thwarting taste of the mulberry. Vital green, as if sunlight is zipping up your spinal column.

In other factories, we've heard, there are foremen and managers and whistles to announce and regulate the breaks. Here the clocks and whistles are in our bodies. The thread itself is our boss. There is a fifteen-minute period between the mulberry orgy—"call it *the evening meal*, please, don't be disgusting," Dai pleads, her saliva still gleaming on the floor—and the regeneration of the thread. During this period, we sit in a circle in the center of the room, an equal distance from our bedding and the Machine. Stubbornly we reel backward: Takayama town. Oyaka village. Toku. Kiyo. Nara. Fudai. Sho. Radishes and pickles. Laurel and camphor smells of Shikoku. Father. Mother. Mount Fuji. The Inland Sea.

All Japan is undergoing a transformation—we *kaiko-joko* are not alone in that respect. I watched my grandfather become a sharecropper on his own property. A dependent. He was a young man when the Black Ships came to Edo. He grew foxtail millet and red buckwheat. Half his crop he paid in rent; then two-thirds; finally, after two bad harvests, he owed his entire yield. That year, our capital moved in a ceremonial, and real, procession from Kyoto to Edo, now Tokyo, the world shedding names under the carriage wheels, and the teenage emperor in his palanquin traveling over the mountains like an imperial worm.

In the first decade of the Meiji government, my grandfather was forced into bankruptcy by the land tax. In 1873, he joined the farmer's revolt in Chūbu. Along with hundreds of others of the newly bankrupted and dispossessed from Chūbu, Gifu, Aichi, he set fire to the creditor's offices where his debts were recorded. After the rebellion failed, he hanged himself in our barn. The gesture was meaningless. The debt still existed, of course.

My father inherited the debts of his father.

There was no dowry for me.

In my twenty-third year, my mother died, and my father turned white, lay flat. Death seeded in him and began to grow tall, like grain, and my brothers carried Father to the Inaba Shrine for the mountain cure.

It was at precisely this moment that the Recruitment Agent arrived at our door.

The Agent visited after a thundershower. He had a parasol from London. I had never seen such a handsome person in my life, man or woman. He had blue eyelids, a birth defect, he said, but it had worked out to his extraordinary advantage. He let me sniff at his vial of French cologne. It was as if a rumor had materialized inside the dark interior of our farmhouse. He wore Western dress. He also had—and I found this incredibly appealing—mid-ear sideburns and a mustache.

"My father is sick," I told him. I was alone in the house. "He is in the other room, sleeping."

"Well, let's not disturb him." The Agent smiled and stood to go.

"I can read," I said. For years I'd worked as a servant in the summer retreat of a Kobe family. "I can write my name."

Show me the contract, I begged him.

And he did. I couldn't run away from the factory and I couldn't die, either, explained the Recruitment Agent—and perhaps I looked at him a little dreamily, because I remember that he repeated this injunction in a hard voice, tightening up the grammar: "If you die, your father will pay." He was peering deeply into my face; it was April, and I could see the rain in his mustache. I met his gaze and giggled, embarrassing myself.

"Look at you, blinking like a firefly! Only it's very serious—"

He lunged forward and grabbed playfully at my waist, causing my entire face to darken in what I hoped was a womanly blush. The Agent, perhaps fearful that I was choking on a radish, thumped my back.

"There, there, Kitsune! You will come with me to the model factory? You will reel for the realm, for your emperor? For me, too," he added softly, with a smile.

I nodded, very serious myself now. He let his fingers brush softly against my knuckles as he drew out the contract.

"Let me bring it to Father," I told the Agent. "Stand back. Stay here. His disease is contagious."

The Agent laughed. He said he wasn't used to being bossed by a *joko*. But he waited. Who knows if he believed me?

My father would never have signed the document. He would not have agreed to let me go. He blamed the new government for my grandfather's death. He was suspicious of foreigners. He would have demanded to know, certainly, where the factory was located. But I could work whereas he could not. I saw my father coming home, cured, finding the five-yen advance. I had never used an ink pen before. In my life as a daughter and a sister, I had never felt so powerful. No woman in Gifu had ever brokered such a deal on her own. KITSUNE TAJIMA, I wrote in the slot for the future worker's name, my heart pounding in my ears. When I returned it, I apologized for my father's unsteady hand.

On our way to the *kaiko*-tea ceremony, I was so excited that I could barely make my questions about the factory intelligible. He took me to a summer guesthouse in the woods behind the Miya River, which he told me was owned by a Takayama merchant family and, at the moment, empty.

Something is wrong, I knew then. This knowledge sounded with such clarity that it seemed almost independent of my body, like a bird calling once over the trees. But I proceeded, following the Agent toward a dim staircase. The first room I glimpsed was elegantly furnished, and I felt my spirits lift again, along with my caution. I counted fourteen steps to the first landing, where he opened the door onto a room that reflected none of the downstairs refinement. There was a table with two stools, a bed; otherwise the room was bare. I was surprised to see a large brown blot on the mattress. One porcelain teapot. One cup. The Agent lifted the tea with an unreadable expression, frowning into the pot; as he poured, I thought I heard a little splash; then he cursed, excused himself, said he needed a fresh ingredient. I heard him continuing up the staircase. I peered into the cup and saw that there was something alive inside it—writhing, dying—a fat white *kaiko*. I shuddered but I didn't fish it out.

What sort of tea ceremony was this? Maybe, I thought, the Agent is testing me, to see if I am squeamish, weak. Something bad was coming—the stench of a bad and thickening future was everywhere in that room. The bad thing was right under my nose, crinkling its little legs at me.

I pinched my nostrils shut, just as if I were standing in the mud a heartbeat from jumping into the Miya River. Without so much as consulting the Agent, I squinched my eyes shut and gulped.

The other workers cannot believe I did this willingly. Apparently, one sip of the *kaiko*-tea is so venomous that most bodies go into convulsions. Only through the Agent's intervention were they able to get the tea down. It took his hands around their throats.

I arranged my hands in my lap and sat on the cot. Already I was feeling a little dizzy. I remember smiling with a sweet vacancy at the door when he returned.

"You—drank it."

I nodded proudly.

Then I saw pure amazement pass over his face—I passed the test, I thought happily. Only it wasn't that, quite. He began to laugh.

"No *joko*," he sputtered, "not one of you, ever—" He was rolling his eyes at the room's corners, as if he regretted that the hilarity of this moment was wasted on me. "No girl has ever gulped a pot of it!"

Already the narcolepsy was buzzing through me, like a hive of bees stinging me to sleep. I lay guiltily on the mat—why couldn't I sit up? Now the Agent would think I was worthless for work. I opened my mouth to explain that I was feeling ill but only a smacking sound came out. I held my eyes open for as long as I could stand it.

Even then, I was still dreaming of my prestigious new career as a factory reeler. Under the Meiji government, the hereditary classes had been abolished, and I even let myself imagine that the Agent might marry me, pay off my family's debts. As I watched, the Agent's genteel expression underwent a complete transformation; suddenly it was as blank as a stump. The last thing I saw, before shutting my eyes, was his face.

I slept for two days and woke on a dirty tatami in this factory with Dai applauding me; the green thread had erupted through my palms in my sleep—the metamorphosis unusually accelerated. I was lucky, as Chiyo says. Unlike Tooka and Etsuyo and so many of the others I had no limbo period, no cramps from my guts unwinding, changing; no time at all to meditate on what I was becoming—a secret, a furred and fleshy silk factory.

What would Chiyo think of me, if she knew how much I envy her initiation story? That what befell her—her struggle, her screams—I long for? That I would exchange my memory for Chiyo's in a heartbeat? Surely this must be the final, inarguable proof that I am, indeed, a monster.

Many workers here have a proof of their innocence, some physical trace, on the body: scar tissue, a brave spot. A sign of struggle that is ineradicable. Some girls will push their white fuzz aside to show you: Dai's pocked hands, Mitsuki's rope burns around her neck. Gin has wiggly lines around her mouth, like lightning, where she was scalded by the tea that she spat out.

And me?

There was a moment, at the bottom of the stairwell, and a door that I could easily have opened back into the woods of Gifu. I alone, it seems, out of twenty-two workers, signed my own contract.

"Why did you drink it, Kitsune?"

I shrug.

"I was thirsty," I say.

Roosters begin to crow outside the walls of Nowhere Mill at five a.m. They make a sound like gargled light, very beautiful, which I picture as Dai's red and Gin's orange and Yoshi's pink thread singing on the world's largest reeler. Dawn. I've been lying awake in the dark for hours.

"Kitsune, you never sleep. I hear the way you breathe," Dai says.

"I sleep a little."

"What stops you?" Dai rubs her belly sadly. "Too much thread?"

"Up here." I knock on my head. "I can't stop reliving it: the Agent walking through our fields under his parasol, in the rain . . ."

"You should sleep," says Dai, peering into my eyeball. "Yellowish. You don't look well."

Midmorning, there is a malfunction. Some hitch in the Machine causes my reeler to spin backward, pulling the thread from my fingers so quickly that I am jerked onto my knees; then I'm dragged along the floor toward the Machine's central wheel like an enormous, flopping fish. The room fills with my howls. With surprising calm, I become aware that my right arm is on the point of being wrenched from its socket. I lift my chin and begin, with a naturalness that belongs entirely to my terror, to swivel my head around and bite blindly at the air; at last I snap the threads with my *kaiko-*jaws and fall sideways. Under my wrist, more thread kinks and scrags. There is a terrible stinging in my hands and my head. I let my eyes close: for some reason I see the space beneath my mother's cedar chest, where the moonlight lay in green splashes on our floor. I used to hide there as a child and sleep so soundly that no one in our one-room house could ever find me. No such luck today: hands latch onto my shoulders. Voices are calling my name—"Kitsune! Are you awake? Are you okay?"

"I'm just clumsy," I laugh nervously. But then I look down at my hand. Short threads extrude from the bruised skin of my knuckles. They are the wrong color. Not my green. Ash.

Suddenly I feel short of breath again.

It gets worse when I look up. The silk that I reeled this morning is bright green. But the more recent thread drying on the bottom of my reeler is black. Black as the sea, as the forest at night, says Hoshi euphemistically. She is too courteous to make the more sinister comparisons.

I swallow a cry. Am I sick? It occurs to me that five or six of these black threads dragged my entire weight. It had felt as though my bones would snap in two before my thread did.

"Oh no!" gasp Tooka and Etsuyo. Not exactly sensitive, these sisters from Sakegawa. "Oh, poor Kitsune! Is that going to happen to us, too?"

"Anything you want to tell us?" Dai prods. "About how you are feeling?"

"I feel about as well as you all look today," I growl.

"I'm not worried," says Dai in a too-friendly way, clapping my shoulder. "Kitsune just needs sleep."

But everybody is staring at the spot midway up the reel where the green silk shades into black.

My next mornings are spent splashing through the hot water basin, looking for fresh fibers. I pull out yards of the greenish-black thread. Soiled silk. Hideous. Useless for kimonos. I sit and reel for my sixteen hours, until the Machine gets the last bit out of me with a shudder.

My thread is green three days out of seven. After that, I'm lucky to get two green outflows in a row. This transformation happens to me alone. None of the other workers report a change in their colors. It must be my own illness then, not *kaiko*-evolution. If we had a foreman here, he would quarantine me. He might destroy me, the way silkworms infected with the blight are burned up in Katamura.

And in Gifu? Perhaps my father has died at the base of Mount Inaba. Or he has made a full recovery, journeyed home with my brothers, and cried out with joyful astonishment to find my five-yen advance? Let it be that, I pray. My afterlife will be whatever he chooses to do with that money.

Today marks the forty-second day since we last saw the Agent. In the past he has reliably surprised us with visits, once or twice per month. Factory inspections, he calls them, scribbling notes about the progress of our transformations, the changes in our weight and shape, the quality of our silk production. He's never stayed away so long before. The thought of the Agent, either coming or not coming, makes me want to retch. Water sloshes in my head. I lie on the mat with my eyes shut tight and watch the orange tea splash into my cup . . . "I hear you in there, Kitsune. I know what you're doing. You didn't sleep."

Dai's voice. I keep my eyes shut.

"Kitsune, stop thinking about it. You are making yourself sick."

"Dai, I can't."

Today my stomach is so full of thread that I'm not sure I'll be able to stand. I'm afraid that it will all be black. Some of us are now forced to crawl on our hands and knees to the Machine, toppled by our ungainly bellies. I can smell the basins heating. A thick, greasy steam fills the room. I peek up at Dai's face, then let my eyes flutter shut again.

"Smell that?" I say, more nastily than I intend to. "In here we're dead already. At least on the stairwell I can breathe forest air."

"Unwinding one cocoon for an eternity," she snarls. "As if you had only a single memory. Reeling in the wrong direction."

Dai looks ready to slap me. She's angrier than I've ever seen her. Dai is the Big Mother but she's also a samurai's daughter, and sometimes that combination gives rise to a ferocious kind of caring. She's tender with the little ones, but if an older *joko* plummets into a mood or ill health, she'll scream at us until our ears split. Furious, I suppose, at her inability to defend us from ourselves.

"The others also suffered in their pasts," she says. "But we sleep, we get up, we go to work, some crawl forward if there is no other way..."

"I'm not like the others," I insist, hating the baleful note in my voice but desperate to make Dai understand this. Is Dai blind to the contrast? Can she not see that the innocent recruits—the ones who were signed over to the Agent by their fathers and their brothers—produce pure colors, in radiant hues? Whereas my thread looks rotten, greeny black.

"Sleep can't wipe me clean like them. I chose this fate. I can't blame a greedy uncle, a gullible father. I drank the tea of my own free will."

"Your free will," says Dai, so slowly that I'm sure she's about to mock me; then her eyes widen with something like joy. "Ah! So: use that to stop drinking it at night, in your memory. Use your will to stop thinking about the Agent."

Dai is smiling down at me like she's won the argument.

"Oh, yes, very simple!" I laugh angrily. "I'll just stop. Why didn't I think of that? Say, here's one for you, Dai," I snap. "Stop reeling for the Agent at your workbench. Stop making the thread in your gut. Try that, I'm sure you'll feel better."

Then we are shouting at each other, our first true fight; Dai doesn't understand that this memory reassembles itself in me mechanically, just as the thread swells in our new bodies. It's nothing I control. I see the Agent arrive; my hand trembling; the ink lacing my name across the contract. My regret: I know I'll never get to the bottom of it. I'll never escape either place, Nowhere Mill or Gifu. Every night, the cup refills in my mind.

"Go reel for the empire, Dai. Make more silk for him to sell. Go throw the little girls another party! Make believe we're not slaves here."

Dai storms off, and I feel a mean little pleasure.

For two days we don't speak, until I worry that we never will again. But on the second night, Dai finds me. She leans in and whispers that she has accepted my challenge. At first I am so happy to hear her voice that I only laugh, take her hand. "What challenge? What are you talking about?"

"I thought about what you said," she tells me. She talks about her samurai father's last stand, the Satsuma Rebellion. In the countryside, she says, there are peasant armies who protest "the blood tax," refuse to sow new crops. I nod with my eyes shut, watching my grandfather's hat floating through our fields in Gifu.

"And you're right, Kitsune—we have to stop reeling. If we don't, he'll get every year of our futures. He'll get our last breaths. The silk belongs to us, *we* make it. We can use that to bargain with the Agent."

The following morning, Dai announces that she won't move from her mat.

"I'm on strike," she says. "No more reeling."

By the second day, her belly has grown so bloated with thread that we are begging her to work. The mulberry leaves arrive, and she refuses to eat them.

"No more room for that." She smiles.

Dai's face is so swollen that she can't open one eye. She lies with her arms crossed over her chest, her belly heaving.

By the fourth day, I can barely look at her.

"You'll die," I whisper.

She nods resolutely.

"I'm escaping. He might still stop me. But I'll do my best."

We send a note for the Agent with the blind woman. "Please tell him to come."

"Join me," Dai begs us, and our eyes dull and lower, we sway. For five days, Dai doesn't reel. She never eats. Some of us, I'm sure, don't mind the extra fistful of leaves. (A tiny voice I can't gag begins to babble in the background: *If x-many others strike, Kitsune, there will be x-much more food for you . . .*)

Guiltily, I set her portion aside, pushing the leaves into a little triangle. *There*, I think. The flag of Dai's resistance. Something flashes on one—a real silkworm. Inching along in its wet and stupid oblivion. My stomach flips to see all the little holes its hunger has punched into the green leaf.

During our break, I bring Dai my blanket. I try to squeeze some of the water from the leaf-velvet onto her tongue, which she refuses. She doesn't make a sound, but I hiss—her belly is grotesquely distended and stippled with lumps, like a sow's pregnant with a litter of ten piglets. Her excess thread is packed in knots. Strangling Dai from within. Perhaps the Agent can call on a Western veterinarian, I find myself thinking. Whatever is happening to her seems beyond the ken of Emperor Meiji's own doctors.

"Start reeling again!" I gasp. "Dai, please."

"It looks worse than it is. It's easy enough to stop. You'll see for yourself, I hope."

Her skin has an unhealthy translucence. Her eyes are standing out in her shrunken face, as if every breath costs her. Soon I will be able to see the very thoughts in her skull, the way red thread fans into tiny veiny view under her skin. Dai gives me her bravest smile. "Get some rest, Kitsune. Stop poisoning yourself on the stairwell of Gifu. If I can stop reeling, surely you can, too."

When she dies, all the silk is still stubbornly housed in her belly, "stolen from the factory," as the Agent alleges. "This girl died a thief."

Three days after her death, he finally shows up. He strides over to Dai and touches her belly with a stick. When a few of us grab for his legs, he makes a face and kicks us off.

"Perhaps we can still salvage some of it," he grumbles, rolling her into his sack.

A great sadness settles over our whole group and doesn't lift. What the Agent carried off with Dai was everything we had left: Chiyo's clouds and mountains, my farmhouse in Gifu, Etsuyo's fiancé. It's clear to us now that we can never leave this room—we can never be away from the Machine for more than five days. Unless we live here, where the Machine can extract the thread from our bodies at speeds no human hand could match, the silk will build and build and kill us in the end. Dai's experiment has taught us that.

You never hear a peep in here about the New Year anymore.

I'm eating, I'm reeling, but I, too, appear to be dying. Thread almost totally black. The denier too uneven for any market. In my mind I talk to Dai about it, and she is very reassuring: "It's going to be fine, Kitsune. Only, please, you have to stop—"

Stop thinking about it. This was Dai's final entreaty to me.

I close my eyes. I watch my hand signing my father's name again. I am at the bottom of a stairwell in Gifu. The first time I made this ascent I felt weightless, but now the wood groans under my feet. Just as a single cocoon contains a thousand yards of silk, I can unreel a thousand miles from my memory of this one misstep.

Still, I'm not convinced that you were right, Dai—that it's such a bad thing, a useless enterprise, to reel and reel out my memory at night. Some part of me, the human part of me, is kept alive by this, I think. Like water flushing a wound, to prevent it from closing. I am a lucky one, like Chiyo says. I made a terrible mistake. In Gifu, in my raggedy clothes, I had an unreckonable power. I didn't know that at the time. But when I return to the stairwell now, I can feel them webbing around me: my choices, their infinite variety, spiraling out of my hands, my invisible thread. Regret is a pilgrimage back to the place where I was free to choose. It's become my sanctuary here in Nowhere Mill. A threshold where I still exist.

One morning, two weeks after Dai's strike, I start talking to Chiyo about her family's cottage business in Chichibu. Chiyo complains about the smells in her dry attic, where they destroy the silkworm larvae in vinegary solutions. Why do they do that? I want to know. I've never heard this part before. Oh, to stop them from undergoing the transformation, Chiyo says. First, the silkworms stop eating. Then they spin their cocoons. Once inside, they molt several times. They grow wings and teeth. If the caterpillars are allowed to evolve, they change into moths. Then these moths bite through the silk and fly off, ruining it for the market.

Teeth and wings, wings and teeth, I keep hearing all day under the whine of the cables.

That night, I try an experiment. I let myself think the black thoughts all evening. Great wheels inside me turn backward at fantastic, groaning velocities. What I focus on is my shadow in the stairwell, falling slantwise behind me, like silk. I see the ink spilling onto the contract, my name bloating monstrously.

And when dawn comes, and I slug my way over to the workbench and plunge my hands into the boiling vat, I see that the experiment was a success. My new threads are stronger and blacker than ever; silk of some nameless variety we have never belly-spun before. I crank them out of my wrist and onto the dowel. There's not a fleck of green left, not a single frayed strand. "Moonless," says Hoshi, shrinking from them. Opaque. Midnight at Nowhere Mill pales in comparison. Looking down into the basin, I feel a wild excitement. I made it that color. So I'm no mere carrier, no diseased *kaiko*—I can channel these dyes from my mind into the tough new fiber. I can change my thread's denier, control its production. Seized by a second inspiration, I begin to unreel at speeds I would have just yesterday thought laughably impossible. Not even Yuna can produce as much thread in an hour. I ignore the whispers that pool around me on the workbench:

"Kitsune's fishing too deep—look at her finger slits!"

"They look like gills." Etsuyo shudders.

"Someone should stop her. She's fishing right down to the bone."

"What is she making?"

"What are you making?"

"What are you going to do with all that, Kitsune?" Tooka asks nervously.

"Oh, who knows? I'll just see what it comes to."

But I *do* know. Without my giving a thought to what step comes next, my hands begin to fly.

The weaving comes so naturally to me that I am barely aware I am doing it, humming as if in a dream. But this weaving is instinctual. What takes effort, what requires a special kind of concentration, is generating the right density of the thread. To do so, I have to keep forging my father's name in my mind, climbing those stairs, watching my mistake unfurl. I have to drink the toxic tea and feel it burn my throat, lie flat on the cot while my organs are remade by the Agent for the factory, thinking only, *Yes, I chose this.* When these memories send the fierce regret spiraling through me, I focus on my heartbeat, my throbbing palms. Fibers stiffen inside my fingers. Grow strong, I direct the thread. Go black. Lengthen. Stick. And then, when I return to the vats, what I've produced is exactly the necessary denier and darkness. I sit at the workbench, at my ordinary station. And I am so happy to discover that I can do all this myself: the silk generation, the separation, the dyeing, the reeling. Out of the same intuition, I discover that I know how to alter the Machine. "Help me, Tsuki," I say, because I want her to watch what I am doing. I begin to explain, but she is already disassembling my reeler. "I know, Kitsune," she says, "I see what you have in mind." Words seem to be unnecessary now between me and Tsuki—we beam thoughts soundlessly across the room. Perhaps speech will be the next superfluity in Nowhere Mill. Another step we *kaiko*-girls can skip.

Together we adjust the feeder gears, so that the black thread travels in a loop; after getting wrung out and doubled on the Machine's great wheel, it shuttles back to my hands. I add fresh fibers, drape the long skein over my knees. It is going to be as tall as a man, six feet at least.

Many girls continue feeding the Machine as if nothing unusual is happening. Others, like Tsuki, are watching to see what my fingers are doing. For the past several months, every time I've reminisced about the Agent coming to Gifu, bile has risen in my throat. It seems to be composed of every bitterness: grief and rage, the acid regrets. But then, in the middle of my weaving, obeying a queer impulse, I spit some onto my hand. This bile glues my fingers to my fur. Another of nature's wonders. So even the nausea of regret can be converted to use. I grin to Dai in my head. With this dill-colored glue, I am a last able to rub a sealant over my new thread and complete my work.

It takes me ten hours to spin the black cocoon.

The first girls who see it take one look and run back to the tatami.

The second girls are cautiously admiring.

Hoshi waddles over with her bellyful of blue silk and screams.

I am halfway up the southern wall of Nowhere Mill before I realize what I am doing; then I'm parallel to the woodpecker's window. The gluey thread collected on my palms sticks me to the glass. For the first time I can see outside: from this angle, nothing but clouds and sky, a blue eternity. *We will have wings soon*, I think, and ten feet below me I hear Tsuki laugh out loud. Using my thread and the homemade glue, I attach the cocoon to a wooden beam; soon, I am floating in circles over the Machine, suspended by my own line. "Come down!" Hoshi yells, but she's the only one. I secure the cocoon and then I let myself fall, all my weight supported by one thread. Now the cocoon sways over the Machine, a furled black flag, creaking slightly. I think of my grandfather hanging by the thick rope from our barn door.

More black thread spasms down my arms.

"Kitsune, please. You'll make the Agent angry! You shouldn't waste your silk that way—pretty soon they'll stop bringing you the leaves! Don't forget the trade, it's silk for leaves, Kitsune. What happens when he stops feeding us?"

But in the end I convince all of the workers to join me. Instinct obviates the need for a lesson—swiftly the others discover that they, too, can change their thread from within, drawing strength from the colors and seasons of their memories. Before we can begin to weave our cocoons, however, we first agree to work night and day to reel the ordinary silk, doubling our production, stockpiling the surplus skeins. Then we seize control of the machinery of Nowhere Mill. We spend the next six days dismantling and reassembling the Machine, using its gears and reels to speed the production of our own shimmering cocoons. Each dusk, we continue to deliver the regular number of skeins to the zookeeper, to avoid arousing the Agent's suspicions. When we are ready for the next stage of our revolution, only then will we invite him to tour our factory floor.

Silkworm moths develop long ivory wings, says Chiyo, bronzed with ancient designs. Do they have antennae, mouths? I ask her. Can they see? Who knows what the world will look like to us if our strike succeeds? I believe we will emerge from it entirely new creatures. In truth there is no model for what will happen to us next. We'll have to wait and learn what we've become when we get out.

The old blind woman really is blind, we decide. She squints directly at the wrecked and rerouted Machine and waits with her arms extended for one of us to deposit the skeins. Instead, Hoshi pushes a letter through the grate.

"We don't have any silk today."

"Bring this to the Agent."

"Go. Tell. Him."

As usual, the old woman says nothing. The mulberry sacks sit on the wagon. After a moment she claps to show us that her hands are empty, kicks the wagon away. Signals: no silk, no food. Her face is slack. On our side of the grate, I hear girls smacking their jaws, swallowing saliva. Fresh forest smells rise off the sacks. But we won't beg, will we? We won't turn back. Dai lived without food for five days. Our faces press against the grate. Several of our longest whiskers tickle the zookeeper's withered cheeks; at last, a dark cloud passes over her face. She barks with surprise, swats the air. Her wrinkles tighten into a grimace of fear. She backs away from our voices, her fist closed around our invitation to the Agent.

"NO SILK," repeats Tsaiko slowly.

The Agent comes the very next night.

"Hello?"

He raps at our grated door with a stick, but he remains in the threshold. For a moment I am sure that he won't come in.

"They're gone, they're gone," I wail, rocking.

"What!"

The grate slides open and he steps onto the factory floor, into our shadows.

"Yes, they've all escaped, every one of them, all your *kaiko-joko*—"

Now my sisters drop down on their threads. They fall from the ceiling on whistling lines of silk, swinging into the light, and I feel as though I am dreaming—it is a dreamlike repetition of our initiation, when the Agent dropped the infecting *kaiko* into the orange tea. Watching his eyes widen and his mouth stretch into a scream, I too am shocked. We have no mirrors here in Nowhere Mill, and I've spent the past few months convinced that we were still identifiable as girls, women—no beauty queens, certainly, shaggy and white and misshapen, but at least half human; it's only now, watching the Agent's reaction, that I realize what we've become in his absence. I see us as he must: white faces, with sunken noses that look partially erased. Eyes insect-huge. Spines and elbows incubating lace for wings. My muscles tense, and then I am airborne, launching myself onto the Agent's back—for a second I get a thrilling sense of what true flight will feel like, once we complete our transformation. I alight on his shoulders and hook my legs around him. The Agent grunts beneath my weight, staggers forward.

"These wings of ours are invisible to you," I say directly into the Agent's ear. I clasp my hands around his neck, lean into the whisper. "And in fact you will never see them, since they exist only in our future, where you are dead and we are living, flying."

I then turn the Agent's head so that he can admire our silk. For the past week every worker has used the altered Machine to spin her own cocoon—they hang from the far wall, coral and emerald and blue, ordered by hue, like a rainbow. While the rest of Japan changes outside the walls of Nowhere Mill, we'll hang side by side, hidden against the bricks. Paralyzed inside our silk, but spinning faster and faster. Passing into our next phase. Then, we'll escape. (Inside his cocoon, the Agent will turn blue and suffocate.)

"And look," I say, counting down the wall: twenty-one workers, and twenty-two cocoons. When he sees the black sac, I feel his neck stiffen. "We have spun one for you." I smile down at him. The Agent is stumbling around beneath me, babbling something that I admit I make no great effort to understand. The glue sticks my knees to his shoulders. Several of us busy ourselves with getting the gag in place, and this is accomplished before the Agent can scream once. Gin and Nishi bring down the cast-iron grate behind him.

The slender Agent is heavier than he looks. It takes four of us to stuff him into the socklike cocoon. I smile at the Agent and instruct the others to leave his eyes for last, thinking that he will be very impressed to see our skill at reeling up close. Behind me, even as this attack is under way, the other *kaiko-joko* are climbing into their cocoons. Already there are girls half swallowed by them, winding silk threads over their knees, sealing the outermost layer with glue.

Now our methods regress a bit, get a little old-fashioned. I reel the last of the black cocoon by hand. Several *kaiko-joko* have to hold the Agent steady so that I can orbit him with the thread. I spin around his chin and his cheekbones, his lips. To get over his mustache requires several revolutions. Bits of my white fur drift down and disappear into his nostrils. His eyes are huge and black and void of any recognition. I whisper my name to him, to see if I can jostle my old self loose from his memory: Kitsune Tajima, of Gifu Prefecture.

Nothing.

So then I continue reeling upward, naming the workers of Nowhere Mill all the while: "Nishi. Yoshi. Yuna. Uki. Etsuyo. Gin. Hoshi. Raku. Chiyoko. Mitsuko. Tsaiko. Tooka. Dai.

"Kitsune," I repeat, closing the circle. The last thing I see before shutting his eyes is the reflection of my shining new face.

Politics

The writers in this section grapple with the question of how women take action in the wider world. Whether explicitly or implicitly, these selections ask how women's experiences and beliefs affect communal life—how women act and react in what has been called the "public" sphere.

In her story "Recitatif" (1983), **Toni Morrison** (1931–) depicts the growth of two girls, one black and one white, who meet while living in a children's home but whose beliefs and social actions are very different.

Poet **Joy Harjo** (1951–), whose work is influenced by her Muskogee Creek heritage, writes in "When the World as We Knew It Ended" (2002) of life before, during, and after the World Trade Center attacks.

In her essay "Bad Feminist: Take One" (2014), **Roxane Gay** (1974–) describes her battle with the term "feminist" and asks how women can speak publicly about sexual and racial equality without being labeled—or labeling each other—"bad."

In her poem "Woodchucks" (1972), **Maxine Kumin** (1925–2014) gives us the first-person perspective of a woman who has decided to intervene in the natural world—with a deadly directness.

In "Reading Lessons" (2005), **Edwidge Danticat** (1969–) depicts a young Haitian American teacher at a low-income school who struggles with her ambivalence and temper as she teaches children and adults who are immigrants from her home country.

Denise Levertov (1923–1997) investigates what it means to be a conqueror or a conquest in her poem "Ways of Conquest" (1975). Using a first-person voice, Levertov explores whether invasion is necessarily intentional and at what point the invader becomes the invaded.

"Recitatif"

Toni Morrison

My mother danced all night and Roberta's was sick. That's why we were taken to St. Bonny's. People want to put their arms around you when you tell them you were in a shelter, but it really wasn't bad. No big long room with one hundred beds like Bellevue. There were four to a room, and when Roberta and me came, there was a shortage of state kids, so we were the only ones assigned to 406 and could go from bed to bed if we wanted to. And we wanted to, too. We changed beds every night and for the whole four months we were there we never picked one out as our own permanent bed.

It didn't start out that way. The minute I walked in and the Big Bozo introduced us, I got sick to my stomach. It was one thing to be taken out of your own bed early in the morning—it was something else to be stuck in a strange place with a girl from a whole other race. And Mary, that's my mother, she was right. Every now and then she would stop dancing long enough to tell me something important and one of the things she said was that they never washed their hair and they smelled funny. Roberta sure did. Smell funny, I mean. So when the Big Bozo (nobody ever called her Mrs. Itkin, just like nobody ever said St. Bonaventure)—when she said, "Twyla, this is Roberta. Roberta, this is Twyla. Make each other welcome," I said, "My mother won't like you putting me in here."

"Good," said Bozo. "Maybe then she'll come and take you home."

How's that for mean? If Roberta had laughed I would have killed her, but she didn't. She just walked over to the window and stood with her back to us.

"Turn around," said the Bozo. "Don't be rude. Now Twyla. Roberta. When you hear a loud buzzer, that's the call for dinner. Come down to the first floor. Any fights and no movie." And then, just to make sure we knew what we would be missing, *"The Wizard of Oz."*

Roberta must have thought I meant that my mother would be mad about my being put in the shelter. Not about rooming with her, because as soon as Bozo left she came over to me and said, "Is your mother sick too?"

"No," I said. "She just likes to dance all night."

"Oh." She nodded her head and I liked the way she understood things so fast. So for the moment it didn't matter that we looked like salt and pepper standing there and that's what the other kids called us sometimes. We were eight years old and got Fs all the time. Me because I couldn't remember what I read or what the teacher said. And Roberta because she couldn't read at all and didn't even listen to the teacher. She wasn't good at anything except jacks, at which she was a killer: pow scoop pow scoop pow scoop.

We didn't like each other all that much at first, but nobody else wanted to play with us because we weren't real orphans with beautiful dead parents in the sky. We were dumped. Even the New York City Puerto Ricans and the upstate Indians ignored us. All kinds of kids were in there, black ones, white ones, even two Koreans. The food was good, though. At least I thought so. Roberta hated it and left whole pieces of things on her plate: Spam, Salisbury steak—even Jell-O with fruit cocktail in it, and she didn't care if I ate what she wouldn't. Mary's idea of supper was popcorn and a can of Yoo-hoo. Hot mashed potatoes and two weenies was like Thanksgiving for me.

It really wasn't bad, St. Bonny's. The big girls on the second floor pushed us around now and then. But that was all. They wore lipstick and eyebrow pencil and wobbled their knees while they watched TV. Fifteen, sixteen, even, some of them were. They were put-out girls, scared runaways most of them. Poor little girls who fought their uncles off but looked tough to us, and mean. God, did they look mean. The staff tried to keep them separate from the younger children, but sometimes they caught us watching them in the orchard where they played radios and danced with each other. They'd light out after us and pull our hair or twist our arms. We were scared of them, Roberta and me, but neither of us wanted the other one to know it. So we got a good list of dirty names we could shout back when we ran from them through the orchard. I used to dream a lot and almost always the orchard was there. Two acres, four maybe, of these little apple trees. Hundreds of them. Empty and crooked like beggar women when I first came to St. Bonny's but fat with flowers when I left. I don't know why I dreamt about that orchard so much. Nothing really happened there. Nothing all that important, I mean. Just the big girls dancing and playing the radio. Roberta and me watching. Maggie fell down there once. The kitchen woman with legs like parentheses. And the big girls laughed at her. We should have helped her up, I know, but we were scared of those girls with lipstick and eyebrow pencil. Maggie couldn't talk. The kids said she had her tongue cut out, but I think she was just born that way: mute. She was old and sandy-colored and she worked in the kitchen. I don't know if she was nice or not. I just remember her legs like parentheses and how she rocked when she walked. She worked from early in the morning till two o'clock, and if she was late, if she had too much cleaning and didn't get out till two fifteen or so, she'd cut through the orchard so she wouldn't miss her bus and have to wait another hour. She wore this really stupid little hat—a kid's hat with ear flaps—and she wasn't much taller than we were. A really awful little hat. Even for a mute, it was dumb—dressing like a kid and never saying anything at all.

"But what about if somebody tries to kill her?" I used to wonder about that. "Or what if she wants to cry? Can she cry?"

"Sure," Roberta said. "But just tears. No sounds come out."

"She can't scream?"

"Nope. Nothing."

"Can she hear?"

"I guess."

"Let's call her," I said. And we did.

"Dummy! Dummy!" She never turned her head.

"Bow legs! Bow legs!" Nothing. She just rocked on, the chin straps of her baby-boy hat swaying from side to side. I think we were wrong. I think she could hear and didn't let on. And it shames me even now to think there was somebody in there after all who heard us call her those names and couldn't tell on us.

We got along all right, Roberta and me. Changed beds every night, got Fs in civics and communication skills and gym. The Bozo was disappointed in us, she said. Out of 130 of us state cases, 90 were under twelve. Almost all were real orphans with beautiful dead parents in the sky. We were the only ones dumped and the only ones with Fs in three classes including gym. So we got along—what with her leaving whole pieces of things on her plate and being nice about not asking questions.

I think it was the day before Maggie fell down that we found out our mothers were coming to visit us on the same Sunday. We had been at the shelter twenty-eight days (Roberta twenty-eight and a half) and this was their first visit with us. Our mothers would come at ten o'clock in time for chapel, then lunch with us in the teachers' lounge. I thought if my dancing mother met her sick mother it might be good for her. And Roberta thought her sick mother would get a big bang out of a dancing one. We got excited about it and curled each other's hair. After breakfast we sat on the bed watching the road from the window. Roberta's socks were still wet. She washed them the night before and put them on the radiator to dry. They hadn't, but she put them on anyway because their tops were so pretty—scalloped in pink. Each of us had a purple construction-paper basket that we had made in craft class. Mine had a yellow crayon rabbit on it. Roberta's had eggs with wiggly lines of color. Inside were cellophane grass and just the jelly beans because I'd eaten the two marshmallow eggs they gave us. The Big Bozo came herself to get us. Smiling she told us we looked very nice and to come downstairs. We were so surprised by the smile we'd never seen before, neither of us moved.

"Don't you want to see your mommies?"

I stood up first and spilled the jelly beans all over the floor. Bozo's smile disappeared while we scrambled to get the candy up off the floor and put it back in the grass.

She escorted us downstairs to the first floor, where the other girls were lining up to file into the chapel. A bunch of grown-ups stood to one side. Viewers mostly. The old biddies who wanted servants and the fags who wanted company looking for children they might want to adopt. Once in a while a grandmother. Almost never anybody young or anybody whose face wouldn't scare you in the night. Because if any of the real orphans had young relatives they wouldn't be real orphans. I saw Mary right away. She had on those green slacks I hated and hated even more now because didn't she know we were going to chapel? And that fur jacket with the pocket linings so ripped she had to pull to get her hands out of them. But her face was pretty—like always—and she smiled and waved like she was the little girl looking for her mother, not me.

I walked slowly, trying not to drop the jelly beans and hoping the paper handle would hold. I had to use my last Chiclet because by the time I finished cutting everything out, all the Elmer's was gone. I am left-handed and the scissors never worked for me. It didn't matter, though; I might just as well have chewed the gum. Mary dropped to her knees and grabbed me, mashing the basket, the jelly beans, and the grass into her ratty fur jacket.

"Twyla, baby. Twyla, baby!"

I could have killed her. Already I heard the big girls in the orchard the next time saying, "Twyyyyyla, baby!" But I couldn't stay mad at Mary while she was smiling and hugging me and smelling of Lady Esther dusting powder. I wanted to stay buried in her fur all day.

To tell the truth I forgot about Roberta. Mary and I got in line for the traipse into chapel and I was feeling proud because she looked so beautiful even in those ugly green slacks that made her behind stick out. A pretty mother on earth is better than a beautiful dead one in the sky even if she did leave you all alone to go dancing.

I felt a tap on my shoulder, turned, and saw Roberta smiling. I smiled back, but not too much lest somebody think this visit was the biggest thing that ever happened in my life. Then Roberta said, "Mother, I want you to meet my roommate, Twyla. And that's Twyla's mother."

I looked up it seemed for miles. She was big. Bigger than any man and on her chest was the biggest cross I'd ever seen. I swear it was six inches long each way. And in the crook of her arm was the biggest Bible ever made.

Mary, simpleminded as ever, grinned and tried to yank her hand out of the pocket with the raggedy lining—to shake hands, I guess. Roberta's mother looked down at me and then looked down at Mary too. She didn't say anything, just grabbed Roberta with her Bible-free hand and stepped out of line, walking quickly to the rear of it. Mary was still grinning because she's not too swift when it comes to what's really going on. Then this light bulb goes off in her head and she says "That bitch!" really loud and us almost in the chapel now. Organ music whining; the Bonny Angels singing sweetly. Everybody in the world turned around to look. And Mary would have kept it up—kept calling names if I hadn't squeezed her hands as hard as I could. That helped a little, but she still twitched and crossed and uncrossed her legs all through service. Even groaned a couple of times. Why did I think she would come there and act right? Slacks. No hat like the grandmothers and viewers, and groaning all the while. When we stood for hymns she kept her mouth shut. Wouldn't even look at the words on the page. She actually reached in her purse for a mirror to check her lipstick. All I could think of was that she really needed to be killed. The sermon lasted a year, and I knew the real orphans were looking smug again.

We were supposed to have lunch in the teachers' lounge, but Mary didn't bring anything, so we picked fur and cellophane grass off the mashed jelly beans and ate them. I could have killed her. I sneaked a look at Roberta. Her mother had brought chicken legs and ham sandwiches and oranges and a whole box of chocolate-covered grahams. Roberta drank milk from a thermos while her mother read the Bible to her.

Things are not right. The wrong food is always with the wrong people. Maybe that's why I got into waitress work later—to match up the right people with the right food. Roberta just let those chicken legs sit there, but she did bring a stack of grahams up to me later when the visit was over. I think she was sorry that her mother would not shake my mother's hand. And I liked that and I liked the fact that she didn't say a word about Mary groaning all the way through the service and not bringing any lunch.

Roberta left in May when the apple trees were heavy and white. On her last day we went to the orchard to watch the big girls smoke and dance by the radio. It didn't matter that they said, "Twyyyyyla, baby." We sat on the ground and breathed. Lady Esther. Apple blossoms. I still go soft when I smell one or the other. Roberta was going home. The big cross and the big Bible was coming to get her and she seemed sort of glad and sort of not. I thought I would die in that room of four beds without her and I knew Bozo had plans to move some other dumped kid in there with me. Roberta promised to write every day, which was really sweet of her because she couldn't read a lick so how could she write anybody? I would have drawn pictures and sent them to her but she never gave me her address. Little by little she faded. Her wet socks with the pink scalloped tops and her big serious-looking eyes—that's all I could catch when I tried to bring her to mind.

I was working behind the counter at the Howard Johnson's on the Thruway just before the Kingston exit. Not a bad job. Kind of a long ride from Newburgh, but okay once I got there. Mine was the second night shift, eleven to seven. Very light until a Greyhound checked in for breakfast around six thirty. At that hour the sun was all the way clear of the hills behind the restaurant. The place looked better at night—more like shelter—but I loved it when the sun broke in, even if it did show all the cracks in the vinyl and the speckled floor looked dirty no matter what the mop boy did.

It was August and a bus crowd was just unloading. They would stand around a long while: going to the john, and looking at gifts and junk-for-sale machines, reluctant to sit down so soon. Even to eat. I was trying to fill the coffeepots and get them all situated on the electric burners when I saw her. She was sitting in a booth smoking a cigarette with two guys smothered in head and facial hair. Her own hair was so big and wild I could hardly see her face. But the eyes. I would know them anywhere. She had on a powder-blue halter and shorts outfit and earrings the size of bracelets. Talk about lipstick and eyebrow pencil. She made the big girls look like nuns. I couldn't get off the counter until seven o'clock, but I kept watching the booth in case they got up to leave before that. My replacement was on time for a change, so I counted and stacked my receipts as fast as I could and signed off. I walked over to the booth, smiling and wondering if she would remember me. Or even if she wanted to remember me. Maybe she didn't want to be reminded of St. Bonny's or to have anybody know she was ever there. I know I never talked about it to anybody.

I put my hands in my apron pockets and leaned against the back of the booth facing them.

"Roberta? Roberta Fisk?"

She looked up. "Yeah?"

"Twyla."

She squinted for a second and then said, "Wow."

"Remember me?"

"Sure. Hey. Wow."

"It's been awhile," I said, and gave a smile to the two hairy guys.

"Yeah. Wow. You work here?"

"Yeah," I said. "I live in Newburgh."

"Newburgh? No kidding?" She laughed then, a private laugh that included the guys but only the guys, and they laughed with her. What could I do but laugh too and wonder why I was standing there with my knees showing out from under that uniform. Without looking I could see the blue-and-white triangle on my head, my hair shapeless in a net, my ankles thick in white oxfords. Nothing could have been less sheer than my stockings. There was this silence that came down right after I laughed. A silence it was her turn to fill up. With introductions, maybe, to her boyfriends or an invitation to sit down and have a Coke. Instead she lit a cigarette off the one she'd just finished and said, "We're on our way to the Coast. He's got an appointment with Hendrix." She gestured casually toward the boy next to her.

"Hendrix? Fantastic," I said. "Really fantastic. What's she doing now?"

Roberta coughed on her cigarette and the two guys rolled their eyes up at the ceiling.

"Hendrix. Jimi Hendrix, asshole. He's only the biggest—Oh, wow. Forget it."

I was dismissed without anyone saying good-bye, so I thought I would do it for her.

"How's your mother?" I asked. Her grin cracked her whole face. She swallowed. "Fine," she said. "How's yours?"

"Pretty as a picture," I said and turned away. The backs of my knees were damp. Howard Johnson's really was a dump in the sunlight.

James is as comfortable as a house slipper. He liked my cooking and I liked his big loud family. They have lived in Newburgh all of their lives and talk about it the way people do who have always known a home. His grandmother has a porch swing older than his father and when they talk about streets and avenues and buildings they call them names they no longer have. They still call the A&P Rico's because it stands on property once a mom-and-pop store owned by Mr. Rico. And they call the new community college Town Hall because it once was. My mother-in-law puts up jelly and cucumbers and buys butter wrapped in cloth from a dairy. James and his father talk about fishing and baseball and I can see them all together on the Hudson in a raggedy skiff. Half the population of Newburgh is on welfare now, but to my husband's family it was still some upstate paradise of a time long past. A time of ice houses and vegetable wagons, coal furnaces and children weeding gardens. When our son was born my mother-in-law gave me the crib blanket that had been hers.

But the town they remembered had changed. Something quick was in the air. Magnificent old houses, so ruined they had become shelter for squatters and rent risks, were bought and renovated. Smart IBM people moved out of their suburbs back into the city and put shutters up and herb gardens in their backyards. A brochure came in the mail announcing the opening of a Food Emporium. Gourmet food, it said—and listed items the rich IBM crowd would want. It was located in a new mall at the edge of town and I drove out to shop there one day—just to see. It was late in June. After the tulips were gone and the Queen Elizabeth roses were open everywhere. I trailed my cart along the aisle tossing in smoked oysters and Robert's sauce and things I knew would sit in my cupboard for years. Only when I found some Klondike ice cream bars did I feel less guilty about spending James's fireman's salary so foolishly. My father-in-law ate them with the same gusto little Joseph did.

Waiting in the checkout line I heard a voice say, "Twyla!"

The classical music piped over the aisles had affected me and the woman leaning toward me was dressed to kill. Diamonds on her hand, a smart white summer dress. "I'm Mrs. Benson," I said.

"Ho. Ho. The Big Bozo," she sang.

For a split second I didn't know what she was talking about. She had a bunch of asparagus and two cartons of fancy water.

"Roberta!"

"Right."

"For heaven's sake. Roberta."

"You look great," she said.

"So do you. Where are you? Here? In Newburgh?"

"Yes. Over in Annandale."

I was opening my mouth to say more when the cashier called my attention to her empty counter.

"Meet you outside." Roberta pointed her finger and went into the express line.

I placed the groceries and kept myself from glancing around to check Roberta's progress. I remembered Howard Johnson's and looking for a chance to speak only to be greeted with a stingy "wow." But she was waiting for me and her huge hair was sleek now, smooth around a small, nicely shaped head. Shoes, dress, everything lovely and summery and rich. I was dying to know what happened to her, how she got from Jimi Hendrix to Annandale, a neighborhood full of doctors and IBM executives. Easy, I thought. Everything is so easy for them. They think they own the world.

"How long," I asked her. "How long have you been here?"

"A year. I got married to a man who lives here. And you, you're married too, right? Benson, you said."

"Yeah. James Benson."

"And is he nice?"

"Oh, is he nice?"

"Well, is he?" Roberta's eyes were steady as though she really meant the question and wanted an answer.

"He's wonderful, Roberta. Wonderful."

"So you're happy."

"Very."

"That's good," she said and nodded her head. "I always hoped you'd be happy. Any kids? I know you have kids."

"One. A boy. How about you?"

"Four."

"Four?"

She laughed. "Step kids. He's a widower."

"Oh."

"Got a minute? Let's have a coffee."

I thought about the Klondikes melting and the inconvenience of going all the way to my car and putting the bags in the trunk. Served me right for buying all that stuff I didn't need. Roberta was ahead of me.

"Put them in my car. It's right here."

And then I saw the dark blue limousine.

"You married a Chinaman?"

"No," she laughed. "He's the driver."

"Oh, my. If the Big Bozo could see you now."

We both giggled. Really giggled. Suddenly, in just a pulse beat, twenty years disappeared and all of it came rushing back. The big girls (whom we called gar girls—Roberta's misheard word for the evil stone faces described in a civics class) there dancing in the orchard, the ploppy mashed potatoes, the double weenies, the Spam with pineapple. We went into the coffee shop holding on to one another and I tried to think why we were glad to see each other this time and not before. Once, twelve years ago, we passed like strangers. A black girl and a white girl meeting in a Howard Johnson's on the road and having nothing to say. One in a blue-and-white triangle waitress hat, the other on her way to see Hendrix. Now we were behaving like sisters separated for much too long. Those four short months were nothing in time. Maybe it was the thing itself. Just being there, together. Two little girls who knew what nobody else in the world knew—how not to ask questions. How to believe what had to be believed. There was politeness in that reluctance and generosity as well. Is your mother sick too? No, she dances all night. Oh—and an understanding nod.

We sat in a booth by the window and fell into recollection like veterans.

"Did you ever learn to read?"

"Watch." She picked up the menu. "Special of the day. Cream of corn soup. Entrées. Two dots and a wriggly line. Quiche. Chef salad, scallops. . . ."

I was laughing and applauding when the waitress came up.

"Remember the Easter baskets?"

"And how we tried to *introduce* them?"

"Your mother with that cross like two telephone poles."

"And yours with those tight slacks."

We laughed so loudly heads turned and made the laughter hard to suppress.

"What happened to the Jimi Hendrix date?"

Roberta made a blow-out sound with her lips.

"When he died I thought about you."

"Oh, you heard about him finally?"

"Finally. Come on, I was a small-town country waitress."

"And I was a small-town country dropout. God, were we wild. I still don't know how I got out of there alive."

"But you did."

"I did. I really did. Now I'm Mrs. Kenneth Norton."

"Sounds like a mouthful."

"It is."

"Servants and all?"

Roberta held up two fingers.

"Ow! What does he do?"

"Computers and stuff. What do I know?"

"I don't remember a hell of a lot from those days, but Lord, St. Bonny's is as clear as daylight. Remember Maggie? The day she fell down and those gar girls laughed at her?"

Roberta looked up from her salad and stared at me. "Maggie didn't fall," she said.

"Yes, she did. You remember."

"No, Twyla. They knocked her down. Those girls pushed her down and tore her clothes. In the orchard."

"I don't—that's not what happened."

"Sure it is. In the orchard. Remember how scared we were?"

"Wait a minute. I don't remember any of that."

"And Bozo was fired."

"You're crazy. She was there when I left. You left before me."

"I went back. You weren't there when they fired Bozo."

"What?"

"Twice. Once for a year when I was about ten, another for two months when I was fourteen. That's when I ran away."

"You ran away from St. Bonny's?"

"I had to. What do you want? Me dancing in that orchard?"

"Are you sure about Maggie?"

"Of course I'm sure. You've blocked it, Twyla. It happened. Those girls had behavior problems, you know."

"Didn't they, though. But why can't I remember the Maggie thing?"

"Believe me. It happened. And we were there."

"Who did you room with when you went back?" I asked her as if I would know her. The Maggie thing was troubling me.

"Creeps. They tickled themselves in the night."

My ears were itching and I wanted to go home suddenly. This was all very well but she couldn't just comb her hair, wash her face, and pretend everything was hunky-dory. After the Howard Johnson's snub. And no apology. Nothing.

"Were you on dope or what that time at Howard Johnson's?" I tried to make my voice sound friendlier than I felt.

"Maybe, a little. I never did drugs much. Why?"

"I don't know, you acted sort of like you didn't want to know me then."

"Oh, Twyla, you know how it was in those days: black—white. You know how everything was."

But I didn't know. I thought it was just the opposite. Busloads of blacks and whites came into Howard Johnson's together. They roamed together then: students, musicians, lovers, protesters. You got to see everything at Howard Johnson's, and blacks were very friendly with whites in those days. But sitting there with nothing on my plate but two hard tomato wedges wondering about the melting Klondikes it seemed childish remembering the slight. We went to her car and, with the help of the driver, got my stuff into my station wagon.

"We'll keep in touch this time," she said.

"Sure," I said. "Sure. Give me a call."

"I will," she said, and then, just as I was sliding behind the wheel, she leaned into the window. "By the way. Your mother. Did she ever stop dancing?"

I shook my head. "No. Never."

Roberta nodded.

"And yours? Did she ever get well?"

She smiled a tiny sad smile. "No. She never did. Look, call me, okay?"

"Okay," I said, but I knew I wouldn't. Roberta had messed up my past somehow with that business about Maggie. I wouldn't forget a thing like that. Would I?

Strife came to us that fall. At least that's what the paper called it. Strife. Racial strife. The word made me think of a bird—a big shrieking bird out of 1,000,000,000 BC. Flapping its wings and cawing. Its eye with no lid always bearing down on you. All day it screeched and at night it slept on the rooftops. It woke you in the morning, and from the *Today* show to the eleven o'clock news it kept you an awful company. I couldn't figure it out from one day to the next. I knew I was supposed to feel something strong, but I didn't know what, and James wasn't any help. Joseph was on the list of kids to be transferred from the junior high school to another one at some far-out-of-the-way place and I thought it was a good thing until I heard it was a bad thing. I mean I didn't know. All the schools seemed dumps to me, and the fact that one was nicer looking didn't hold much weight. But the papers were full of it and then the kids began to get jumpy. In August, mind you. Schools weren't even open yet. I thought Joseph might be frightened to go over there, but he didn't seem scared so I forgot about it, until I found myself driving along Hudson Street out there by the school they were trying to integrate and saw a line of women marching. And who do you suppose was in line, big as life, holding a sign in front of her bigger than her mother's cross? MOTHERS HAVE RIGHTS TOO! it said.

I drove on and then changed my mind. I circled the block, slowed down, and honked my horn.

Roberta looked over and when she saw me she waved. I didn't wave back, but I didn't move either. She handed her sign to another woman and came over to where I was parked.

"Hi."

"What are you doing?"

"Picketing. What's it look like?"

"What for?"

"What do you mean, 'What for?' They want to take my kids and send them out of the neighborhood. They don't want to go."

"So what if they go to another school? My boy's being bussed too, and I don't mind. Why should you?"

"It's not about us, Twyla. Me and you. It's about our kids."

"What's more *us* than that?"

"Well, it is a free country."

"Not yet, but it will be."

"What the hell does that mean? I'm not doing anything to you."

"You really think that?"

"I know it."

"I wonder what made me think you were different."

"I wonder what made me think you were different."

"Look at them," I said. "Just look. Who do they think they are? Swarming all over the place like they own it. And now they think they can decide where my child goes to school. Look at them, Roberta. They're Bozos."

Roberta turned around and looked at the women. Almost all of them were standing still now, waiting. Some were even edging toward us. Roberta looked at me out of some refrigerator behind her eyes. "No, they're not. They're just mothers."

"And what am I? Swiss cheese?"

"I used to curl your hair."

"I hated your hands in my hair."

The women were moving. Our faces looked mean to them of course and they looked as though they could not wait to throw themselves in front of a police car or, better yet, into my car and drag me away by my ankles. Now they surrounded my car and gently, gently began to rock it. I swayed back and forth like a sideways yo-yo. Automatically I reached for Roberta, like the old days in the orchard when they saw us watching them and we had to get out of there, and if one of us fell the other pulled her up and if one of us was caught the other stayed to kick and scratch, and neither would leave the other behind. My arm shot out of the car window but no receiving hand was there. Roberta was looking at me sway from side to side in the car and her face was still. My purse slid from the car seat down under the dashboard. The four policemen who had been drinking Tab in their car finally got the message and strolled over, forcing their way through the women. Quietly, firmly they spoke. "Okay, ladies. Back in line or off the streets."

Some of them went away willingly; others had to be urged away from the car doors and the hood. Roberta didn't move. She was looking steadily at me. I was fumbling to turn on the ignition, which wouldn't catch because the gearshift was still in drive. The seats of the car were a mess because the swaying had thrown my grocery coupons all over and my purse was sprawled on the floor.

"Maybe I am different now, Twyla. But you're not. You're the same little state kid who kicked a poor old black lady when she was down on the ground. You kicked a black lady and you have the nerve to call me a bigot."

The coupons were everywhere and the guts of my purse were bunched under the dashboard. What was she saying? Black? Maggie wasn't black.

"She wasn't black," I said.

"Like hell she wasn't, and you kicked her. We both did. You kicked a black lady who couldn't even scream."

"Liar!"

"You're the liar! Why don't you just go on home and leave us alone, huh?"

She turned away and I skidded away from the curb.

The next morning I went into the garage and cut the side out of the carton our portable TV had come in. It wasn't nearly big enough, but after a while I had a decent sign: red spray-painted letters on a white background—AND SO DO CHILDREN****. I meant just to go down to the school and tack it up somewhere so those cows on the picket line across the street could see it, but when I got there, some ten or so others had already assembled—protesting the cows across

"Recitatif"

the street. Police permits and everything. I got in line and we strutted in time on our side while Roberta's group strutted on theirs. That first day we were all dignified, pretending the other side didn't exist. The second day there was name calling and finger gestures. But that was about all. People changed signs from time to time, but Roberta never did and neither did I. Actually my sign didn't make sense without Roberta's. "And so do children what?" one of the women on my side asked me. Have rights, I said, as though it was obvious.

Roberta didn't acknowledge my presence in any way, and I got to thinking maybe she didn't know I was there. I began to pace myself in the line, jostling people one minute and lagging behind the next, so Roberta and I could reach the end of our respective lines at the same time and there would be a moment in our turn when we would face each other. Still, I couldn't tell whether she saw me and knew my sign was for her. The next day I went early before we were scheduled to assemble. I waited until she got there before I exposed my new creation. As soon as she hoisted her MOTHERS HAVE RIGHTS TOO I began to wave my new one, which said, HOW WOULD YOU KNOW? I know she saw that one, but I had gotten addicted now. My signs got crazier each day, and the women on my side decided that I was a kook. They couldn't make heads or tails out of my brilliant screaming posters.

I brought a painted sign in queenly red with huge black letters that said, IS YOUR MOTHER WELL? Roberta took her lunch break and didn't come back for the rest of the day or any day after. Two days later I stopped going too and couldn't have been missed because nobody understood my signs anyway.

It was a nasty six weeks. Classes were suspended and Joseph didn't go to anybody's school until October. The children—everybody's children—soon got bored with that extended vacation they thought was going to be so great. They looked at TV until their eyes flattened. I spent a couple of mornings tutoring my son, as the other mothers said we should. Twice I opened a text from last year that he had never turned in. Twice he yawned in my face. Other mothers organized living room sessions so the kids would keep up. None of the kids could concentrate, so they drifted back to *The Price is Right* and *The Brady Bunch*. When the school finally opened there were fights once or twice and some sirens roared through the streets every once in a while. There were a lot of photographers from Albany. And just when ABC was about to send up a news crew, the kids settled down like nothing in the world had happened. Joseph hung my HOW WOULD YOU KNOW? sign in his bedroom. I don't know what became of AND SO DO CHILDREN****. I think my father-in-law cleaned some fish on it. He was always puttering around in our garage. Each of his five children lived in Newburgh, and he acted as though he had five extra homes.

I couldn't help looking for Roberta when Joseph graduated from high school, but I didn't see her. It didn't trouble me much what she had said to me in the car. I mean the kicking part. I know I didn't do that, I couldn't do that. But I was puzzled by her telling me Maggie was black. When I thought about it I actually couldn't be certain. She wasn't pitch black, I knew, or I would have remembered that. What I remember was the kiddie hat and the semicircle legs. I tried to reassure myself about the race thing for a long time until it dawned on me that the truth was already there, and Roberta knew it. I didn't kick her; I didn't join in with the gar girls and kick that lady, but I sure did want to. We watched and never tried to help her and never called for help. Maggie was my dancing mother. Deaf, I thought, and dumb. Nobody inside. Nobody who would hear you if you cried in the night. Nobody who could tell you anything important that you could use. Rocking, dancing, swaying as she walked. And when the gar girls pushed her down and started roughhousing, I knew she wouldn't scream, couldn't—just like me—and I was glad about that.

We decided not to have a tree, because Christmas would be at my mother-in-law's house, so why have a tree at both places? Joseph was at SUNY New Paltz and we had to economize, we said. But at the last minute, I changed my mind. Nothing could be that bad. So I rushed around town looking for a tree, something small but wide. By the time I found a place, it was snowing and very late. I dawdled like it was the most important purchase in the world and the tree man was fed up with me. Finally I chose one and had it tied onto the trunk of the car. I drove away slowly because the sand trucks were not out yet and the streets could be murder at the beginning of a snowfall. Downtown the streets were wide and rather empty except for a cluster of people coming out of the Newburgh Hotel. The one hotel in town that wasn't built out of cardboard and Plexiglas. A party, probably. The men huddled in the snow were dressed in tails and the women had on furs. Shiny things glittered from underneath their coats. It made me tired to look at them. Tired, tired, tired. On the next corner was a small diner with loops and loops of paper bells in the window. I stopped the car and went in. Just for a cup of coffee and twenty minutes of peace before I went home and tried to finish everything before Christmas Eve.

"Twyla?"

There she was. In a silvery evening gown and dark fur coat. A man and another woman were with her, the man fumbling for change to put in the cigarette machine. The woman was humming and tapping on the counter with her fingernails. They all looked a little bit drunk.

"Well. It's you."

"How are you?"

I shrugged. "Pretty good. Frazzled. Christmas and all."

"Regular?" called the woman from the counter.

"Fine," Roberta called back and then, "Wait for me in the car."

She slipped into the booth beside me. "I have to tell you something, Twyla. I made up my mind if I ever saw you again, I'd tell you."

"I'd just as soon not hear anything, Roberta. It doesn't matter now, anyway."

"No," she said. "Not about that."

"Don't be long," said the woman. She carried two regulars to go and the man peeled his cigarette pack as they left.

"It's about St. Bonny's and Maggie."

"Oh, please."

"Listen to me. I really did think she was black. I didn't make that up. I really thought so. But now I can't be sure. I just remember her as old, so old. And because she couldn't talk—well, you know, I thought she was crazy. She'd been brought up in an institution like my mother was and like I thought I would be too. And you were right. We didn't kick her. It was the gar girls. Only them. But, well, I wanted to. I really wanted them to hurt her. I said we did it, too.

You and me, but that's not true. And I don't want you to carry that around. It was just that I wanted to do it so bad that day—wanting to is doing it."

Her eyes were watery from the drinks she'd had, I guess. I know it's that way with me. One glass of wine and I start bawling over the littlest thing.

"We were kids, Roberta."

"Yeah. Yeah. I know, just kids."

"Eight."

"Eight."

"And lonely."

"Scared, too."

She wiped her cheeks with the heel of her hand and smiled. "Well, that's all I wanted to say."

I nodded and couldn't think of any way to fill the silence that went from the diner past the paper bells on out into the snow. It was heavy now. I thought I'd better wait for the sand trucks before starting home.

"Thanks, Roberta."

"Sure."

"Did I tell you? My mother, she never did stop dancing."

"Yes. You told me. And mine, she never got well." Roberta lifted her hands from the tabletop and covered her face with her palms. When she took them away she really was crying. "Oh, shit, Twyla. Shit, shit, shit. What the hell happened to Maggie?"

When the World as We Knew It Ended

Joy Harjo

We were dreaming on an occupied island at the farthest edge
of a trembling nation when it went down.

Two towers rose up from the east island of commerce and touched
the sky. Men walked on the moon. Oil was sucked dry
by two brothers. Then it went down. Swallowed
by a fire dragon, by oil and fear.
Eaten whole.

It was coming.

We had been watching since the eve of the missionaries in their
long and solemn clothes, to see what would happen.

We saw it
from the kitchen window over the sink
as we made coffee, cooked rice and
potatoes, enough for an army.

We saw it all, as we changed diapers and fed
the babies. We saw it,
through the branches
of the knowledgeable tree
through the snags of stars, through
the sun and storms from our knees
as we bathed and washed
the floors.

Joy Harjo

The conference of the birds warned us, as they flew over
destroyers in the harbor, parked there since the first takeover.
It was by their song and talk we knew when to rise
when to look out the window
to the commotion going on—
the magnetic field thrown off by grief.

We heard it.
The racket in every corner of the world. As
the hunger for war rose up in those who would steal to be president
to be king or emperor, to own the trees, stones, and everything
else that moved about the earth, inside the earth
and above it.

We knew it was coming, tasted the winds who gathered intelligence
from each leaf and flower, from every mountain, sea
and desert, from every prayer and song all over this tiny universe
floating in the skies of infinite
being.

And then it was over, this world we had grown to love
for its sweet grasses, for the many-colored horses
and fishes, for the shimmering possibilities
while dreaming.

But then there were the seeds to plant and the babies
who needed milk and comforting, and someone
picked up a guitar or ukulele from the rubble
and began to sing about the light flutter
the kick beneath the skin of the earth
we felt there, beneath us

a warm animal
a song being born between the legs of her;
a poem.

Bad Feminist: Take One

Roxane Gay

My favorite definition of "feminist" is one offered by Su, an Australian woman who, when interviewed for Kathy Bail's 1996 anthology *DIY Feminism*, said feminists are "just women who don't want to be treated like shit." This definition is pointed and succinct, but I run into trouble when I try to expand that definition. I fall short as a feminist. I feel like I am not as committed as I need to be, that I am not living up to feminist ideals because of who and how I choose to be.

I feel this tension constantly. As Judith Butler writes in her 1988 essay "Performative Acts and Gender Constitution," "Performing one's gender wrong initiates a set of punishments both obvious and indirect, and performing it well provides the reassurance that there is an essentialism of gender identity after all." This tension—the idea that there is a right way to be a woman, a right way to be the most essential woman—is ongoing and pervasive.

We see this tension in socially dictated beauty standards—the right way to be a woman is to be thin, to wear makeup, to wear the right kind of clothes (not too slutty, not too prudish—show a little leg, ladies), and so on. Good women are charming, polite, and unobtrusive. Good women work but are content to earn 77 percent of what men earn or, depending on whom you ask, good women bear children and stay home to raise those children without complaint. Good women are modest, chaste, pious, submissive. Women who don't adhere to these standards are the fallen, the undesirable; they are bad women.

Butler's thesis could also apply to feminism. There is an essential feminism or, as I perceive this essentialism, the notion that there are right and wrong ways to be a feminist and that there are consequences for doing feminism wrong.

Essential feminism suggests anger, humorlessness, militancy, unwavering principles, and a prescribed set of rules for how to be a proper feminist woman, or at least a proper white, heterosexual feminist woman—hate pornography, unilaterally decry the objectifications of women, don't cater to the male gaze, hate men, hate sex, focus on career, don't shave. I kid, mostly, with that last one. This is nowhere near an accurate description of feminism, but the movement has been warped by misperception for so long that even people who should know better have bought into this essential image of feminism.

Consider Elizabeth Wurtzel, who, in a June 2012 *Atlantic* article, says, "Real feminists earn a living, have money and means of their own." By Wurtzel's thinking, women who don't "earn a living, have money and means of their own," are fake feminists, undeserving of the label, a disappointment to the sisterhood. She takes the idea of essential feminism even further in a September 2012 *Harper's Bazaar* article, where she suggests that a good feminist works hard to be beautiful. She says, "Looking great is a matter of feminism. No liberated woman would misrepresent the cause by appearing less than hale and happy." It's too easy to dissect the error of such thinking. She is suggesting that a woman's worth is, in part, determined by her beauty, which is one of the very things feminism works against.

The most significant problem with essential feminism is how it doesn't allow for the complexities of human experience or individuality. There seems to be little room for multiple or discordant points of view. Essential feminism has, for example, led to the rise of the phrase "sex-positive feminism," which creates a clear distinction between the feminists who are positive about sex and feminists who aren't—which, in turn, creates a self-fulfilling essentialist prophecy.

I sometimes cringe when I am referred to as a feminist, as if I should be ashamed of my feminism or as if the word "feminist" is an insult. The label is rarely offered in kindness. I am generally called a feminist when I have the nerve to suggest that the misogyny so deeply embedded in our culture is a real problem requiring relentless vigilance. The essay in this collection about Daniel Tosh and rape jokes originally appeared in *Salon*. I tried not to read the comments because they get vicious, but I couldn't help but note one commenter who told me I was an "angry blogger woman," which is simply another way of saying "angry feminist." All feminists are angry instead of, say, passionate.

A more direct reprimand came from a man I was dating during a heated discussion that wasn't quite an argument. He said, "Don't you dare raise your voice to me," which was strange because I had not raised my voice. I was stunned because no one had ever said such a thing to me. He expounded, at length, about how women should talk to men. When I dismantled his pseudotheories, he said, "You're some kind of feminist, aren't you?" There was a tone to his accusation, making it clear that to be a feminist was undesirable. I was not being a good woman. I remained silent, stewing. I thought, *Isn't it obvious I am a feminist, albeit not a very good one?* I also realized I was being chastised for having a certain set of beliefs. The experience was disconcerting, at best.

I'm not the only outspoken woman who shies away from the feminist label, who fears the consequences of accepting the label.

In an August 2012 interview with *Salon*'s Andrew O'Hehir, actress Melissa Leo, known for playing groundbreaking female roles, said, "Well, I don't think of myself as a feminist at all. As soon as we start labeling and categorizing ourselves and others, that's going to shut down the world. I would never say that. Like, I just did that episode with Louis C.K." Leo is buying into a great many essential feminist myths with her comment. We are categorized and labeled from the moment we come into this world by gender, race, size, hair color, eye color, and so forth. The older we get, the more labels and categories we collect. If labeling and categorizing ourselves is going to shut the world down, it has been a long time coming. More disconcerting, though, is the assertion that a feminist wouldn't take a role on Louis C.K.'s sitcom, *Louie*, or that a feminist would be unable to find C.K.'s brand of humor amusing. For Leo, there are feminists and then there are women who defy categorization and are willing to embrace career opportunities.

Trailbreaking female leaders in the corporate world tend to reject the feminist label too. Marissa Mayer, who was appointed president and CEO of Yahoo in July 2012, said in an interview,

> I don't think that I would consider myself a feminist. I think that I certainly believe in equal rights, I believe that women are just as capable, if not more so in a lot of different dimensions, but I don't, I think, have sort of the militant drive and the sort of, the chip on the shoulder that sometimes comes with that. And I think it's too bad, but I do think that "feminism" has become in many ways a more negative word. You know, there are amazing opportunities all over the world for women, and I think that there is more good that comes out of positive energy around that than comes out of negative energy.

For Mayer, even though she is a pioneering woman, feminism is associated with militancy and preconceived notions. Feminism is negative, and despite the feminist strides she has made through her career at Google and now Yahoo, she'd prefer to eschew the label for the sake of so-called positive energy.

Audre Lorde once stated, "I am a Black Feminist. I mean I recognize that my power as well as my primary oppressions come as a result of my blackness as well as my womanness, and therefore my struggles on both of these fronts are inseparable." As a woman of color, I find that some feminists don't seem terribly concerned with the issues unique to women of color—the ongoing effects of racism and postcolonialism, the status of women in the Third World, the fight against the trenchant archetypes black women are forced into (angry black woman, mammy, Hottentot, and the like).

White feminists often suggest that by believing there are issues unique to women of color, an unnatural division occurs, impeding solidarity, sisterhood. Other times, white feminists are simply dismissive of these issues. In 2008, prominent blogger Amanda Marcotte was accused of appropriating ideas for her article "Can a Person Be Illegal?" from the blogger "brownfemipower," who posted a speech she gave on the same subject a few days prior to the publication of Marcotte's article. The question of where original thought ends and borrowed concepts begin was complicated significantly in this case by the sense that a white person had yet again taken the creative work of a person of color.

The feminist blogosphere engaged in an intense debate over these issues, at times so acrimonious black feminists were labeled "radical black feminists," were accused of overreacting and, of course, "playing the race card."

Such willful ignorance, such willful disinterest in incorporating the issues and concerns of black women into the mainstream feminist project, makes me disinclined to own the feminist label until it embraces people like me. Is that my way of essentializing feminism, of suggesting there's a right kind of feminism or a more inclusive feminism? Perhaps. This is all murky for me, but a continued insensitivity, within feminist circles, on the matter of race is a serious problem.

There's also this. Lately, magazines have been telling me there's something wrong with feminism or women trying to achieve a work-life balance or just women in general. The *Atlantic* has led the way in these lamentations. In the aforementioned June 2012 article, Elizabeth Wurtzel, author of *Prozac Nation*, wrote a searing polemic about "1% wives" who are hurting feminism and the progress of women by choosing to stay at home rather than enter the workplace. Wurtzel begins the essay provocatively, stating,

> When my mind gets stuck on everything that is wrong with feminism, it brings out the 19th century poet in me: *Let me count the ways*. Most of all, feminism is pretty much a nice girl who really, really wants so badly to be liked by everybody—ladies who lunch, men who hate women, all the morons who demand choice and don't understand responsibility—that it has become the easy lay of social movements.

There are problems with feminism. Wurtzel says so, and she is vigorous in defending her position. Wurtzel knows the right way for feminism. In that article, Wurtzel goes on to state there is only one kind of equality, economic equality, and until women recognize that and enter the workforce en masse, feminists, and wealthy feminists in particular, will continue to fail. They will continue to be bad feminists, falling short of essential ideals of feminism. Wurtzel isn't wrong about the importance of economic equality, but she is wrong in assuming that with economic equality, the rest of feminism's concerns will somehow disappear.

In the July/August 2012 *Atlantic*, Anne-Marie Slaughter wrote more than twelve thousand words about the struggles of powerful, successful women to "have it all." Her article was interesting and thoughtful, for a certain kind of woman—a wealthy woman with a very successful career. She even parlayed the piece into a book deal. Slaughter was speaking to a small, elite group of women while ignoring the millions of women who don't have the privilege of, as Slaughter did, leaving high-powered positions at the State Department to spend more time with their sons. Many women who work do so because they have to. Working has little to do with having it all and much more to do with having food on the table.

Slaughter wrote,

> I'd been the woman congratulating herself on her unswerving commitment to the feminist cause, chatting smugly with her dwindling number of college or law-school friends who had reached and maintained their place on the highest rungs of their profession. I'd been the one telling young women at my lectures that you *can* have it all and do it all, regardless of what field you are in.

The thing is, I am not at all sure that feminism has ever suggested women can have it all. This notion of being able to have it all is always misattributed to feminism when really, it's human nature to want it all—to have cake and eat it too without necessarily focusing on how we can get there and how we can make "having it all" possible for a wider range of people and not just the lucky ones.

Alas, poor feminism. So much responsibility keeps getting piled on the shoulders of a movement whose primary purpose is to achieve equality, in all realms, between men and women. I keep reading these articles and getting angry and tired because they suggest there's no way for women to ever *get it right*. These articles make it seem like, as Butler suggests, there is, in fact, a right way to be a woman and a wrong way to be a woman. The standard for the right way to be a woman and/or a feminist appears to be ever changing and unachievable.

In the weeks leading up to the publication of Sheryl Sandberg's *Lean In*, critics had plenty to say about the Facebook chief operating officer's ideas about being a woman in the workplace—even though few had actually read the tome. Many of the resulting discussions bizarrely mischaracterized *Lean In*, tossing around misleading headlines, inaccurate facts, and unfair assumptions.

As it turns out, not even a fairly average entry into the world of corporate advice books is immune from double standards.

Sandberg intersperses personal anecdotes from her remarkable career (a vice presidency at Google, serving as the US Treasury's chief of staff during the Clinton administration) with observations, research, and pragmatic advice for how women can better achieve professional and personal success. She urges women to "lean in" to their careers and to be "ambitious in any pursuit." *Lean In* is competently written, blandly interesting, and it does repeat a great deal of familiar research—although it isn't particularly harmful to be reminded of the challenges women face as they try to get ahead.

Intentionally or not, much of the book is a stark reminder of the many obstacles women face in the workplace. I cannot deny that parts resonated, particularly in Sandberg's discussion about "impostor syndrome" and how women are less willing to take advantage of potential career opportunities unless they feel qualified.

But Sandberg is rigidly committed to the gender binary, and *Lean In* is exceedingly heteronormative. Professional women are largely defined in relation to professional men; *Lean In*'s loudest unspoken advice seems to dictate that women should embrace traditionally masculine qualities (self-confidence, risk taking, aggression, etc.). Occasionally, this advice backfires because it seems as if Sandberg is advocating, *If you want to succeed, be an asshole.* In addition, Sandberg generally assumes a woman will want to fulfill professional ambitions while also marrying a man and having children. Yes, she says, "Not all women want careers. Not all women want children. Not all women want both. I would never advocate that we should all have the same objectives." But she contradicts herself by placing every single parable within the context of heterosexual women who want a wildly successful career and a rounded-out nuclear family. Accepting that Sandberg is writing to a very specific audience, and has little to offer those who don't fall within that target demographic, makes enjoying the book a lot easier.

One of the main questions that has arisen in the wake of *Lean In*'s publication is whether Sandberg has a responsibility to women who don't fall within her target demographic. Like Slaughter, Sandberg is speaking to a rather narrow group of women. In the *New York Times*, Jodi Kantor writes, "Even [Sandberg's] advisers acknowledge the awkwardness of a woman with double Harvard degrees, dual stock riches (from Facebook and Google, where she also worked), a 9,000-square-foot house and a small army of household help urging less fortunate women to look inward and work harder."

At times, the inescapable evidence of Sandberg's fortune is grating. She casually discusses her mentor Larry Summers, working for the Treasury department, her doctor siblings, and her equally successful husband, David Goldberg. (As CEO of SurveyMonkey, Goldberg moved the company headquarters from Portland to the Bay Area so he could more fully commit to his family.) She gives the impression that her movement from one ideal situation to the next is easily replicable.

Sandberg's life is so absurd a fairy tale, I began to think of *Lean In* as a snow globe, where a lovely little tableau was being nicely preserved for my delectation and irritation. I would not be so bold as to suggest Sandberg has it all, but I need to believe she is pretty damn close to whatever "having it all" might look like. Common sense dictates that it is not realistic to assume anyone could achieve Sandberg's successes simply by "leaning in" and working harder—but that doesn't mean Sandberg has nothing to offer, or that *Lean In* should be summarily dismissed.

Cultural critics can get a bit precious and condescending about marginalized groups, and in the debate over *Lean In* "working-class women" have been lumped into a vaguely defined group of women who work too hard for too little money. But very little consideration has been given to these women as actual people who live in the world, and who maybe, just maybe, have ambitions too.

There has been, unsurprisingly, significant pushback against the notion that leaning in is a reasonable option for working-class women, who are already stretched woefully thin. Sandberg is not oblivious to her privilege, noting:

> I am fully aware that most women are not focused on changing social norms for the next generation but simply trying to get through each day. Forty percent of employed mothers lack sick days and vacation leave, and about 50 percent of employed mothers are unable to take time off to care for a sick child. Only about half of women receive any pay during maternity leave. These policies can have severe consequences; families with no access to paid family leave often go into debt and can fall into poverty. Part-time jobs with fluctuating schedules offer little chance to plan and often stop short of the forty-hour week that provides basic benefits.

It would have been useful if Sandberg offered realistic advice about career management for women who are dealing with such circumstances. It would also be useful if we had flying cars. Assuming Sandberg's advice is completely useless for working-class women is just as shortsighted as claiming her advice needs to be completely applicable to all women. And let's be frank: if Sandberg chose to offer career advice for working-class women, a group she clearly knows little about, she would have been just as harshly criticized for overstepping her bounds.

The critical response to *Lean In* is not entirely misplaced, but it is emblematic of the dangers of public womanhood. Public women, and feminists in particular, have to be everything to everyone; when they aren't, they are excoriated for their failure. In some ways, this is understandable. We have come far, but we have so much further to go. We need so very much, and we hope women with a significant platform might be everything we need—a desperately untenable position. As Elizabeth Spiers notes in the *Verge*,

> When's the last time someone picked up a Jack Welch (or Warren Buffett, or even Donald Trump) bestseller and complained that it was unsympathetic to working class men who had to

> work multiple jobs to support their families? . . . And who reads a book by Jack Welch and defensively feels that they're being told that they have to adopt Jack Welch's lifestyle and professional choices or they are lesser human beings?

Lean In cannot and should not be read as a definitive text, or a book offering universally applicable advice to all women, everywhere. Sandberg is confident and aggressive in her advice, but the reader is under no obligation to do everything she says. Perhaps we can consider *Lean In* for what it is—just one more reminder that the rules are always different for girls, no matter who they are and no matter what they do.

Woodchucks

Maxine Kumin

Gassing the woodchucks didn't turn out right.
The knockout bomb from the Feed and Grain Exchange
was featured as merciful, quick at the bone
and the case we had against them was airtight,
both exits shoehorned shut with puddingstone,
but they had a sub-sub-basement out of range.

Next morning they turned up again, no worse
for the cyanide than we for our cigarettes
and state-store Scotch, all of us up to scratch.
They brought down the marigolds as a matter of course
and then took over the vegetable patch
nipping the broccoli shoots, beheading the carrots.

The food from our mouths, I said, righteously thrilling
to the feel of the .22, the bullets' neat noses.
I, a lapsed pacifist fallen from grace
puffed with Darwinian pieties for killing,
now drew a bead on the little woodchuck's face.
He died down in the everbearing roses.

Ten minutes later I dropped the mother. She
flipflopped in the air and fell, her needle teeth
still hooked in a leaf of early Swiss chard.
Another baby next. O one-two-three
the murderer inside me rose up hard,
the hawkeye killer came on stage forthwith.

Maxine Kumin

There's one chuck left. Old wily fellow, he keeps
me cocked and ready day after day after day.
All night I hunt his humped-up form. I dream
I sight along the barrel in my sleep.
If only they'd all consented to die unseen
gassed underground the quiet Nazi way.

Reading Lessons

Edwidge Danticat

The first time Danielle remembers ever being aware of her breasts was when she was thirteen and her mother told her to rub crushed butterflies on them to make them grow. Not already dead butterflies but live ones, plucked from flower petals by her own hands. Saturns were preferable because it was easy to tell the pale females, which she needed, from the darker males, which she did not. Swallowtails and other species with black spots were considered unlucky. And she was not, no matter what, to mistake a thick-antennaed moth for a butterfly, for if she rubbed a poisonous moth on her dot of a nipple not only would she get a rash but she wouldn't see another centimeter of growth for the rest of her life.

She was already an expert lizard hunter—she preferred the kink-tailed ones to any other kind—so the butterflies proved to be easy prey, but because she was used to more struggle than they were capable of she'd sometimes press too hard. Either their wings would crumble, leaving a fine, sticky dust under her fingernails, or the butterflies would simply fall apart and she'd pile the corpses in a jar, a kaleidoscopic, see-through mausoleum, too horrifying to keep in her mother's cosmetics cabinet yet too beautiful to discard.

The day her mother was shot by a young man no older than Danielle—a classmate of hers, according to some witnesses—as she was coming home from her textile shop, Danielle simply uncovered her jar of butterflies and threw its contents to the two iguanas she kept in a small cage in her parents' bamboo-hedged, hibiscus-lined garden. And, because she'd taken her mother's advice, her breasts did grow, so much so that, years after she had left adolescence and left Haiti with her father and was working as a first-grade teacher at a small experimental school in Miami's Little Haiti, she discovered in the shower one morning a chestnut-size lump in one of them, the right one, which seemed to have bloomed overnight, as if her mammary glands had been soaked in a butterfly bath while she slept.

She had told the story of her mother and the butterfly potion to the two Haitian women who showed up in her classroom that very evening to learn to read. Surrounded by hand-drawn maps of their Little Haiti neighborhood, real maps of what Danielle and the kids called Big Haiti, a globe that showed the whole world, and drawings made with parents and refrigerator doors in mind, both women sat stiffly in the adult desks towering over the children's bureaus, which, for the evening, had been pushed to the outer corners.

Danielle had been drafted to teach one of the school's so-called twilight literacy classes after the principal, her clandestine boyfriend of two and a half years, came up with the idea of helping the students by giving the parents a taste of the American educational system. The school had a 99 percent Haitian student body—the one "foreign" boy had, like the school's principal, been born of Haitian parents in Burundi—so she expected the same of her evening class. She was dreading her first moments before the Creole-speaking mothers and fathers, who, unlike their children, wouldn't simply look up at her with helpless glee but would rate her on things that she suddenly found difficult to conceal, like her rapid loss of enthusiasm for her job, or her growing discomfort at keeping a secret that could be either harmless or devastating.

Before the two women had shown up, she'd been thinking of just going through the motions, replicating with them some of what she attempted from morning to afternoon with their kids—the alphabet singsongs, the vowel and consonant drills, the color charts, the math demonstrations with Popsicle sticks. She might even repeat for them some of the questions the children constantly asked: What is a refugee? Why do my parents need money? What is a *bouzen*? What is a vagabond? Every once in a while, she planned to tell the parents, she was delighted when a child made a more puerile inquiry: How does a kite fly? How does an airplane stay up in the air? Where are my tears hiding when I'm not crying?

When forty-three parents enrolled for the classes, two of whom Principal Boyfriend, as Danielle liked to call him, quickly discovered couldn't read in any language at all, he bypassed his small group of eager recent Ed-school graduates and deposited the two, for more intimate instruction, in her care. Besides, he pointed out, each had a child in her class. The younger parent, Fania, a willowy woman in a sleeveless crimson dress, was mother to Vanya, a scrawny girl whose hair was always braided in what seemed to be a hundred yarnlike plaits, each individually fastened with a different-colored barrette. Vanya's barrettes reminded Danielle of the flecked aphids that had invaded her mother's garden during the summer months of her childhood, sucking the moisture out of her banana trees until they were drier than paper.

Lorvane, a strapping, stoic-looking, blue-uniformed hotel maid, had three children at the school. One of them was indeed Danielle's pupil—Paul, a restless, rambunctious boy, who at the beginning of the year had lost two front milk teeth that showed no signs of being replaced by adult ones.

"What's in this for me?" Danielle had asked Principal Boyfriend when he'd playfully dangled a time sheet in front of her that afternoon.

"Aside from the extra money?" He still had the same French accent, he'd told Danielle, with which he'd spoken since he left Burundi at sixteen. "Of course, the endless satisfaction of being a miracle worker, of making the blind see."

There were times when his projects annoyed her so much that she thought she might hit him, not hard and not often, just once. But there were also times when she found herself feeling grateful to him, for even as he orchestrated his grand pedagogical schemes he never overlooked the details of her own life. He'd signed her up to teach that class, for example, as if he knew exactly what she would need that evening: not to be alone in their vast yet sparsely furnished Brickell Avenue condo, staring into a mirror, prodding anxious fingers at her flesh.

Her two evening students had only nodded to each other once when they'd arrived; both looked equally exhausted after long days at what Danielle assumed were physically taxing jobs. Even before the class had officially started, they could barely keep their eyes open.

"Why do you want to learn to read?" Danielle asked them.

Lorvane shrugged, then replied, "Because I don't want people to take me for an imbecile."

"For my daughter," Fania said, her close-set eyes growing misty and full.

"I have another reason you might want to keep in your mind," Danielle said, leaning back into the same red rocking chair from which she read daily to her first graders. "Do the two of you ever travel between Haiti and here?"

"Now and then," Fania answered.

Lorvane nodded coyly, as if uncertain where Danielle was taking them.

"You remember what it's like when it's time to fill out your customs and immigration forms? You probably ask the person who happens to be sitting next to you on the plane to do it for you, right?"

Fania kept her eyes on the cover of her brand-new composition notebook while Lorvane bobbed her head, her droopy chin sinking into her chest.

"Some of the seatmates are not always in the mood, or able to help you," Danielle continued, "so they wave you off, forcing you to ask the steward or stewardess, who has other duties but must quickly do this small favor for you as the whole plane watches. Reading and writing can spare you this type of humiliation."

She had prepared the speech beforehand and wanted to give them both a concrete goal to aspire to, the dream of one day completing questionnaires for themselves and for others. But to round things off, Danielle—whose furniture-maker father had snickered at his illiterate plane-mates during the flight that had brought them to Miami—also told Fania and Lorvane about ancient civilizations whose indigenous populations never knew how to read or write but, instead, used hieroglyphs with which it was easy to recognize water as a series of wavy lines, and a man or a bird as a drawing of such. And she reminded them both of the well-known Haitian saying *"Analfabèt pa bèt,"* one of Principal Boyfriend's recent favorites, which, though it did not rhyme in English, could be translated as "Illiterates are not stupid." Then, before proceeding to help the women trace and retrace the first letter of what suddenly seemed like a very long alphabet, she told Fania and Lorvane, whose mouth opened into a giant *O* as she occasionally nodded off, about breasts and butterflies and mothers lost too young. She volunteered to answer their questions, which, it turned out, were not so different from the ones often asked by her younger students: How long with this take? When will I go home?

That night, after class, the two women made a trip to Principal Boyfriend's office to tell him that they had learned only how to write the letter *A* in their first session with Danielle. She never opened a book and wrote only that single letter on the board toward the end of class. The rest of the time, she had just talked and talked like some crazy woman, and not always in English, which they hoped to learn, but in Creole, which they already spoke a whole lot better than she did. They asked to be transferred to someone else.

"Screw them," she told Principal Boyfriend when he recounted all this to her in bed. He held one of her hands under the sheets. She dangled the other over the side of the bed and, after a sudden rush of blood to her fingertips, felt it go numb.

She wished sometimes that she'd agreed to his suggestion to paste a glow-in-the-dark constellation to the ceiling. He'd told her soon after they moved in together that when he was a boy he was afraid of really dark nights, nights that in Cankuzo were called "Who are you?" nights because it was hard even to recognize a friend. She hadn't wanted their bedroom to look like a child's bunker, but now she thought she might reconsider, for if she had planets and galaxies, half-moons and shooting stars to stare up at on nights like this it might be easier to pretend that she was somewhere else, in her mother's garden, perhaps, on a warm summer evening, with soft blades of grass stroking her cheeks.

Before going to bed, she had checked again and her lump was still there. It had neither grown nor shrunk since the morning, when she'd come across it like a strange presence in a familiar place, a sudden sixth finger near a perfect set of five, an amorphous birthmark on a swanlike neck. She was beginning to think of it, this thing inside her, as a fragile egg that might crack. It was essential that he not touch it, especially with amorous intent, as loving touches might nourish it or release it from its shell to roam freely to other parts of her body.

"Maybe I should send those two women to someone else," he said. He released her fingers to run his hand across her flat, muscle-rippled abdomen. When his elbow accidentally touched the lacy padded bra she had kept on, she moved it away and carefully lowered his arm onto his gut, a small mass of a beer belly filled with foods and sweets and liquors that she had also enjoyed.

"I love you, you know," he whispered. His words surprised her. She couldn't remember the last time he'd said that to her. Maybe six months before, in the little garden café near the school, where he'd boldly taken her to lunch to celebrate their two-year anniversary as a "secret" couple before asking her to move in with him. Apart from her father, he was the only man she felt she could follow anywhere, yet she could never bring herself to tell him this. She had already shown her loyalty by joining the staff of his school, by agreeing to carry on a live-in romance that all her colleagues suspected but could not prove.

She didn't reply to his declaration of love, just reached over and took his hand and put it back on her stomach.

"We have an investigation going at school," he said. He moved his face closer to hers and stared at her in the dark. She wanted to turn away, but instead she pressed her eyelids together to make another kind of sky, a sky full of fireflies, tiny little torches lighting dead mothers' paths.

"Is it something big?" She wished she could paste fireflies to their bedroom ceiling, ones that she could let loose around the room now and then. But even when she was a girl, and immersed in the insect world, she had never trapped fireflies. Unlike the butterflies she kept until they turned to glittery dust, once the fireflies were dead she was no longer interested in them.

"One of our kids told an aide that he was slapped by a teacher," he said. I asked Chantal Cazeau to look into it."

Chantal Cazeau: that grim-faced twenty-four-year-old doctoral student who was volunteering at the school for the year. On the wall above her desk in the office that she shared with three other aides was a giant poster filled with despondent-looking kids across whose faces were printed the words "children need advocates," followed by a dozen exclamation marks. Like all the other teachers, Danielle had sat through many of Chantal Cazeau's lunchtime professional-development seminars.

"The children are sacred" was the theme of every one of her talks. "They deal with all kinds of shit at home: poverty, drugs, indifference, absent parents working two or three jobs to make the rent. We don't want to add to their trauma here."

In addition to her role as school counselor, Chantal Cazeau had suddenly become the school's attorney general, cracking down on lesson-plan violators, inattentive testers, and abusive teachers. Principal Boyfriend had a lot to do with this. With the children's salvation as his ultimate end, he could turn the least bit of enthusiasm into zeal, and had quickly made Chantal Cazeau a fanatic. Even though he shared little of his private life with his staff, he never hesitated to tell them that he loved them. He'd probably told Chantal Cazeau in some way that he loved her, just as he had the cafeteria workers, the janitors, the security guards, his secretary, even the soccer coach. And in return they all worshipped him enough, he hoped, to serve the children even better.

It wasn't meant to be a slap, just the wave of a hand, like a conductor guiding members of an orchestra, each with the same goal in mind but different instruments in hand. Toothless Paul, as even the other children with missing teeth called him, was one of the most disruptive boys in her class. He had long legs, which he constantly knocked together, and a loud, jittery laugh. Of her faithful twelve, her disciples, he interrupted her the most, both with his clamorous mirth and his impertinent questions. Whenever she tried to silence him by giving him some extra task or forcing him to stand alone in the back of the room, she was reminded that, unlike the other children, who had some weaknesses in either English or Creole, Paul was equally fluent in both and knew a long list of mumble-ready cuss words in each.

He was in the habit of reaching over and, with both hands, grabbing the top of the chair in front of him, and rocking the little girl in it back and forth. Her name was Ruth, and she always wore elaborately ruffled Sunday dresses to class. Danielle had once called her parents to advise them to dress her more casually, but Ruth's father had informed her that they didn't take school casually and did not want to attire their daughter in a way that might encourage her to do so. Also, he said, they were Pentecostals and their religion prohibited them from letting their child wear most of the other clothes that were in stores these days.

Danielle could now see that Paul's rowdiness might have something to do with his mother's inability to either engage or restrain him, for he always seemed eager, hungry even, for distractions beyond anything around him. Perhaps she should have called the mother in, or referred him to Chantal Cazeau for evaluation, but she had thought herself capable of handling him.

That particular morning, she was reading a version of Hans Christian Andersen's "The Snow Queen" to the class. Concerned that the children might not fully understand the story, she had avoided it before. But Principal Boyfriend had encouraged her to make it a part of her reading lesson, to show her students, he said, that people from other cultures also valued tales filled with ugly demons and little girls who spoke to flowers, rivers, and birds.

She had found herself enthralled with the sound of her own wistful voice. *The most beautiful landscapes looked like boiled spinach, and the nicest people appeared loathsome, or they seemed to stand on their heads with their stomachs missing and their faces so twisted that you couldn't tell who they were. If someone had a freckle, you can be sure that it would spread over his nose and mouth.* For a while, she had even managed to ignore Paul, who mimicked her facial expressions and lip movements and grimaced to distract the others. *How grey and hard the wide world was!* But the more Paul was ignored the more animated his impersonation became, until most of the children stopped listening to laugh at him. Or were they laughing at her?

The room was completely silent when Danielle put the book down and headed for Paul's desk. As Danielle approached, he straightened his body and looked straight ahead, avoiding her glare.

Even as she was standing beside him, she had not yet decided what to do with him. Where would she send him this time? To the back of the room? Or, as a new measure, to the principal's office?

She had meant only to accentuate whatever command she gave him by pounding on his desk with her open palm, but when a familiar toothless smirk flashed across his face, one he desperately tried to control, she found herself wanting to erase it, the way she did the words and numbers from the blackboard at the end of each school day.

She realized that she'd hit him only when she heard the other children gasp. Paul reached up and rubbed the side of his face, but only for a moment. There were no finger marks that she could see, no blood streaming past his lips. He didn't cry. Instead, he went on smirking, his toothless gap growing wider, until Danielle walked back to her red rocking chair and continued her reading lesson.

The next morning, Principal Boyfriend left before she did, for he had duties, as he constantly reminded her, which required that he arrive at school ahead of the staff, even the cafeteria workers. On this day, this new day, she would neglect the lump, not check for it at all. She would pretend that in her sleep some magic clock had been turned back to the days when her body was still her own.

She was certain now that he knew about Paul. He was simply waiting for her to confess.

"We owe each other that much," she could imagine him saying. Or perhaps, "You owe young Paul that much."

"And what does anyone owe me?" she might say, but probably wouldn't.

She couldn't face them yet. Not him. Not Paul. Not Chantal Cazeau. So she called his machine at work and said that her father wasn't feeling well and she was going to see him.

Her father still lived in the same town house in the gated lakeside community where she'd spent her late-teen and college years. Aside from her education, it was the only lavish expense he'd allowed himself, after selling their house, his furniture business, and her mother's textile shop in Haiti. Between her college and graduate school years, he had remarried twice, first to a retired nurse, who went to Port-au-Prince on a medical mission and decided to stay, then to a young beauty-salon owner who had wanted him to cut off all contact with Danielle.

Whenever she came to visit her now-single father, she loved lying on his gingham, feather-stuffed couch with her head on his lap, as they caught up on each other's life. He no longer smelled the way he did when she was a girl, like the lemon-and-alcohol-scented furniture varnish, which had given an orange tint to his callused palms. Now he smelled like wet soil, crabgrass and other weeds, tree barks, and insect carcasses, like his lakeside garden. He had worked as a carpenter and landscaper for years and was happy, as he often said, to have no other responsibilities but to watch the sun rise and set. He didn't leave the house much, except when Danielle begged him to join her and Principal Boyfriend for the occasional dinner and holiday meals.

After both his wives had left, he began draping the walls with fabric so that his living room looked exactly like the showroom of her mother's textile shop, where crêpe, calico, gabardine, satin, and organza filled every spot. But in her father's house the cloth swayed in the midday breeze.

"You did what?" her father asked, gently running his fingers through her hair.

"I slapped one of the boys in my class yesterday," she said.

"Any blood?"

"No blood."

"Then?"

"Then maybe I should quit."

"Why?" he asked, without even lifting his fingers out of her hair. "Don't you remember how hard your mother used to beat you because you liked playing with insects so much, because you were like a boy?"

She did remember, as a matter of fact. Not all the time, but every now and then she did. What she remembered most vividly, though, was her mother's odd advice, suggesting that in some way she could transform herself by rubbing the insects against her chest. It seemed harmless now, that advice, even fantastical. But back then she had taken it seriously. Could her body have, too?

"Your mother loved you so much," her father went on. He'd spent that whole first night after the shooting in a chair, shaking, and hadn't said more than three or four words at a time to anyone. "It can't be. It is not possible."

From where her head lay on his lap, Danielle could see what in the midday light seemed like two lines of crystal tears sliding down his face.

"When she was pregnant with you," he said, "she didn't even want to raise her arms too far above her head, because someone had told her that it could cause the umbilical cord to be wrapped around your neck. She didn't hit you because she hated you. She wanted you to be better."

"Better than what?" she asked as she reached up to wipe the tears.

"Better than dirt," he said. "Better than your classmate who killed her. Better, probably, than the boy you slapped yesterday."

Where was that classmate now, about whom all she could remember was that he spent his summers in Canada and could sing along with the radio in three languages?

She had become a teacher, her father knew, in order to find these types of boys early, to detect and save them. But the moment she slapped Paul she'd felt neither guilt nor remorse but retribution, justice.

That afternoon, after school, they were all in her classroom, just as his secretary said they would be. Sometimes when she walked into a place like her classroom or their apartment, a place she'd helped decorate, she felt as though she had breached the threshold of her imagination and was inside her own head.

Principal Boyfriend was sitting behind the small mahogany desk they'd picked out together at a flea market. She had wanted something other than the bland, district-assigned desk, something that reflected her own taste.

On her labeled locker, in the same row as the children's, she'd pasted laminated replicas of her diplomas and certificates of advanced-training courses from the University of Miami, where they'd met. He had told her to put them out in full view, to assure the parents that their children were being taught by well-qualified staff.

When Danielle walked in, she tried to envision how many others had already been there that day. The kids, of course, and the day's substitute teacher. After school, there might also have been counselors and aides, making suggestions about what measures should be taken.

They had chosen to meet in her classroom, his secretary had said, so that Paul could feel more comfortable telling his story, reenacting the incident even, if he had to. But her own familiarity with everything there confused her. It was as though some of the children had grown up and had become these adults, who were all suddenly irate with her.

Chantal Cazeau sat slouched in the rocking chair, immediately across from Principal Boyfriend. She was flipping through a legal pad filled with notes scribbled in her diminutive handwriting. Paul was at his own desk next to Lorvane, who was wedged into another child's chair. Lorvane, who had probably been called from work, wore her white-collared indigo uniform. The four of them seemed flat and rigid, like the Velcro figures Danielle sometimes used to mime stories for the children.

Principal Boyfriend seemed torn between his roles, his eyes swerving back and forth to look at each of them. Danielle could see that he was choosing his words carefully. Finally, he simply asked her, "Are you OK?"

"Let's get started." Chantal Cazeau tapped the legal pad against her palm. "We have quite a bit to cover here."

It was obvious that she was in charge. He had yielded total control to her for these particular proceedings. Good leadership, he liked to say, like good loving, was knowing when to surrender.

Lorvane got up and reached back to massage her behind, where the chair had left a damp crease.

They were all standing now, all except Paul, who remained quietly at his desk, gripping both sides with clenched fists. He tapped his sneakers against the floor without making any noise.

"First of all, I'd like to let Paul know that it was very brave of him to come forward," Chantal said, nodding in the child's direction.

"The principal and I are committed to making sure that something like this never happens again."

"Miss?" Lorvane took a few small, hesitant steps toward Danielle. "They say you slapped my son?"

Lorvane kept moving closer, until Danielle could feel her warm breath on her face, could almost describe, if pressed, what Lorvane had eaten for lunch.

"Yesterday I came to learn to read from you." Lorvane pursed her lips, just as her son sometimes did during those rare moments when he was still.

"I wanted to come because my son told me what a good teacher you are," Lorvane continued. "He told me you are patient with him and all the other children. He says you talk to them and explain many things and read all kinds of stories to them every day. I said to myself, 'I have much to learn from this teacher, this wonderful teacher.'"

Lorvane reached toward Paul's desk and, without taking her eyes off Danielle, grabbed him by the shoulders and plopped him between herself and Danielle. His body was obedient and lifeless; his arms hung limply at his sides.

"Am I lying, son?" Lorvane raised the boy's face toward them. Paul shook his head no. His mouth was closed, but his lips trembled and it seemed to Danielle that, for the first time since she'd known him, he might start to cry.

"Let's all sit down and talk about this," Chantal Cazeau said, her voice a few decibels higher than usual.

"You see, Miss," Lorvane went on, ignoring Chantal. "I would give you the permission to spank my son anytime if he needed it, if it would help him."

"That's not the way we do things here," Principal Boyfriend finally interjected. "We would never hit your son at this school," he assured Lorvane. "Do you understand?"

"I would sign a paper, if I have to, for spanking," Lorvane insisted. "But I would never let anyone slap my son."

Lorvane gently moved Paul aside. Freed, he buried his face behind one of the chairs. Stepping back, Lorvane took a deep breath, then aimed for Danielle.

The slap landed on Danielle's cheek before she could see it coming. Her head swung so quickly that both of her ears tapped against each of her shoulders for a moment. Her cheek throbbed. It felt hot, then warm, then deadened, so that if Lorvane slapped her again she probably wouldn't feel a thing.

Now she understood the concept of turning the other cheek. It wasn't so much directed at your neighbor; it was allowing yourself to experience even further pain. Acted out, it would indeed be an extraordinary sacrifice.

"We are finished now," Lorvane said. "No more meetings. No police. Just teach my child. And remember, 'Kids are not stupid.'"

Lorvane grabbed Paul's hand and yanked him across the room toward the door. Her voice remained suspended in the room like one of the children's runaway balloons, the kind they brought to school for birthdays and holidays but never managed to hold on to.

On his way out, with the contented look of the vindicated warrior, Paul turned to face Danielle, opened his mouth, and flashed his bare gums in his version of a celebratory smile.

Danielle heard herself breathing loudly as she tried to massage some sensation back into her cheekbone. The door slammed behind Lorvane and Paul, their loud exchange fading as they moved down the hall.

Chantal Cazeau laid her pad on the desk in front of Principal Boyfriend and motioned for Danielle to sit down in the rocking chair. Principal Boyfriend's gaze was fixed on Danielle as though she and he were alone in one of those dark rooms of his childhood, and he was trying to figure out who she was.

A droning sound, like a telephone dial tone, was ringing in Danielle's ear, but she thought she heard Principal Boyfriend ask once more, "Are you OK?"

Ways of Conquest

Denise Levertov

You invaded my country by accident,
not knowing you had crossed the border.
Vines that grew there touched you.
                                   You ran past them,
shaking raindrops off the leaves—you or the wind.
It was toward the hills you ran,
inland—

I invaded your country with all my
'passionate intensity,'
pontoons and parachutes of my blindness.
But living now in the suburbs of the capital
incognito,
           my will to take the heart of the city
           has dwindled. I love
its unsuspecting life,
its adolescents who come to tell me their dreams in the dusty park
among the rocks and benches,
I the stranger who will listen.
I love
the wild herons who return each year to the marshy outskirts.
What I invaded has
invaded me.

About Shared Inquiry

A Shared Inquiry™ discussion begins when the leader of the discussion group poses an interpretive question to participants about the meaning of a reading selection. The question is substantial enough that no single answer can resolve it. Instead, several answers—even answers that are in conflict—may be valid. In effect, the leader is telling the group: "Here is a problem of meaning that seems important. Let's try to resolve it."

From that moment on, participants are free to offer answers and opinions to the group, to request clarification of points, and to raise objections to the remarks of other participants. They also discuss specific passages in the selection that bear on the interpretive question and compare their differing ideas about what these passages mean. The leader, meanwhile, asks additional questions, clarifying and expanding the interpretive question and helping group members to arrive at more cogent answers. All participants don't have to agree with all of the answers—each person can decide which answer seems most convincing. This process is called Shared Inquiry.

In Shared Inquiry discussion, three kinds of questions can be raised about a reading selection: factual questions, interpretive questions, and evaluative questions. Interpretation is central to a Shared Inquiry discussion but factual questions can bring to light evidence in support of interpretations and can clear up misunderstandings. On the other hand, evaluative questions invite participants to compare the experiences and opinions of an author with their own and can introduce a personal dimension into the discussion.

About Shared Inquiry

In order for discussions to be most rewarding, it is strongly recommended that a significant amount of time be spent coming to an understanding of what the authors are saying. The following guidelines will help keep the conversation focused on the text and assure all the participants a voice:

1. **Read the selection carefully before participating in the discussion.** This ensures that all participants are equally prepared to talk about the ideas in the reading.

2. **Discuss the ideas in the selection, and try to understand them fully.** Reflecting as individuals and as a group on what the author says makes the exploration of both the selection and related issues that will come up in the discussion more rewarding.

3. **Support interpretations of what the author says with evidence from the reading, along with insights from personal experience.** This provides focus for the group on the selection that everyone has read and builds a strong foundation for discussing related issues.

4. **Listen to other participants and respond to them directly.** Shared Inquiry is about the give and take of ideas, the willingness to listen to others and talk with them respectfully. Directing your comments and questions to other group members, not always to the leader, will make the discussion livelier and more dynamic.

5. **Expect the leader to mainly ask questions.** Effective leaders help participants develop their own ideas, with everyone gaining a new understanding in the process. When participants hang back and wait for the leader to suggest answers, discussion tends to falter.

Discussion Questions

"WHAT DO WOMEN WANT?" | Kim Addonizio

Why does the speaker say she wants a red dress that is "flimsy and cheap"? (5)

1. Why does the author appropriate Freud's question, "What do women want?" for her title?

2. Why does the speaker want her dress to be made so that "no one has to guess / what's underneath"?

3. Why does the speaker want to walk past different businesses?

4. Why does the speaker want to "walk like I'm the only / woman on earth and I can have my pick"?

5. Why does the speaker want the dress to "confirm / your worst fears about me"?

6. How does the red dress show "how little I care about you / or anything except what / I want"?

7. Why is the act of finding the dress like "choosing a body / to carry me into this world"?

8. Why does the speaker declare she will wear the dress "like bones, like skin"?

9. Why does the speaker end by claiming the dress will be "the goddamned / dress they bury me in"?

Discussion Questions

AT ODDS | Julia Serano

Why does Serano believe that she must choose between a female identity and her sexual attraction to girls?

1. Why does Serano believe her sexual orientation and becoming female are conflicting desires?
2. In junior high school, why is Serano sure that her dreams of being a girl are dangerous and sinful?
3. Why is Serano finally able to give herself "permission to experience the girl thoughts"? (9)
4. In light of the conflicts faced by Serano, why does she say, "Sometimes we do that to ourselves—we pit our desires against one another"? (15)
5. Why is Serano able, fifteen years later, to "fulfill both desires simultaneously"? (15)

Why does Serano describe her particular experience in adolescence as being "thrown to the wolves"? (10)

1. Why does Serano "remember wanting to simply shrink into nothingness" whenever she went into the boys' locker room? (11)
2. Why does Serano compare growing up as a boy while feeling female to "bleeding to death from a million small cuts"? (11)
3. When Serano fantasizes about being turned into a girl against her will, why does she feel "a strange combination of both humiliation and elation"? (11)
4. Why does seeing girls flirting with her friends at the baseball game give Serano the intense experience of *"knowing"* she would get a sex change? (13)
5. After this experience of intuition, why does Serano go on to date girls without telling them of her struggle with gender identity?

Discussion Questions

ENDING POEM | Aurora Levins Morales and Rosario Morales

Why is "Ending Poem" written in alternating lines of roman and italicized type? (17–18)

1. Why do the speakers begin by listing their varied geographic and ethnic origins?

2. Why do the speakers then limit the degree to which they identify themselves with these origins?

3. Why does the second speaker say, "*We didn't know our forbears' names with a certainty*"?

4. Why do the speakers use images of nature to describe Africa and the Taíno, but not Europe?

5. Why does the table have "a cloth woven by one, dyed by another, / *embroidered by another still*"?

6. Why do the speakers say of their "many mothers," "*They have kept it all going /* All the civilizations erected on their backs"?

7. Why does the first speaker say, "Come, lay that dishcloth down. Eat, dear, eat"?

8. Why does the second speaker say, "*History made us*"?

9. What does the first speaker mean when she says, "We will not eat ourselves up inside anymore"?

10. Why does the poem end with the statement, "*And we are whole*"?

EVEN THE QUEEN | Connie Willis

Is the story saying that the Liberation freed women or oppressed them?

1. Why is the elimination of menstruation referred to as "the Liberation"?

279

Discussion Questions

2. Why does Traci describe the law of personal sovereignty as "the inherent right of citizens in a free society to make complete jackasses of themselves"? (23)

3. Is Traci serious or ironic when she repeatedly refers to the time before the Liberation as "days of dark oppression"?

4. Why is it the prospect of no longer having to menstruate that unites women into an effective political force?

5. Does the story support Evangeline's statement that the Liberation separated women "from the natural rhythms of your life, the very wellspring of your femaleness"? (30)

6. Why does Karen agree with Traci that "getting rid of your period" would be worth giving up your freedom? (34)

Does the story side with Traci and her family, with the Cyclists, or make equal fun of both?

1. Why are Traci, Traci's mother, Karen, and Viola horrified by the prospect of Perdita joining the Cyclists?

2. Does the story present the floratarian restaurant as charming or ridiculous?

3. Why does Traci's mother compare not having a shunt to going back to "concubinage, cholera, and corsets"? (28)

4. Do Evangeline's explanations of the Cyclists' principles and practices make them seem admirable or absurd?

5. Why does Evangeline say that all the women's comments about the discomfort of menstruating "reflect the self-loathing thrust on you by the patriarchy"? (33)

6. Why does the story end with Perdita deciding not to join the Cyclists because she didn't realize cramps and bleeding were involved?

Discussion Questions

ROWING | Anne Sexton

Why does the speaker repeat "I grew" throughout the poem? (37)

1. Why does the poem open with "A story, a story!/(Let it go. Let it come.)"?

2. What is the speaker trying to convey about childhood through her choice of imagery?

3. Why does the speaker say she was "stamped out like a Plymouth fender"?

4. What does the speaker mean when she says "touch is all"?

5. Why does the speaker say, "I grew,/like a pig in a trenchcoat I grew"?

6. Why does the speaker continue to grow despite the "strange apparitions"?

7. Why does the speaker start rowing in her middle age?

8. What does "the gnawing pestilential rat" represent to the speaker?

9. How does the African proverb at the close of the poem affect the meaning of the story the speaker has told?

10. Why does the poem conclude, "This story ends with me still rowing"?

I GO BACK TO MAY 1937 | Sharon Olds

Why does the speaker at first want to tell her parents, "Stop,/don't do it"? Why does she then change her mind? (43)

1. Why does the speaker imagine her parents at the gates of their respective colleges?

2. Why does the speaker include details about both the mother's and the father's gate?

3. Why does the speaker describe her parents as "dumb"?

Discussion Questions

4. In what ways are the parents described as being the same? How are they different?

5. Why does the speaker imagine entering the scene and having her parents turn to her?

6. Why does the speaker "take them up like the male and female / paper dolls and bang them together"?

7. Why does the speaker imagine banging the paper dolls together "as if to / strike sparks from them"?

8. Why does the speaker end by saying, "Do what you are going to do, and I will tell about it"?

FREEDOM FIGHTER | Perri Klass

Why does Jan think of herself as "a rebel, an iconoclast, a strange and estranged and angry freedom fighter"? (48)

1. Why does Jan tell her clinic patients that this baby is her third "with a certain smugness"? (46)

2. For what does Jan feel "obscurely" forgiven when Marcie likes the robe Jan offers her? (51)

3. Why can't Jan help being "impressed with the serendipity" of Marcie's new career? (52)

4. Why do Marcie and Jan enjoy taking care of Ellie, the hitchhiker?

5. At the end of the story, why does Marcie agree with Jan that being pregnant for the third time is Jan's "revolutionary gesture"? (64)

6. When Jan asks what Marcie's revolutionary gesture is, why does Marcie gesture "widely" but not speak? (64)

Discussion Questions

Why does Jan think so much about how Marcie may be reacting to her?

1. Why does Jan imagine saying to Marcie, "Talk to me of things I know nothing about, and listen while I draw to your attention the wonder of my own adventure"? (47)

2. Why does Jan say, "Let's hit the lingerie shop," when she "sees Marcie watching her watch the woman with all the snowsuits"? (50)

3. Why can Jan only "nod emphatically" when she is hurt by Marcie's refusal to talk about her son, Ricky? (53)

4. Why is Jan "most conscious of Marcie's ironic eye" during her phone conversation with Alan? (56)

5. Why does Jan think of Marcie as "regal and beautiful, admirable and unknowable"? (64)

6. Why does Klass include italicized scene openers (*"Jan and Marcie go away for the weekend," "Jan and Marcie stop to do some shopping,"* etc.)?

MY FATHER'S CHINESE WIVES | Sandra Tsing Loh

Why do Jenna and Kaitlin find it hard to believe that someone would want to marry their father?

1. Why is Jenna bothered by her father's insistence that his wife be Chinese?

2. Why does Kaitlin conclude that her father's intention to marry a Chinese woman is a form of punishment?

3. Why do Jenna and Kaitlin decide to meet their stepmother Zhou Ping?

4. Why is Kaitlin "flipping out" over the birthday card and gifts? (72)

5. Why does Jenna repeatedly stifle the pain of remembering her childhood experiences?

Discussion Questions

Why is some version of the line "He is old now" articulated at various points throughout the story?

1. What does Jenna mean when she says that one would refer to her father as Old Dragon Whiskers "not just because it is a picturesque Oriental way of speaking"? (65)

2. Why does Jenna describe herself and Kaitlin as their father's "odd American experiment"? (75)

3. Why does Kaitlin expect her father to provide a reason for his anger "all those years"? (76)

4. Why does Jenna conclude that her father has no answer for his anger?

5. What does Jenna's interpretation of Zhou Ping's song tell us about Jenna's feelings toward her father?

STORIES DON'T HAVE ENDINGS | Janice Gould

Why does the narrator find it problematic that "stories don't have endings"? (79)

1. Why does the narrator see "no ending" even in her mother's death? (79)

2. What does the word "abnormal" mean to the narrator? (79)

3. Why does the narrator say of her father that "it must have taken him a load of courage to lie down" with her dying mother? (79)

4. Why does the narrator continue to dream of herself and Sharon "riding our horses out by the bluffs"? (83)

5. Now that her mother has died, does the narrator know her plans for the future?

How do different characters experience shame in the story?

1. Why does the narrator believe that the female customer at the diner "saw what she wanted to see"? (80)

2. Why was it "a matter of principle" and "a matter of superstition" for the narrator to never look at herself in the mirror? (81)

3. After spending the night in Sharon's bed, why does the narrator never go back?

4. What does the narrator mean when she remembers, "I never gave anything with my body in those days"? (84)

5. Why does the narrator feel the need to "explain those things" that she hopes her mother "now knows"? (84)

THE BOX HOUSE AND THE SNOW | Cristina Henríquez

Why does the mother acquiesce to the father's decision to make their daughter hold up the house?

1. Why does the mother reassure the father that his pride in the house is "joyous" and therefore acceptable? (85)

2. Why does the mother bite her tongue when the father says it would take too long to teach the girl to do the mother's job?

3. Why does the mother tell the father that the house is *"more* perfect" because it faces a challenge? (91)

4. Why does the mother's dream end with her "choking on snow"? (94)

5. Why does the mother leave the daughter at home alone, even after the daughter repeatedly tells her mother she is tired?

Why does the father blame the daughter for ruining the house?

1. Why is the house "the father's favorite thing in the world"? (85)

2. Why does the father believe that the news story will focus on the house?

3. Why is the father so insistent that the reporters not speak to the daughter?

Discussion Questions

4. Why does the father insist, "She let it through"? (96)

5. At the end of the story, why does the father insist the house is ruined?

A BOY MY SISTER DATED IN HIGH SCHOOL | Emily Mitchell

Years after being slapped by a boy she dated, why does the narrator's sister feel increasingly guilty about her reaction?

1. Why does the narrator's sister wait years to tell the story of being slapped by her boyfriend?

2. After he slaps her, why does the narrator's sister imagine that the boy might be frozen in one position forever "in punishment for what he had done"? (102)

3. After the boy apologizes for slapping her, why does the narrator's sister say, "I guess you should take me home"? (102)

4. Why doesn't the narrator's sister want to give the boy the satisfaction of being "a terrible, unforgivable villain"? (102)

5. Once the boy and the narrator's sister smile at each other, why do they feel "they were back on solid ground, back in the world they knew"? (103)

Did the narrator's sister believe that getting slapped was "really, truly no big deal"? (103)

1. Why does the narrator's sister think her mother "would only overreact" if she were told what had happened? (103)

2. Why does the narrator's sister begin to feel, much later, that "she had let herself down by the way she had reacted"? (104)

3. Why does the narrator's sister think that the guilt she carries is a stone that is "small and round, but heavy"? (104)

Discussion Questions

4. Why does the narrator's sister hope that talking about what happened will make the guilt "smaller, maybe even make it vanish"? (104)

5. Why does the narrator think that sharing the story might reduce the guilt, but could also "make it multiply"? (104)

APPLE PICKING | Laura Negrete

At the end of the poem, why does the speaker say that the Virgen de Guadalupe "ruined it for the rest of us. Not Eve"? (107)

1. Why does the poem begin with the speaker and her family "gathered / in the living room" with a Bible salesman?

2. Why does the salesman watch the speaker, her sisters, and Elena as he "sermon[s] about the woman's role"?

3. Why does Mamá Andrea regard her breasts as "useless / and in the way"?

4. Why is the dialogue between Juan (John) and Felipe (Phillip) used twice, once in Spanish and later in English?

5. Why does the speaker say her mother was stolen by her father?

6. Why does the speaker call her trip to the Basilica "a duty-bound pilgrimage" made "unintentionally"?

7. Why does the speaker wait until mass is over to see the Virgen de Guadalupe?

8. Why does the speaker say that it is her dignity that wanted to taste the Virgen de Guadalupe's "cherry sweet skin"?

9. Why does the speaker say that her skin would burn the Virgen de Guadalupe's "throat like cheap whisky"?

10. Why is the poem entitled "Apple Picking"?

Discussion Questions

DRINKING COFFEE ELSEWHERE | ZZ Packer

During the freshmen orientation game, why does Dina say, "I guess I'd be a revolver"? (110)

1. Why does Dina think that "Russian roulette sounded like a better way to go" than trusting the "white boys" to catch her? (109)
2. Why is Dina so determined not to reveal anything important about her life to Dr. Raeburn?
3. Why does Dina leave the grocery bag on the sidewalk after she drops it while running away from the boy with the nice shoes?
4. Why is Dina "hooked on to that one word, pretending"? (127)
5. Why does Dina feel as though she had her "own locks to click shut"? (129)

Why doesn't Dina go to Vancouver with Heidi?

1. Why does Dina finally decide to let Heidi into her room?
2. Why does Dina think she "began to love Heidi that night in the dish room"? (123)
3. Why does Dina describe spending time in her room with Heidi as a "pleasant trap of silence"? (125)
4. After Heidi tells Dina about her mother's car, why does Dina say to Heidi, "It's all right. It's not a big deal"? (126)
5. Why does the story end with Dina imagining Heidi coming to visit?

THE BURNING HEART | Louise Glück

Does the voice asking if "the fire hurts" ever get the kind of answer it wants? (132)

1. Why does the first speaker begin, "Ask her if she regrets anything"?

Discussion Questions

2. What does the woman say is forgotten "when you're touched"?

3. When asked again about touch, why does the woman answer, "I didn't ask for anything;/everything was given"?

4. What does being "hauled into the underworld" suggest about the woman's experience?

5. In remembering her situation, why does the woman say, "I thought/we were not responsible/any more than we were responsible/for being alive"?

6. Why does she describe herself as a "pariah"?

7. Why does the woman ask, "If I didn't change, wasn't my action/in the character of that young girl?"

8. What made the woman tremble?

9. How does the woman feel about "being both/fire and eternity" with her husband?

10. Does the woman *"regret her life"*?

RE-FORMING THE CRYSTAL | Adrienne Rich

Why does the speaker begin by saying "I am trying to imagine/how it feels to you/to want a woman"? (133)

1. Why does the speaker liken "desire without discrimination" to "a fix"?

2. Why is desire described as "the sudden knowledge . . . that the body is sexual"?

3. Why does the speaker say that her energy "could be used a hundred ways, and going to meet you could be one of them"?

4. Why does the speaker note that "all the old roads that used to wander the country" have been lost?

Discussion Questions

5. Why does the speaker say, "Tonight I understand/my photo on the license is not me,/my/name on the marriage-contract was not mine"?

6. What does the speaker mean when she says, "The woman/I needed to call my mother/was silenced before I was born"?

7. Why does the speaker want to understand her "fear both of the machine and of the accidents of nature"?

8. Why does the speaker say, "My desire for you is not trivial"?

9. Why does the speaker differentiate between her desire and "the energy it draws on"?

10. Why does the poem end with the speaker imagining various ways to use her energy?

MIND-BODY STORY | Nina Barrett

Why is a job interview with the *New York Times* the moment Barrett "fell out of [her] story"? (140)

1. Why does Barrett identify with feminism despite how complicated the definition of feminism is for her?

2. Why hadn't Barrett given her pregnancy "much thought in regard to the interview"? (140)

3. Why does Barrett measure herself by her academic and professional success?

4. Why does Barrett think that her identity "existed most *really* on paper"? (141)

5. Why is staring at the Victorian houses the time when Barrett's "childhood ended, and [her] résumé began"? (152)

Discussion Questions

Why has Barrett spent so many years trying to "minimize the significance of having a female body"? (152–153)

1. After the interview, why does Barrett say, "I had forgotten that my mind was attached to a physical form that could betray me at any moment"? (141)

2. Why does Barrett decide not to say, "the penis was a mere afterthought of fetal development" during the debate? (143)

3. Why does Barrett come to think of her academic triumph in eighth grade as evidence that the school had succeeded in making her "more of a Man each day"? (145)

4. At age thirteen, why does Barrett believe that her brain is her "means of salvation"? (146)

5. Why does Barrett decide to date the boy even though she "didn't especially like him"? (147)

ONE OUT OF TWELVE: WRITERS WHO ARE WOMEN IN OUR CENTURY (selection) | Tillie Olsen

According to Olsen, why is there "one woman writer of achievement for every twelve men writers so ranked"? (157)

1. Why does Olsen focus more on the lives of women writers than she does on their literary works?

2. Why does Olsen say of the ratio of men to women writers, *"Any figure but one to one would insist on query: Why?"* (157)

3. Why does Olsen list so many ways in which women have historically been treated as "Unclean; taboo"? (158)

4. When speaking of how much it takes to become a writer, why does Olsen say that it is "difficult for any male not born into a class that breeds such confidence. Almost impossible for a girl, a woman"? (160)

5. Why are some young women writers able to be "fed indeed by the very glories of some of this literature that puts them down"? (161)

Discussion Questions

6. Why does Olsen say that she "would not—if I could—have killed the caring part" of the angel in the house? (170)

7. How much control does Olsen think women writers have over the factors that restrict them?

Why does Olsen think that it is so important to have more recognized women writers?

1. Why does Olsen think more women don't draw directly on the specifically female aspects of their experiences in their writing?

2. Does Olsen think that the demands of motherhood are inherently incompatible with those of the writer?

3. Why does Olsen state, "I hope and I fear for what will result" from women "assuming as their right fullness of work *and* family life?" (164)

4. Why does Olsen say of children's needs, "The very fact that these are needs of love, not duty, that one feels them as one's self; *that there is no one else to be responsible for these needs*, gives them primacy"? (165)

5. Does Olsen believe that the demands of motherhood are inevitably going to have a negative impact on women writers?

6. Why does Olsen want to resist focusing on the *"only's"*? (171)

BABY GOTTA EAT, PARTS I-V | Kima Jones

Why does Jones see her bills as both a symbol of her financial burden and a testament of her "independence and will to choose"? (173)

1. Why does Jones say that having a dying orchid as her "only companion" is also a choice? (174)

2. Why does Jones say that her novel "feels rich"? (174)

Discussion Questions

3. Why does Jones ask herself, "Is my work worth my own time?" (175)

4. Why does Jones write, "I want poems that will keep me in love and stay with me"? (176)

5. Why does Jones say that her poems are "their own people"? (176)

6. Why does Jones repeat that poetry is her whole life and "everything else" is ruining it? (176)

7. Why does Jones advise, "Eat your fruit as if it is still hanging from its tree / Eat your fruit often and to the pit"? (180)

8. What do the notes Jones includes in Part V reveal about her priorities and how they change?

9. Why does Jones end by sharing how much she earned as a writer in 2014?

LOWERING YOUR STANDARDS FOR FOOD STAMPS | Sheryl Luna

Why does the speaker say "I'm far from poems"? (187)

1. What is the speaker's situation and state of mind as the poem opens?

2. What does the speaker mean by, "Maslow's got everything on me"?

3. What does the speaker mean when she says, "I have no / poem to carry, no material illusions"?

4. Why does the speaker say that she is "unlearning America's languages"?

5. What circumstances give "killing time" a new meaning?

6. What does the speaker experience "at night" when "black space has [her] dizzy"?

293

Discussion Questions

7. What does the speaker mean by, "Words some say are weeping twilight and sunrise"?

8. Why is the speaker "drawn to dramas"?

9. What does the speaker mean by "911: no metered aubade"?

10. What does the title of the poem have to do with the speaker's observation at the close?

COLOR BLIND OR COLOR BRAVE? | Mellody Hobson

Why does Hobson believe it is important to be "color brave" rather than "color blind"?

1. Why does Hobson begin by sharing her and her colleague's experience of being mistaken for servers when they arrived at the editorial board lunch?

2. Why is Hobson's response when her friend rushes in, "Now, don't you think we need more than one black person in the U.S. Senate?" (189)

3. Why does Hobson say, "The numbers do not lie," and include statistics about how wealth and positions of influence are distributed by race? (190)

4. Why does her mother's question, "How did they treat you?" still hang in the air for Hobson? (191)

5. Why does Hobson say we should have honest conversations about race, "not because it's the right thing to do, but because it's the smart thing to do"? (192)

6. Why does Hobson describe diversity as a "competitive advantage"? (192)

7. Why does Hobson admire her mother's "brutal pragmatism"? (193)

REELING FOR THE EMPIRE | Karen Russell

Why is it by remembering how she signed herself into slavery that Kitsune is able to create the cocoon that will transform her?

1. Why do the reelers make up different stories about their pasts?

2. Why does Kitsune feel pride, "in spite of everything," about the quality of the silk she and the others can produce? (200)

3. Why won't Kitsune answer Tooka's question, "Are we monsters now?" (201)

4. During the short break while the thread regenerates, why do the women stubbornly "reel backward" by remembering places and people from their pasts? (203)

5. Why does Kitsune drink the Agent's tea willingly, even though she senses "the stench of a bad and thickening future"? (206)

6. Why is Kitsune able to convince all of the other women to join her?

7. Why does Kitsune feel "regret is a pilgrimage back to the place where I was free to choose"? (213)

Why is the idea of silk-reeling as an "imperial vocation" so compelling in this society? (197)

1. Why do the men "nearly always sign the contract" for their daughters or wives? (198)

2. Why does Hoshi repeat the Agent's statement that "we are the treasures of the realm"? (202)

3. Why is Dai willing to die rather than begin reeling again?

4. When Kitsune and the other reelers drop from the ceiling in front of the Agent, why does she think it is "a dreamlike repetition of our initiation"? (217)

5. Why does Kitsune recite the names of the reelers as she seals off the Agent in the cocoon?

Discussion Questions

"RECITATIF" | Toni Morrison

At the end of the story, why does Roberta cry and ask, "What the hell happened to Maggie?" (244)

1. Why does Twyla believe that Maggie fell down until Roberta tells her the gar girls "pushed [Maggie] down and tore her clothes"? (236)

2. When Twyla and Roberta meet during the protests, why does Roberta tell Twyla they kicked Maggie?

3. Why does Twyla think of Maggie as her "dancing mother"? (242)

4. At the end of the story, why is Roberta so determined to tell Twyla what she has remembered about Maggie?

5. Why does Roberta tell Twyla that Maggie was black, and then later say that she "can't be sure" if Maggie was black? (243)

Why do Twyla and Roberta each often ask about the other's mother?

1. While having coffee with Roberta after they meet at the Food Emporium, why does Twyla want "to go home suddenly"? (237)

2. When she first sees Roberta protesting outside the school, why does Twyla decide to turn around and talk to her?

3. Why is Twyla's first protest sign one that "didn't make sense without Roberta's"? (241)

4. Why can't Twyla "help looking for Roberta" at Joseph's high school graduation? (242)

5. Why is the story called "Recitatif"?

Discussion Questions

WHEN THE WORLD AS WE KNEW IT ENDED | Joy Harjo

After the world is "over," why does the speaker say there are still "the seeds to plant and the babies/who needed milk and comforting"? (246)

1. Why does the speaker begin with the idea of an "occupied island"? Who are the occupiers?
2. Why does the speaker describe the two towers as, "Swallowed/by a fire dragon, by oil and fear"?
3. What does the speaker mean when she says, "It was coming"?
4. Why does the speaker say her community "had been watching since the eve of the missionaries" to see what would happen?
5. What is it that the members of the community saw while they cooked, raised children, and cleaned?
6. Why were the members of the community warned by "the conference of the birds" before the fall of the two towers?
7. To what is the speaker referring when she speaks of "the first takeover"?
8. What does the speaker mean when she says, "And then it was over, this world we had grown to love"? In what ways is the world "over"?

BAD FEMINIST: TAKE ONE | Roxane Gay

Does Gay believe that it is enough to define feminists as "just women who don't want to be treated like shit"? (247)

1. Why does Gay "run into trouble" when she tries to expand the definition of feminism beyond this point? (247)
2. According to Gay, what are the "consequences for doing feminism wrong"? (248)
3. Who or what does Gay blame for there being "little room for multiple or discordant points of view" within feminism? (248)

Discussion Questions

4. After the argument with her boyfriend, why does Gay react by thinking, *"Isn't it obvious I am a feminist, albeit not a very good one?"* (249)

5. Why does Gay disagree with Wurtzel's argument that economic equality will make feminism's concerns disappear?

Why does Gay answer her question about whether she is essentializing feminism herself with "perhaps"? (251)

1. According to Gay, why has feminism been "warped by misperception for so long that even people who should know better" have bought into an essentialist definition of feminism? (248)

2. According to Gay, why is there "willful disinterest in incorporating the issues and concerns of black women into the mainstream feminist project"? (251)

3. Does Gay believe that a woman writing about feminism has "a responsibility to women who don't fall within her target demographic"? (254)

4. Why does Gay characterize *Lean In* as a "snow globe"? (254)

5. In Gay's view, why must "public women, and feminists in particular" be "everything to everyone; when they aren't, they are excoriated for their failure"? (255)

WOODCHUCKS | Maxine Kumin

Why does the speaker wish that the woodchucks had "consented to die unseen/gassed underground the quiet Nazi way"? (258)

1. Why does the speaker in the poem say, "Gassing the woodchucks didn't turn out right"?

2. What does it mean when the speaker says that the case against the woodchucks "was airtight"?

Discussion Questions

3. Why does the speaker decide to shoot the woodchucks after they "turned up again" the next morning?

4. Why does the speaker say the woodchucks were "no worse / for the cyanide than we for our cigarettes / and state-store Scotch"?

5. Why does the speaker describe herself as "a lapsed pacifist fallen from grace"?

6. When the speaker shoots the baby woodchuck, why does she say, "He died down in the everbearing roses"?

7. What does the speaker mean when she says "the hawkeye killer came on stage forthwith"?

8. Why does the speaker keep hunting the chuck described as the "Old wily fellow"?

9. Does the speaker learn anything about herself from her experience killing the woodchucks?

READING LESSONS | Edwidge Danticat

Why does Danielle think of her mother's advice about rubbing butterflies on her breasts at several moments in the story?

1. Why does Danielle tell her adult students "about breasts and butterflies and mothers lost too young"? (263)

2. Why does Danielle think of the lump in her breast as a "fragile egg that might crack"? (264)

3. Why does Danielle not reply when Principal Boyfriend tells her he loves her?

4. While reading Hans Christian Andersen's story "The Snow Queen," why does Danielle find herself "enthralled with the sound of her own wistful voice"? (266)

5. Why does Danielle decide to "pretend that in her sleep some magic clock had been turned back to the days when her body was still her own"? (267)

299

Discussion Questions

6. Why does Danielle imagine a conversation with Principal Boyfriend in which she might, "but probably wouldn't" say, "And what does anyone owe me?" (267)

7. Why does Danielle's father say, "Don't you remember how hard your mother used to beat you because you liked playing with insects so much, because you were like a boy?" (268)

Why does Danielle hit Paul?

1. Why does Danielle tell Fania and Lorvane that literacy can spare them "humiliation" when completing customs forms? (262)

2. When she slaps Paul, why does Danielle feel "neither guilt nor remorse but retribution, justice"? (269)

3. Why does Lorvane say, "I would sign a paper, if I have to, for spanking. . . . But I would never let anyone slap my son"? (271)

4. After Lorvane slaps Danielle, why does Danielle feel she comes to understand "the concept of turning the other cheek"? (272)

5. Why does Lorvane tell Danielle, "And remember, 'Kids are not stupid'"? (272)

6. Why is the story called "Reading Lessons"?

WAYS OF CONQUEST | Denise Levertov

Why does the speaker say, "You invaded my country by accident"? (273)

1. Why does the invader run past the vines that touched him or her?

2. Why does the speaker say the raindrops were shaken off the leaves by "you or the wind"?

3. Is the line "I invaded your country with all my 'passionate intensity'" spoken by the same voice as the one in the first stanza or a different one?

Discussion Questions

4. What are the "pontoons and parachutes of my blindness" the speaker refers to?

5. Why does living "in the suburbs of the capital / incognito" cause the speaker's "will to take the heart of the city" to dwindle?

6. Why is the speaker "the stranger who will listen" to the adolescents' dreams?

7. Why does the speaker "love / the wild herons who return each year to the marshy outskirts"?

8. With what emotion does the speaker say, "What I invaded has / invaded me"?

301

Acknowledgments

All possible care has been taken to trace ownership and secure permission for each selection in this anthology. The Great Books Foundation wishes to thank the following authors, publishers, and representatives for permission to reproduce copyrighted material:

"What Do Women Want?," from TELL ME, by Kim Addonizio. Copyright © 2000 by Kim Addonizio. Reproduced by permission of the Permissions Company on behalf of BOA Editions, Ltd.

At Odds, by Julia Serano, from DESIRE: WOMEN WRITE ABOUT WANTING. Copyright © 2007 by Julia Serano. Reproduced by permission of the author.

Ending Poem, from GETTING HOME ALIVE, by Aurora Levins Morales and Rosario Morales. Copyright © 1986 by Aurora Levins Morales and Rosario Morales. Reproduced by permission of the Permissions Company on behalf of Aurora Levins Morales.

Even the Queen, from THE BEST OF CONNIE WILLIS, by Connie Willis. Copyright © 2013 by Connie Willis. Reproduced by permission of the Lotts Agency, Ltd., on behalf of Connie Willis.

Rowing, from THE AWFUL ROWING TOWARD GOD, by Anne Sexton. Copyright © 1975 by Loring Conant Jr., Executor of the Estate of Anne Sexton. Reproduced by permission of Houghton Mifflin Harcourt Publishing Company and Sterling Lord Literistic, Inc.

I Go Back to May 1937, from THE GOLD CELL, by Sharon Olds. Copyright © 1987 by Sharon Olds. Reproduced by permission of Alfred A. Knopf, an imprint of the Knopf Doubleday Publishing Group, a division of Penguin Random House LLC.

Freedom Fighter, from LOVE AND MODERN MEDICINE, by Perri Klass. Copyright © 2001 by Perri Klass. Reproduced by permission of Houghton Mifflin Harcourt Publishing Company and Elaine Markson Literary Agency.

My Father's Chinese Wives, by Sandra Tsing Loh, from *Quarterly West*. Copyright © 1994 by Sandra Tsing Loh. Reproduced by permission of ICM Partners on behalf of the author.

Stories Don't Have Endings, by Janice Gould, from SPIDER WOMAN'S GRANDDAUGHTERS. Copyright © 1989 by Janice Gould. Reproduced by permission of the author.

The Box House and the Snow, from COME TOGETHER, FALL APART: A NOVELLA AND STORIES, by Cristina Henríquez. Copyright © 2006 by Cristina Henríquez. Reproduced by permission of Riverhead, an imprint of Penguin Publishing Group, a division of Penguin Random House LLC.

A Boy My Sister Dated in High School, from VIRAL: STORIES, by Emily Mitchell. Copyright © 2015 by Emily Mitchell. Reproduced by permission of W. W. Norton & Company, Inc.

Acknowledgments

Apple Picking, by Laura Negrete, from *Columbia Poetry Review*, Spring 2004. Copyright © 2004 by Laura Negrete. Reproduced by permission of the author.

Drinking Coffee Elsewhere, from DRINKING COFFEE ELSEWHERE, by ZZ Packer. Copyright © 2003 by ZZ Packer. Reproduced by permission of Riverhead, an imprint of Penguin Publishing Group, a division of Penguin Random House LLC, and Canongate Books.

The Burning Heart, from VITA NOVA, by Louise Glück. Copyright © 1999 by Louise Glück. Reproduced by permission of HarperCollins Publishers and Carcanet Press, Ltd.

Re-forming the Crystal, from THE FACT OF A DOORFRAME: SELECTED POEMS 1950–2001, by Adrienne Rich. Copyright © 2002 by Adrienne Rich. Copyright © 2001, 1999, 1995, 1991, 1989, 1986, 1984, 1981, 1967, 1963, 1962, 1961, 1960, 1959, 1958, 1957, 1956, 1955, 1954, 1953, 1952, 1951 by Adrienne Rich. Copyright © 1978, 1975, 1973, 1971, 1969, 1966 by W. W. Norton & Company, Inc. Reproduced by permission of W. W. Norton & Company, Inc.

Mind-Body Story, from THE PLAYGROUP, by Nina Barrett. Copyright © 1994 by Nina Barrett. Reproduced by permission of the author.

One Out of Twelve: Writers Who Are Women in Our Century, from SILENCES, by Tillie Olsen. Copyright © 1978 by the Tillie Olsen Trust. Reproduced by permission of Francis Golden Literary Agency, Inc. on behalf of the Tillie Olsen Trust.

Baby Gotta Eat, Parts I–V, by Kima Jones, from *Scratch Magazine*. Copyright © 2014 by Kima Jones. Reproduced by permission of the author.

Lowering Your Standards for Food Stamps, by Sheryl Luna, from *Poetry*, April 2014. Copyright © 2014 Sheryl Luna. Reproduced by permission of the author.

Color Blind or Color Brave?, by Mellody Hobson. Originally delivered as a TED Talk in 2014. Reproduced by permission of TED Conferences, LLC.

Reeling for the Empire, from VAMPIRES IN THE LEMON GROVE, by Karen Russell. Copyright © 2013 by Karen Russell. Reproduced by permission of Alfred A. Knopf, an imprint of the Knopf Doubleday Publishing Group, a division of Penguin Random House LLC, and the Random House Group, Ltd.

"*Recitatif*", by Toni Morrison, from CALLING THE WIND: TWENTIETH-CENTURY AFRICAN-AMERICAN SHORT STORIES. Copyright © 1983 by Toni Morrison. Reproduced by permission of ICM Partners on behalf of the author.

When the World as We Knew It Ended, from HOW WE BECAME HUMAN: NEW AND SELECTED POEMS: 1975–2001, by Joy Harjo. Copyright © 2002 by Joy Harjo. Reproduced by permission of W. W. Norton & Company, Inc.

Bad Feminist: Take One, from BAD FEMINIST, by Roxane Gay. Copyright © 2014 by Roxane Gay. Reproduced by permission of HarperCollins Publishers.

Woodchucks, from SELECTED POEMS 1960–1990, by Maxine Kumin. Copyright © 1972, 1997 by Maxine Kumin. Reproduced by permission of W. W. Norton & Company, Inc. and the Anderson Literary Agency, Inc.

Reading Lessons, by Edwidge Danticat. First published by the *New Yorker*. Copyright © 2005 by Edwidge Danticat. Reproduced by permission of Aragi Inc. on behalf of Edwidge Danticat.

Ways of Conquest, from THE FREEING OF THE DUST, by Denise Levertov. Copyright © 1975 by Denise Levertov. Reproduced by permission of New Directions Publishing Corp.